Manage Your Money
and Live Better

Get the Most from Your Dwindling Dollars

Manage Your Money and Live Better

Get the Most from Your Dwindling Dollars

DAVID L. MARKSTEIN

McGRAW-HILL BOOK COMPANY

New York   St. Louis   San Francisco   Düsseldorf   Johannesburg
Kuala Lumpur   London   Mexico   Montreal   New Delhi
Panama   Rio de Janeiro   Singapore   Sydney   Toronto

MANAGE YOUR MONEY AND LIVE BETTER
Get the Most from Your Dwindling Dollars

07-040428-3

1234567890   BPBP   754321

This book was set in Primer by the Monotype Composition
Co., Inc., and printed on permanent paper and bound by
Book Press. The editors were Dale L. Dutton, Barbara
Church, and Carolyn Nagy. Teresa F. Leaden supervised
production.

*To old friends: Mary and Ivor, Ranny and Jules,
Marian and Joe.*

Contents

Preface

THERE IS A STORY told of a great criminal lawyer who defended a young man on a capital charge and obtained an acquittal.

"Sir," the young man's joyful mother said after the jury had brought in its verdict, "how can we ever thank you?"

"Happily, madam, the Phoenicians anticipated your problem," the attorney replied. "They invented money."

Since that day money has taken the form of shell wampum, obols, drachmae, talents, francs (both Swiss and French), marks, pounds, pieces of eight, war clubs, sacrificial animals, and, not least, the dollars we in the United States and Canada use for the goods we require.

More things about money change than its mere name and form. Essentially, money was invented and continues to be used as a medium of exchange. Without money functioning as such a medium, the carpenter could not use his handiwork to pay for that of the auto worker, the doctor could not remunerate his accountant or investment counselor, and the latter worthies would be unable to buy groceries. Barter would be an alternative. By barter, the carpenter might construct the auto worker's house and the auto worker furnish the car door on which he had worked as a return, while the doctor could treat the children of the investment counselor and CPA whose help he enjoyed, but the M.D. would be unable to compensate the auto worker if he wanted to buy a car made in another city.

Money, then, is the medium by which each of us compensates others and is in turn compensated for goods and services. Our problem is to obtain the most goods and services we can in exchange for what we furnish in the workings of the economic system.

That is what this book is all about. Its aim is to help you obtain more for the money you receive as salary, wage, or business profits.

David L. Markstein

Manage Your Money
and Live Better

Get the Most from Your Dwindling Dollars

1

Work with What You Have

ONE OF MY FRIENDS is a military officer. We talked not long ago about money and standards of living. "I don't think I'll ever be a rich man," he confided, "but I expect to live like one most of my life."

This book won't tell you how to be a rich man (my earlier book *Nine Roads to Wealth** should help toward that objective), but it will tell you how to live like one—more so, at any rate, than you are probably doing right now. Not everyone is qualified by temperament, training, or opportunity to reach a level at which he can play table-stakes poker with Onassis, Hunt, J. Paul Getty, or Lemuel D. Plainfellow, the village rich man who lives down by the lake. Yet most of us, lacking great wealth, can live better on what we have. The secret is money management.

---

* McGraw-Hill Book Company, New York, 1970.

Hampered by set incomes, harried by inflation, bedeviled by increasing wants and needs as our families grow and as the good things of life turned out by technology multiply but seem to stand just out of a reach limited by lack of the wealth of Onassis, Hunt, Getty, or Plainfellow, most of us rock through life with an attitude much like that of one irascible old fellow who was asked what he wanted. *"More,"* he replied. "That's what I want. More. Always more."

How to have more of what you want without more income is the problem. We're going to look at solutions. But first, it is necessary to examine the background conditions under which we live in order to understand both the problem and workable solutions.

The key is money itself: how it is "manufactured"—for that is how it comes into existence in the sophisticated, superheated economy of the seventies—and why inflation can be expected to continue biting into the amount of goods at floating prices your income in fixed dollars will purchase. It is necessary to look at Economics with a capital *E* before delving into the economics (lowercase *e*) of daily living.

Managing personal money is a matter of sound importance in good times. It becomes a question of survival in harder days when unemployment mounts and sales come slower. In 1969, a lid on money-supply growth threatened corporate as will as ordinary citizens' liquidity, slowed building, staggered the stock market, and quickly turned a hot boom into a cold recession. Efforts at expansion in 1970, when the Federal Reserve grew alarmed at what it had wrought in 1969 and turned the dollar spigot back to what inflation fighters called a too-full flow, also spell danger to your way of living. Happily, both offer opportunities to people adept at personal money management to live better without becoming billionaires or even millionaires.

YOUR MONEY

Begin with the thing called a dollar, which you receive as wage, salary, or the profits of a business or professional practice and which you spend for fewer and fewer of the goods and services your family consumes.

In the early days of the industrial revolution, when the complicated society in which we live was emerging, the prophet of finance was an economist named Adam Smith. He wrote a book called *The Wealth of Nations.* Until the Depression of 1929 to 1933 subtracted so much wealth from every nation that people demanded an economic system which would not swing to such wild extremes, *The Wealth of Nations* was a bible of how business should operate. Its "system" was called *"laissez faire."* This French term, roughly translated, means "let it happen." Laissez faire called for minimum interference of government in the workings of the commercial and financial machinery. Its tenet was that businessmen, in their collective wisdom, might stumble but would eventually right themselves and the lurching machine they operated. Generally, they did. Sometimes, they didn't. Then the results were terrible, as anyone who lived in the dark days of the early thirties will remember.

Out of those dark days developed a different kind of economic thinking. It was called the New Economics. Its high priest was a British economist and stock market speculator named John Maynard Keynes. Lord Keynes (pronounced "canes") advocated a combination of fiscal and monetary steps to inflate things during recessions and threatened downturns and to contract them when a boom was blooming. Toward this end, classic Keynesianism called for the government to run budget surpluses at times when things were rocking along at full economic steam, but if the pressure of a boom began to reach alarming proportions, to contract money supply.

Lord Keynes's followers soon tired of this kind of thing. They became "neo-Keynesians" and ditched the British thinker's dictum regarding budget surpluses in good times. During only three of the years since the end of World War II has the United States government run surpluses. There have been deficits in all other years.

Neo-Keynesianism still called for a combination of fiscal and monetary steps for tuning the economy, however. In theory at least, and sometimes in practice, taxes were lowered to fan the fire of a beginning boomlet, and were raised when it was desired to head off an accelerating boom.

Now neo-Keynesianism has become passé. The new gurus directing the economic machine (which still lurches and stumbles despite their efforts, although not to the degree it did in the simpler days when Adam Smith's followers ruled the roosts and rostrums) are sometimes referred to as the Monetary School and occasionally the Chicago School because some of the first thinking along their party line began at that midwestern academic tank. They increasingly refer to their bag as the New, New Economics.

Their thesis is simple. Money governs everything, contend the New, New Economists. Shrink the supply and the economic machine begins to slow and sputter as would an internal-combustion engine fed an ever-thinner fuel mixture. Enrich the gas going into the engine and that economic engine will roar and rattle furiously ahead.

Confrontation between the two ideas came in 1968 when the advocates of both concepts agreed that a slowing of the then boom was necessary. Neo-Keynesians were at the throttle. They applied the fiscal step of a tax increase but let money supply continue to expand. The economic engine behaved as would a car whose surprised driver slammed on the brake pedal to find that the linings were gone and the brakes didn't work. Boom and inflation kept right on going.

Then a Republican administration took office. Its economists tended toward, although they did not always openly avow, the New, New Economics. They promptly stepped on the extra braking systems by stopping growth of money supply. Results were quick. "They proved that their system could make a recession happen where a boom had been in progress before," one economist said. "Whether New, New Economics is able to handle better business conditions without fanning inflation is doubtful."

You don't have to agree with either of the contending economic-thought forces. But you must know that the monetary advocates are in command now. Their steps in either direction affect your ability to live better. To cope with whatever current steps they're taking, you have to understand how they operate. Two free mailings can help you in spotting changes of money-supply strategy. The first is *U.S. Financial Data.* This is issued weekly, and you can secure it by asking the Federal Reserve Bank of St. Louis. The other is called *Federal Reserve Statistical Release, Weekly Summary of Banking and Credit Measures.* It is obtainable from the Federal Reserve Board, Washington, D.C.

The practical effect of monetary changes—not the daily wiggles or the one-week-at-a-time movements, but the big trend changes—is to turn the economy around. In the wake of a tightening of money comes possible recession, probable high-interest costs, and problematical, slower sales. Sometimes prices drop and that's a help. In the wake of an increase in money supply comes (hopefully) a new economic boom and (certainly) eventual increased inflation. You have to take the latter into consideration, or instead of living better on the same money, you might find yourself living more skimpily. Detailed ideas for recognizing and combating inflation are found in my book *How You Can Beat Inflation.**

Writing on "Inflation and Its Cure" in the July, 1970, *Federal Reserve Bank of St. Louis Review,* Norman N. Bowsher noted:

> Inflation has proceeded at a faster and faster rate since 1964. Overall prices, which had been rising less than 1½ per cent a year in the early 1960's, increased 2 per cent in 1965, 3.5 percent in 1966 and 1967, 4 percent in 1968, and 5 per cent in 1969. The acceleration of price advance reflected a rise in total spending for goods and services at an average 8 per cent annual rate from late 1964 to late 1969, or roughly double the rise in production capacity. The excessive rise in total spending was fostered by generally expansive fiscal and monetary actions from 1964 through 1968.
>
> From the third quarter (1969) to the second quarter (1970) over-prices rose at an estimated 5.3 per cent annual rate, even faster than the 5 per cent increase in the previous year. . . . A quick dampening of inflation is even less likely

* McGraw-Hill Book Company, New York, 1970.

now than in the 1953–54, 1957–58 or 1960–61 periods for several reasons: the upward thrust of prices has been much stronger than during the earlier periods; policies to resist inflation have been milder; and their impact on spending has been less . . . the inflation has had, and is likely to continue to have, severe consequences. In brief, inflation reduces the value of money and other dollar-denominated assets relative to the value of other assets, causing a redistribution of wealth and income. The process of adapting to higher and higher rates of inflation, given existing contracts, laws, and other rigidities, causes inefficiencies, inequities, and interruptions to production.

Once inflationary expectations become strong, it is difficult and costly to extinguish them. Commitments made on the expectation of continued inflation become more difficult to fulfill if the inflation is less than anticipated. When excessive spending is dampened, many prices do not move quickly to their equilibrium levels, and declines in production and employment result.

YOURSELF

If you're going to beat this continuing inflation and live increasingly well through the increases and decreases in money supply ordained by our money masters, the New, New Economists, the next step is to understand the material you're working with—yourself. Make a personal inventory as coldbloodedly as a merchant would inventory the shirts, socks, or screwdrivers in his store.

The U.S. Department of Labor has a booklet called *Merchandising Your Job Talents.* Our task is not the finding of a job, but self-inventory toward the end of a richer way of life. The USDL pamphlet suggests you list:

> ■ *Skills and abilities:* What personal qualities do I have? . . . Think back over your job experience and school and volunteer activities and try to be honest with yourself. Are your strong points initiative, imagination, leadership, ability to organize, willingness to follow orders, interest in detail, or ability to work with people?
> ■ *Education:* The schools you attended and the dates, the principal courses you took, and the degrees you received. The

business, vocational, military, on-the-job training, or special
courses you took, the dates, and any certificates you received.
Then ask yourself: What courses or training did I like best
and why? What courses or training did I dislike and why?
Now list your scholarships or honors and your extracurricular
activities.

■ *Interests, talents, and aptitudes:* What are my hobbies or
volunteer activities? What are my special talents or aptitudes? For example, can I fix a car? Play a musical instru-
ment? Speak another language besides English? Am I good
at drawing or painting? What do I learn most easily?

YOUR ASSETS

Financial assets are important, too, and knowledge of your
net worth must come up early in personal money management. The American Bankers Association has defined it this
way:

> Net worth is the difference between what you own and what
> you owe. Do you know what your net worth is today? This
> is an important question to ask yourself once a year. Your
> net worth is a guide for your personal money management
> policy in the coming year, whether you should buy, sell,
> spend, save more, give more, invest, or borrow. Changes in
> your net worth show whether or not you are making financial
> progress. You can determine exactly how and where you
> stand with a financial statement.

What matters in personal money management is how you
put all this information together. The U.S. government runs
on a budget, although it seldom lives within its income
means. You haven't the alternative of a deficit budget. Certainly, no family can sustain repeated deficits as the federal
establishment has done in the last several decades. Be realistic in light of the information developed in your inventories
of personal and financial assets. Your budget should be a
living guide. That means you should make it carefully. None
of the ideas we'll consider in later chapters will be viable unless you have *and live within* a money-management budget.

What I own	Value today	Goal in one year	Value in one year
Cash			
Savings account(s)	————	————	————
Checking account(s)	————	————	————
Other	————	————	————
Life insurance (cash value)	————	————	————
Real estate (market value)			
Home	————	————	————
Other	————	————	————
Personal property (If I had to sell)			
Automobile	————	————	————
Furniture	————	————	————
Furs, jewelry, etc.	————	————	————
Investments (market value)			
Bonds	————	————	————
Stocks	————	————	————
Other	————	————	————
Other assets			
Notes receivable	————	————	————
Accounts receivable	————	————	————
Current bills			
Charge accounts	————	————	————
Other	————	————	————
Instalment debts (Balance due)			
Automobile	————	————	————
Furniture	————	————	————
Appliances	————	————	————
Other	————	————	————
Mortgage debt (Balance due)	————	————	————
Other liabilities			
Notes payable	————	————	————
Accounts payable	————	————	————
Taxes	————	————	————
Total owned	————	————	————

Total owned — total owed = your net worth

Figure 1   (SOURCE: The American Bankers Association.)

YOUR BUDGET

"There are all kinds of forms and accounting systems for handling family money, but the principle of them is the same," according to Mrs. Betty S. Martin, director of the

Women's Division of the Institute of Life Insurance. In her booklet, *A Discussion of Family Money,* Mrs. Martin points out how to start a budget plan:

> You list your definite obligations and find out in this way how much you must put aside to meet these future outlays. From this, you then figure how much money there is for you to spend from day to day and to save.

A budget must be individually tailored. There are "average" budgets seemingly designed to fit a family of some set number of children or having some hypothetical income. But there is no family just like yours, with exactly the same kind of income, the identical home, or precisely the same automotive needs. The number of children may be the same. But the "average" budget's three children don't do the same things, go to the same schools, or keep up with the same juvenile Joneses as your Edith, Ethelred, Frederica, and their father and mother, George and Sophie, don't do the same things or plan meals identical to those of Ronnie, the bachelor next door. On that subject, Lucille F. Mork and Minnie Bell McIntosh of the U.S. Department of Agriculture have said:

> A budget is something you make and remake until it works for you and you are satisfied with the results.
> There is no magic formula.

Nor is there any magic way to foretell the future despite today's wave of interest in the occult, witchcraft, astrology, and tarot cards. Your income, so set and definite today, might recede tomorrow. Or you might be offered better work at higher pay. Your family needs might increase—or drop. You can't do more than estimate future income or outgo. However, the past can be a helpful guide in filling out the suggested worksheet.

Before you fill this out, people who are expert on money planning say that you must set a goal for your budget. Note Mrs. Mork and Mrs. McIntosh of the USDA:

> Some goals are for the distant future. Some are for next year. Some are for right now.

Decide what your family's needs and wants are. List them in the order of importance.

Add to this list and also subtract from it the items that time makes unimportant.

Do not let long-term goals get lost in day-to-day demands. Too many porterhouse steaks this month may crowd out a new dishwasher next year.

Define your goals clearly. Then they will be easier to reach. An example: Long-term goals may be paying off the mortgage, establishing a fund to cover the children's schooling, or

How You Spend Your Money Each Day

Where does your money go? Here is a form to help you keep track of how you spend your money. Write in each day how much you spend under each heading. The headings above the columns are only suggestions. You may want to write in different ones.

At the end of the month, total how much you spent for each item.

This form gives you room for ten days' records. For a month, you will need to add more lines at the bottom of the form. Or, use several copies of the form.

Week or month: _____

	FOOD		CLOTHING		HOUSING				HEALTH	EDUCATION	CONTRIBUTIONS
Date	At home	Away from home	Garments, materials, accessories	Altering and repairing	Rent, repair	Household supplies, utilities, phone, heat	Furnishings and equipment	Doctor, dentist, medicine	Newspapers, magazines, books, tuition	Church, community

TRANS-PORTATION	PERSONAL		RECREA-TION	CLEAN-ING	HELP	GIFTS	INSUR-ANCE	SAVINGS	TAXES	DUES	DEBTS
Car expense, bus, other	Haircuts, allowances, cosmetics	Tobacco, candy, drinks	Movies, hobbies, vacation	Dry cleaning, laundry	House, yard, baby-sitting	Relatives, friends	Life, property, health	Bonds, social security, emergency	Income, Property, others	Union, associ-ations, others	

Total amount spent for the month _____

Money on hand at end of month _____

Money coming in for the month _____

Figure 2   How you spend your money each day. (SOURCE: U.S. Department of Agriculture.)

saving for retirement. Your goal for the next year may be a new car, a living room rug, an encyclopedia, a fine phonograph and records.

Goals differ at different phases of a family's life, just as George and Sophie have different aims from their bachelor friend Ronnie next door. A young married family, a swinging single, a middle-aged couple, and a retired person are like apples, oranges, and bananas—they can't be equated. As you progress through life, some aims are achieved, others prove impossible of accomplishment, and new vistas open as circumstances and tastes change and as inventive American technology dangles newer and better products before your eyes.

At whatever stage you now are, the current budget should be planned by all the family together. If a portion—even three-year-old Frederica—find it unworkable, then it is not likely to prove a viable guide. Advises The American Bankers Association booklet on personal management:

> Make it a joint family effort. Getting your financial facts clear for yourself and for your family can be a beneficial experience. By showing each member of the family just what the financial picture is, everyone will know what's involved and all can pitch in to help. A financial briefing session or business meeting for the entire family can have a good effect. *You're halfway to a solution when your family sees its financial problem clearly and realistically.* Make your wife your personal business partner and let the children participate, too. Learning how to plan with money is an important part of youth training for adult living.
>
> Children will be more cooperative and understanding about family money problems if they are permitted to take part in making the decisions. Burdening them in their early teens with the total picture of the family's use of money might be frightening to them and could result in private family problems being told to outsiders. But when the family is discussing matters which affect them directly, such as purchase of school clothes for the fall term, children of school age should learn that there is a limit to the amount of money that can be used for this purpose and that the rest must go for other things which should be spelled out to them. A child can often

contribute surprisingly sound opinions concerning the way to make the best use of funds.

Such a family conference should consider the difference between needs and wants. Everyone needs food. Most of us want filet mignons. As a pragmatic matter, we can settle for hamburger much of the time. Needs can seldom be cut when the paring knife is taken out to slice enough from the spending list to make it equal the income list. But wants are dispensable.

Note the sources of each item of income: from salary or wage; investment income; insurance payments; retirement pension; USDA payments; business profits; fees received from professional practice; welfare; or social security payments. How dependable is each? How elastic?

Some expenses come up only at quarterly, semiannual, or even yearly intervals, but they have to be paid all the same. A realistic budget should permit a monthly set-aside for these. Even in days of inflation, which is more likely to increase than abate, insurance is necessary and should be allowed for.

And emergencies happen. Ethelred might fall off the carport roof and break his arm; broken arms happen to little boys as part of the growing-up process. Emergency appendectomies come along at hours such as 1 A.M., and the resulting costs are as real as if you'd planned them. An emergency fund is vital. If it is unspent at the end of the year, you are in the happy position of the fellow who insured against fire and the building didn't burn down—except that you still have the emergency "premium" in your pocket. You can invest it, blow some of it on a good restaurant dinner to celebrate the fact that there was a convenient mattress beneath the carport the day Ethelred fell from the roof, or you can soberly add the money to next year's emergency fund in fear that, having escaped catastrophe once, your family might be overdue for it and might experience two arm fractures next year.

If the budget can include it, a monthly or weekly item for

family fun is in order. It renders the keeping of the budget less irksome and is a way of living better on the same money.

Taxes, like death, are inevitable. Less joyous than family blowouts, they must still be provided for.

You will have to decide whether you are the sort of money manager who can keep things straight by lumping all the items into a single savings account or whether it will be better to have separate bank accounts for each. Personally, I'm a lousy bookkeeper. If five projects are underway, I find it necessary to have five special accounts. Others with better accounting methods (and perhaps stronger self-discipline) can do with one.

Self-employed people who do not have the shelter of expected company retirement plans—and others who are on salary but would like to live better than the sometimes-marginal standards on which retirees have to operate—find that items for savings and investment toward retirement are in order.

Regarding expected and unexpected expenses, Mrs. Betty S. Martin of the Institute of Life Insurance advises:

> Food has to be bought and clothing has to be bought and things have to be washed and repaired and replaced. Children have to have shoes and things for school and father has to have lunch money, and if the car's fuel pump has to be fixed, it has to be fixed.
>
> Don't be discouraged because many of these items are "unexpected" expenses. They probably wouldn't be unexpected if you ran a constant inventory on the state of your household and the health of your family and the mathematical chances of a fuel pump wearing out.

People who live on budgets say that the difficult thing is not to figure out probabilities of a fuel pump going bust, but to *keep* to a budget when seemingly desirable things which have not been included in it crop up and when the discipline of money management is new and its raw hemp chafes. Those who have been there say that four steps can help you to keep the budget in operation.

1. *First Make a Trial Budget* Use this to gently fit the harness to your family and your family into the reins that, you hope, will lead it to a richer life through money management. Psychologically, it is easier to say "I'll just do this for a month" during the experimental phase. Those who have cut cigarette smoking or any other habit report that the same tactic helps to smooth the path of any rough initial period. A trial budget allows for radical change if necessary when the trial month or two has shown which things are working and which of the original assumptions were unrealistic.

2. *Review Operations Regularly* When I began publishing a financial newsletter several years ago, four or five dry-run issues were printed to shake out problems that might arise in format, content, or production schedules. "Aha!" I said innocently after this trial run was completed. "Now things will go smoothly." Alas, a year later I was still making changes in the setup dictated by circumstances of operation or the effort to achieve readability and client service. A trial period shows up the more glaring inadequacies of a budget. Periodic review by all the family members who must live within it helps to keep a budget's reins supple.

3. *Rule Out Impulsive Decisions* The family car has broken down and you wonder whether you should invest in a new transmission and four tires for a station wagon that, after the outlay of several hundred dollars has been made, will still be a four-year-old vehicle. "Let's buy a new one," you say impulsively to your wife while together you look at the features, sleek styling, and new paint of the latest model.

It's better to say "Whoa!" than "Whee!" at such a juncture. If the purchase—or even one much smaller than a new car— will fracture your carefully planned budget, invest in that new transmission or wear last year's suit with the narrower lapels. Impulsive buying decisions can wreck a budget on which you depend to make workable the money management steps suggested in future chapters.

4. *Keep Continuing Records* Nobody likes change when things change for the worse, but in a hard world of things as they are instead of as they should be, prices, needs, wants—sometimes incomes—change. The material on which to base realistic decisions at budget-adjustment time must be founded upon continuing records so you won't merely *think* but *know* that tuition costs are increasing or that towels which once cost a quarter (was there ever such a towel?) now run two for $10.

In *A Guide to Budgeting for the Family* (Home and Garden Bulletin No. 108), the U.S. Department of Agriculture offers consumers the following advice:

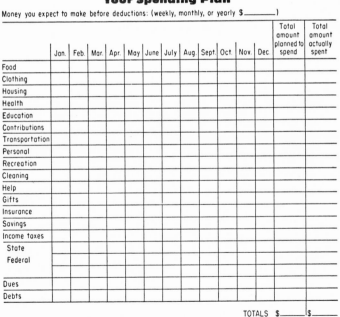

Your Spending Plan

Money you expect to make before deductions: (weekly, monthly, or yearly $_____)

	Jan.	Feb.	Mar.	Apr.	May	June	July	Aug.	Sept.	Oct.	Nov.	Dec.	Total amount planned to spend	Total amount actually spent
Food														
Clothing														
Housing														
Health														
Education														
Contributions														
Transportation														
Personal														
Recreation														
Cleaning														
Help														
Gifts														
Insurance														
Savings														
Income taxes														
State														
Federal														
Dues														
Debts														

TOTALS $_____ $_____

Figure 3 **Your spending plan.** (SOURCE: U.S. Department of Agriculture.)

Keep records. They will tell you if your dollars are giving your family what it really needs and wants.

Make your records simple. You don't need a detailed account of where you spend each nickel. But you do need to know where your money goes.

To keep track of day-to-day expenses . . . make a separate column for each category of expense in your budget. Allow enough space to enter items bought and their cost.

Get frequent reports from everyone who buys for the family. An easy way is to have everyone put receipts and notations of spending on a spindle each day. Or each member of the family can leave a note on file for the "bookkeeper." Some families ask members to note the money they spend and report at a weekly budget session.

At the end of the week, add up the amounts spent and write them in your financial record book. At the end of the month, total the expenditures under each category and compare them with those in your plan. . . . At the end of the budget period, compare what you spent with what you planned to spend.

If your spending was quite different from your plan, find out why. The answer to the question "why" will help you to improve your next plan.

Such constant improvement can provide for improvement in the way you live and for the things you want and will be able to buy, as opposed to things you want now but cannot afford.

YOUR STEPS TO BETTER LIVING

Coming chapters will clue you in on specific money management techniques which in some cases will make it possible for you to have the things you have now at as little as one-half the cost—giving you an opportunity for spending on the things you don't have (as yet).

We'll look into the ways some dollars, even at today's inflated prices, are able to buy $1.10 worth of services and merchandise, and sometimes $1.25, $1.50, or even $2. We will look at ways to employ others' money for our advantage without having to hold up a bank or embezzle money from the corner savings and loan association. These ways will include getting maximum mileage from services which, although not truly "free" in the sense of not costing anything, are "free" in that we have already paid for them through taxation or because they are included (and charged for, whether used or not) in the cost of things we possess.

A dollar which can be saved from the tax collector is available for spending on new things. A tax-saving dollar is even more, since it incurs no new taxes as would a dollar of extra but orthodox income. We will look at the ways corporations maintain liquidity without chicanery by paying bills when due (but not before), and how you can retain sums in your bank account to add to the "float" which the bank considers before assessing charges for its services. We will look at the mathematics of leasing versus buying automobiles, dwellings, etc.; this is not always a winning gambit, but where appropriate to your circumstances, you can sometimes gain considerably. The discussion will include criteria for determining when leasing is a good idea and when it is not.

A dollar can buy more downtown if you know where to shop, how to shop, and when a bargain is truly such and not merely cheap in quality as well as price tag. Chapter Three will also suggest alternate sources of supply which can sometimes bring great savings.

In it we will examine ways to stretch retail credit, securing charge-free purchases—sometimes for extended periods of time—and thus utilizing someone else's funds for extra services and goods. We will look into mail-order buying opportunities to determine when they are opportunities for the purchaser and when they merely afford the seller opportunity to push goods at sometimes inflated prices.

Some purchases turn out badly. This is doubly sad when the seller says, "Sorry—no returns." A coming chapter will discuss ways for obtaining redress (and thus for freeing funds for better living). Supermarkets' nonfood departments sometimes offer rare bargains, and ways are detailed to shave dollars from the drug, appliance, and housewares bills.

The lawn behind your home can become a source of food.

We will explore ways to grow better produce than you can buy and at the same time enjoy backyard farming. Convenience foods are costly; in examples explored in a later chapter you'll see ways to save by sacrificing a little of the kitchen routine.

Some people say "discount" stores have real and rare bargains. Others note that only second-rank merchandise, worth the price tag but no more, can be found on discounters' displays. Both arguments have validity. We will explore ideas for enjoying the real discounts without being taken for off-brand, off-quality goods.

It is on the big-ticket purchases of automobiles, appliances, air conditioners, and the other bulky buys that the biggest savings can be made and the largest sums freed for better living. We're going to examine some ways to get more for less when buying a new car; to save on tires, batteries, and car accessories; to obtain improved gas mileage; to judge the worth of a dealer's warranty on autos and other big-ticket items; and to get what you need from a service contract and not discover, as many have, that "service" is extended only to occurrences that never happen.

In Chapter Five we'll look at how your dwelling dollar can go farther, at leasing a home or apartment or buying into a condominium versus conventional home ownership, at how (sometimes) you can put more money down and take over mortgages negotiated long ago when 4 percent and 5 percent were going interest rates. There are things to look for and look out for in a home or business lease; these can spell lower cost over years to come. There are traps in a conventional mortgage which knowledgeable people avoid. Savings are possible on utility bills, on repairs, on remodeling, and on general dwelling upkeep over the years. We will see ways to find the lowest-cost contractor (who is not necessarily the same fellow who quotes the lowest immediate cost). Available to you are free or minimum-price plans for almost any kind of home addition or new construction you want to undertake. You can rent out part of a house, if this is in conformity with local zoning and other laws, and thereby make an extra apartment pay the whole tab on home notes.

"No one except the very poor and the very rich can afford to be sick in these days of high medical costs and still higher hospital bills," said a recent observer. If you read the suggestions in a coming chapter you will be aware of ways to handle your family's health care without living in dread of bankruptcy from an unexpected lengthy illness, thereby freeing money many families have to save lest the feared ill health or accident becomes reality. The chapter will cite medical and health authorities and give suggestions regarding health insurance policies.

We all dread illness, but vacations are fun and education can lead to better positions and hence higher income for family members. A later chapter will go into ways to vacation at lessened cost, travel for fewer dollars, stay at resorts attended by the wealthy without paying rich men's prices. If you like golf, tennis, bowling, or other sports, it is well to be aware that if you choose the right days and the right seasons for fun, you can save considerably on greens and lanes fees.

In today's science-minded, education-oriented world, the simpler training that would get by in another age won't do. Education costs money. Many people believe—wrongly— that financial aids are made available only to the disadvantaged. Depending upon the university or technical school and upon the courses taken, education can cost remarkably little. Sometimes it costs nothing. A coming chapter details rules and opportunities of the education game.

Certain provisions of law allow you to save toward minors' education by setting aside tax-free funds over the years. The Gifts To Minors acts which make this possible are explained in Chapter Seven.

The next time you seek a loan, ask how much interest the bank will charge. Then inquire whether it is simple interest or whether the banker plans to discount the interest by lopping it off the top. A coming chapter will show the saving you can make by understanding that discount is not interest although the percentage numbers applied to them may be the same. In that chapter you'll find suggestions for negotiating loan rates, for judging whether an offered rate is good under going conditions, and for playing off Banker Bill against Banker Paul down the street. The chapter also goes into alternative loan sources—some lower in cost and longer in payoff terms than banks offer—and suggests ways the bank's routine services can be made to pay off for a man who is in professional practice or who owns a business. You'll see how a knowing few eliminate checking-account charges.

Income you now have can generate extra money on its own. Chapter Nine is devoted to ways you can obtain maximum interest on even small amounts of spare cash while keeping the cash available if you should need it. Moonlighting is a way of life for many. In this chapter you'll find sideline suggestions that can bring in extra money with minimum effort.

Caveat emptor means "buyer beware," and in the free and easy business days of long ago buyers had to beware sharp practices and outright cheating by sellers of many kinds of goods and services. Today, there is increased consumer protection. Our final chapter explains the consumerism movement, its history, and what it has done for more open labeling of products and services. You can obtain value for every dollar if you understand how to call upon governmental and volunteer groups for redress if stuck with unfairly priced or downright gyp goods and services.

TO RECAP

1. Money—the thing which we need to generate better living through management—is not a stable thing. It is inflatable at the will and sometimes the whim of the monetary authorities. Understanding what they are doing and the possible results of monetary contraction/expansion is a first step toward managing for better living.

2. In general, contraction of money supply tends within a

few months to slow a boom and even bring on a recession. Expansion of the supply of dollars tends to brake a drop in the economy and, if continued, to bring about a new boom. Unless carefully managed, such a monetary expansion increases inflation, another factor which your money planning must take into account.

3. Management begins with a personal inventory of talents and assets in order to use personal abilities wisely in programming for better living.

4. This inventory, together with balance sheets of assets, financial and physical, gives a foundation on which to build your personal money management strategy.

5. The budget must be planned to take in a family's wants as well as its needs. Long-range goals must be considered. All family members are affected by a budget; all should be consulted in making it.

6. Keeping a budget is harder than making it. Experts in the field say that certain steps can help: A trial budget spots the wrinkles and irons them out; continuing records show where a budget needs further adjustment over the longer term. A rule against impulse buying avoids wreckage of a carefully considered plan.

2

The Dollar That Buys like Two

THE CHILDREN had filed out of a family conference, two to study their next day's homework while the third went to play in the dying daylight. George and Sophie faced each other across a long coffee table. "We can budget till the end of time," Sophie wailed, "and I'm glad the family has come to agreement on what goes into the budget. But unless you know some way to make $1 do the work of at least $1.25 and I hope as much as $2, this money management plan is not going to work.'

"As they used to say in the old movies—help is on the way," answered George. He swung a leg off the chair arm and poured a thick head on his glass. "There are lots of ways to make one buck do the work of many bucks. Some things come for free, or seem to, although we pay for them in taxes or in the prices of things we purchase anyway. There's extra use in government money. With leasing we can free funds and, often, pay less in the end. There are opportunities to avoid buying altogether. Sometimes, low-cost services are as effective for our purposes as higher-cost services. I talked to Ronnie next door—he's an accountant, and he told me several ways to reduce state, local, and federal taxes. There are things we can do now for which the payoff won't come until retirement, but when it comes it will be big, and will ensure our being able to live, after I stop work, just as if I were still toiling in the commercial vineyards instead of hitting golf balls into the weed patches at the edge of a retirement fairway."

GOVERNMENT MONEY

"There's one thing about the present welfare state that everybody forgets," George continued as he took a long pull that left the beer glass half empty and a mustache of foam around his lips. "The setup is designed to remove any stigma of charity from government aid by making something available to everybody. Even the corporation president who retired with a pension of $100,000 probably collects his social security checks. And you don't have to be retired to eat at the social security table. Many other government aids are available to people above the disadvantaged line. These can help to stretch dollars, and that's important since I see no raise in sight for at least eight months."

As George pointed out, Social Security has broader purposes than the mere pensioning of aged people. Today, according to *Social Security Information for Young Families* (available from the U.S. Department of Health, Education, and Welfare), "the basic idea of Social Security is a simple one."

> During working years employees, their employers, and self-employed people pay social security contributions which are

pooled in three special funds. When earnings stop or are reduced because the worker retires, dies, or becomes disabled, monthly cash benefits are paid from these funds to replace part of the earnings the family has lost.

Part of the contributions go into a hospital insurance fund; and when workers and their dependents reach 65, money from this fund helps pay their hospital bills.

Voluntary medical insurance, also available to people 65 or over, helps pay doctor bills and other medical expenses. Money to pay medical insurance benefits comes from a fourth special fund. Half of the money in this fund comes from the premiums paid by people who have signed up for medical insurance, and the other half is paid by the Federal Government.

"You mean that we've been contributing to help old Uncle Paul all these years when the money might have been provided by Social Security instead?" asked Sophie.

If Uncle Paul was covered by Social Security it would have, freeing funds for better living by families like George's —and yours. Social Security has a wide variety of benefits. It pays to discover which apply to your problems.

Moreover, in the years since World War II, service in Army, Navy, Marine Corps, or Air Force has become a common experience of most young men and a few young women. For this, a grateful government—reminded that elections come up regularly and that veterans' organizations can help to put Congressman Porkbarrel back in office—has provided services which range from hospitalization for service-connected and other injuries to insurance priced at very close to nothing per year.

"But that's wrong!" said Sophie when George outlined the scope of Veterans Administration help. "Nobody should get something for nothing."

"You call our last year's taxes nothing?" snorted George. "We pay for this whether we use it or not. Let's reactivate the life insurance I allowed to lapse after I got out of uniform. It can replace part of the insurance load for which we're presently paying a higher premium. And about Uncle Paul—

wasn't he in World War I or the Spanish-American or maybe the First Punic War? Let's see what VA will do to make Paul's life easier and allow us to withdraw part of the support that's been built into this groaning budget and that can go instead to the better living we're trying to achieve with money management."

WHO NEEDS TO OWN THINGS?

Certainly, not people who have discovered the sometimes magic of leasing.

Companies lease buildings, land, fleets of vehicles, and all manner of things. By doing so, a company can often realize sizable tax advantages (more tax tips later in this chapter). There are other, less significant business advantages, too, which make raw ownership often unrealistic. This works as well for individuals such as you, George, or Ronnie, the bachelor in the next apartment.

"Yes, indeed," answered a tax man to whom I put this question. "Depending upon an individual's occupation and whether some of the things he owns are used to earn a living as well as to live, leasing offers substantial tax advantages. A salesman might use his own car for travel. Say he's compensated by his company on mileage costs, but has to depreciate the car over several years for tax purposes. This means he recovers a frequently unrealistic amount in tax saving each year and, speaking practically, the Treasury on occasion demands depreciation periods which are longer than the term of years over which this salesman will keep the vehicle rolling over country roads and interstate highways. So he is left with a complicated accounting problem when he trades and might, under certain circumstances, have a taxable capital gain on his trade-in. Suppose, however, that he has leased the car. Then he is in a different situation. Every cent he pays out for rent (assuming it is a car employed 100 percent for business travel) becomes deductible in the year it's expended."

Leasing, stripped to its basics, is a financing method. The probability is that our hypothetical salesman might pay the same amount in charges to a loan company or a bank over, for example, a two-year period as he would pay to rent that car for two years. Then it becomes a tax question whether to lease or to buy. Where leasing appears advantageous, there is the added kicker of freeing all capital which would otherwise be tied up in downpayments, etc.

Salesmen are not the only people to whom these tax advantages might apply. A self-employed business man should consider the percentage of business use which applies to any leased asset. Professional people such as dentists, doctors, and architects often use cars (and other private assets) for money-earning purposes part of the time, and under those circumstances they might find leasing a way to live better on the same income by making part of the income available for new spending.

Although the most important single factor in a decision on whether to lease an automobile or living quarters (a leased apartment, for instance, versus a single dwelling or condominium which is owned outright) is the tax angle, there are other factors to be considered before making a decision. These are sideline advantages and serious drawbacks to the leasing bit:

■ *Lower, sometimes no, maintenance.*   A car might carry only the dealer's warranty service, or under certain rental arrangements might have all oil changes, lubrication, etc., included at the lessor's expense.

■ *Easier accounting.*   For a man earning his own keep through self-employment, the advantage of fewer bookkeeping chores can be a sizable one. "This might apply to you and Sophie as individuals despite the fact you are employed by a corporation," Ronnie pointed out, "since all of us have to maintain a lot of ledger work to make our year-end tax accounting balance out."

■ *Freeing of money.*   "By leasing one or two bigger items, I calculate that we'll untie several thousand dollars which are now tied up," George suggested to Sophie after his conference with the accountant. "I might be able to invest that money to bring in added income we can spend for things the family cannot afford at present." (A coming chapter has ideas for this sort of investment to enhance George's and your ability to spend more without making more.)

■ *You forget time's inroads.* Capital assets wear out. A number of them become obsolete because of technological change or because their styling soon begins to have a "last year" look. Renting throws that worry on the lessor's shoulder. When the lease period expires, the lessees (you and George) can demand a later model on signing a new contract.

"All that looks impressive," Sophie said. "But we have to keep one disadvantage in mind before we decide that leasing is the way to find more funds. Remember that at the end of the lease we won't own anything. If we buy and take on the problems of ownership, at the end of whatever might have been a rental period we will still have the asset. It could be beat-up, racked out, obsolete, out of style. But it will be *ours,* and if we do nothing else with it, we can give it to Edith. She's getting to be a big girl and needs grown-up things."

BACK TO THE PEAPOD PATCH

It was late and the last of the children had retired. "Let me freshen your drink, Ron," George said as he reached for ice cubes and the scotch bottle. "We worked out a leasing deal this morning that should save some money, and a celebratory drink is in order."

"Drink to me, then," said Sophie. "While you big brains are telling each other how smart you are, I have figured a method for saving the money we put out in one direction."

Sophie's plan started in the backyard. So can yours.

In that yard, you can grow grass (crab or Bermuda), some altheas, azaleas, and a few crape myrtle trees. You can pave it over and use it as a patio. You can let it run to weeds, mow it regularly, or dig it out to make a swimming pool. Or like Sophie and George, whose muscle power was harnessed to make the plan work, you can grow vegetables.

Says the U.S. Department of Agriculture (*Suburban and Farm Vegetable Gardens*, Home and Garden Bulletin No. 9) about such amateur farming activity by city, suburban, and rural people interested in upping the quality of life on a staid income:

> A good garden adds materially to the well-being of the family by supplying foods that might not otherwise be provided. Fresh vegetables direct from the garden are superior in quality to those generally sold on the market, and in addition are readily available when wanted. As a large number ... now use lockers and home freezers, even more of the vegetables from the garden can be utilized than when canning and fall storage were the only means of preservation. . . . Any gardener needs local information, especially on the earliest and latest safe planting dates for vegetables and any special garden practices and varieties that are best for his location.

People who use home gardens to grow useful, instead of merely ornamental, plants say that the biggest advantage is not the greater quality praised in the USDA publication, but the lower costs. "A packet of seeds costs a quarter," Sophie pointed out that autumn as she and George harvested their home garden, "and after we add some of your sweat, plus a bit of fertilizer, we have many dollars' worth of good eating. Best two-bit deal in the world. I'm going to buy a new cape this winter on the savings."

For maximum savings, a garden grown to eat rather than ornament should be planned with retail prices in mind. It is pointless to plant what is cheap anyway. You want the things likely to be highest in retail price at the time the plants mature. Moreover, as Sophie, George, Edith, Ethelred, and Frederica discovered over their summer of peapod-patch farming, the pleasure of watching things pop out of furrows made in the backyard earth is not least among your gains.

A peapod-patch plan for stretching dollars can involve

clothing as well as food. The coat, dress, or sport jacket you don't replace doesn't cost money, and repairing or making do lets dollars budgeted for clothing spread over other better-living expenditures. A U.S. Department of Agriculture publication, *Clothing Repairs* (Home and Garden Bulletin No. 107) notes:

> You may not enjoy repairing clothes, but it does pay off . . . for the whole family. Now, as always, the stitch-in-time means fewer clothing replacements and more money for other needs. . . . If family members learn respect for their wearables and something about the high cost of rips and tears, that helps."

"Nuts!" said George when Sophie pointed out USDA's words of undying wisdom. "Long ago in England, Beau Brummel said that a tear is something that can happen to any gentleman, but a darn is premeditated poverty. I'm not going to wear darned clothing. Neither will my family. In this competitive world, we can't afford to look poor and the whole purpose of money planning is to live better, not on a downgraded scale."

"Shows how much you know," sniffed Sophie. "See this skirt I'm wearing? Down by the hem is the hole I burned last week when bacon grease splattered on it. I dare you to show me where the hole was. It was rewoven by a professional. And that's what we'll do with all the family's garments, when it is practical to do so, instead of shelling out for new things every time Ethelred catches his trousers on a nail—he seems to look for nails, to judge by the number of times this happens—or Frederica takes a fall on the rough concrete. The 'Y' has a course in basic sewing this fall. I'll invest a few dollars in learning how."

Another USDA Consumer Service pamphlet (Home and Garden Bulletin No. 62) is titled *Removing Stains from Fabrics*. This shows three main types of stains, and lists methods for removing each. It gives poison warnings and shows precautions to take when you set out to save a stained garment instead of replacing it.

THE DOLLAR THAT STRETCHES IN TIME

Even though you have a fixed number of dollars of income, they can go further if you make them move faster. Applied to the overall economy, such an added dimension of money is called velocity. Velocity is added to household dollars when for a time, although not forever, they do double work.

Most corporations pay their debts promptly when due, but not before. Canny company treasurers know that by keeping liquid funds in their own accounts for the maximum length of time, they are enabled to maintain larger "floats" (in family practice this usually means lessened bank charges) and to cover greater area without needing more money. To use this strategy, you should remember that bills are due in twenty-five to thirty days. Payments in less time means that funds you might use for other purposes must be borrowed or the other purposes must be eliminated.

National credit cards such as Master Charge and Bank-Americard assess rates as high as 1½ percent monthly (18 percent a year—no small-change interest) when balances are unpaid for twenty-five days. "This allows a customer to use our money for twenty-five days or longer and not pay any interest at all, provided he is prompt on the twenty-fifth day," pointed out a banker with whom I discussed the practice. "Say he buys a suit on the eighteenth of July. The billing does not go out from our office until the first of August. Payment is due on August 25. Thus the customer who knows how to handle money can stretch his income by employing our funds for a total of thirty-three days (July 18 until August 25) without interest accruing."

The banker went on to point out a time when such a practice would not pay:

"Sometimes, a store or a supplier offers a discount in order to get money in promptly. Such a discount might specify 2 percent off for payment in five or ten days. Your consumer should take advantage of such an offer. Two percent in ten days is 36.5 percent a year return on his money. Even if payable in five days, he'd be realizing half of that, and such earnings don't come along every day."

DON'T BE INSURANCE-POOR

Knowing the four kinds of life insurance can help you to choose a combination that will give maximum protection without running the premium bills so high that you are in the postion of one policyholder who wailed to his agent: "There is one possibility you haven't taken into account. If I die, everybody is well off. But suppose I live? How is my family to eat with such a large hunk of income going to pay your bills?"

In the excellent advisory *Consumers All*, Lawrence A. Jones of the USDA explains the four kinds this way:

> The four basic policies of life insurance are term, whole-life or straight, limited-payment, and endowment.
>
> They differ mainly in whether the insurance is permanent or temporary and the extent to which savings, as well as insurance, are involved. . . . The best insurance for you may be a combination of two or more types.
>
> Term insurance is protection bought for a limited period or term, usually 5 or 10 years. Protection ends at the end of the term, and the policy has no savings or cash value. Because it is strictly for protection, the cost for young people is relatively low, but the cost increases with each renewal and becomes prohibitive at older ages.
>
> Straight life insurance is commonest. Sometimes called whole-life or ordinary insurance, it runs for your lifetime. The premium depends on your age when you first take the insurance and stays the same each year. Part of the premium goes into savings, and the cash value of the policy increases as the years go by. After the need for insurance is past, the cash value can be obtained for retirement or other purposes.
>
> Limited-payment life insurance is similar to straight life insurance, except that you pay premiums only for a stated period, say 20 or 30 years or up to age 65. At the end of the period, the insurance continues as a paid-up policy and no more premium payments are required. It is designed mainly

for people who do not want to pay premiums as they get older. The cash value increases faster than with a straight life policy, but it is more expensive for the protection received.

Endowment insurance is important for its savings features. Money accumulates faster than with other types of policies and at a certain date it is paid as income or in lump sum to the insured, and the insurance protection ends. Should the insured person die before that date, the insurance is paid to his beneficiary. Because savings are emphasized, endowments are the most costly way to buy insurance protection.

The so-called family income plan offered by most life insurance companies combines one of the permanent policies, usually straight life, with gradually decreasing term insurance. For example, a young family covered by a 20-year family income policy of 10 thousand dollars would have that amount of permanent insurance. If the father dies within 20 years after he took out the policy, his family would also receive a stipulated monthly income during the remainder of the 20-year period—a period when income would be most needed.

Figuring out how much insurance you need and how much you can spend for it will also help you decide the kind to buy. If income is extremely short, you might consider term insurance as a temporary measure. Transfer it to permanent, straight life insurance as soon as possible, however. Until your needs for basic protection are met, it is best to postpone taking out endowment or limited-payment life insurance.

Also, keep in mind that to protect dependents in a family, the income earner's life is the one to be insured. Hold off insuring the lives of children until you can afford to do so.

Special uses for insurance should be considered in any money management plan. Business and professional partnerships often carry policies on the life of each partner; they enable the family of a deceased partner to be bought out by surviving partners. Life policies with declining coverage are frequently used to ensure payoff of a home mortgage, so that if George were to die, Sophie and the children could continue in their condominium apartment. Similar policies in conjunction with a savings plan involving mutual funds work so that the estate Ronnie hopes to accumulate over ten years will be paid for and go intact to his sister Gwendolyn, should Ronnie shuffle unexpectedly off this mortal coil. (A warning about insurance: Buy as much as you need. Change the form to fit new circumstances. But don't overinsure. In an age of inflation, no one form of saving or estate building is best.)

Insurance rates are not always the same for the same coverage. This is as true of automobile, casualty, fire, theft, windstorm, etc., as for life insurance. Shop several agencies. Take into consideration the probity of the seller, for, as some Georges and Ronnies have discovered bitterly, the cheapest insurance does not always insure best. Says the Federal Trade Commission in its Consumer Bulletin No. 1, *Pitfalls to Watch for in Mail Order Policies:*

> Insurance policies sent to you through the mails by some companies may contain pitfalls which you should watch out for before deciding whether you want to buy the policy which has been sent to you.
>
> If you receive any letters or other literature in the mail asking you to take out an insurance policy and enclosing copies of the policy, read the policy carefully. If you receive a copy of what appears to be an actual policy with your name already on it, remember that this is still a form of advertising. Read it carefully.
>
> Don't be put off because of the difficulty of understanding the language in which the policy is written. Most insurance policies are written in a style which is difficult for the ordinary layman to understand. This is particularly true for those portions of the policy which describe the limitations and restrictions in the policy or when the company will make payments to you. . . . Perhaps the most important feature of an insurance policy is the kind of risk which it will insure you against. This is the portion of the policy which should be read most carefully. Only you can decide what it is you want but think carefully about it before deciding to buy. It is too late after you have paid the premium for many years to learn that you were not covered for the kinds of risks or losses that you thought you were.

Whether you buy by mail or through Fred the local agent down at the corner, you should be aware of certain ways to save:

1. Don't insure too many small things. This is likely to run up costs unnecessarily. A small loss won't hurt, so take the risk.

2. Most companies sharply depreciate a new car as it gets to its third year. They tend to give "blue book" settlements; that is, instead of paying for all repair costs in situations where, according to the blue book, the worth of the car is less than the cost of putting it back in operation, they reserve the right to pay a policyholder only the depreciated value. You can seldom buy a replacement for this amount. Stop all except liability and property damage coverage after the point where the payoff on an accident won't be in proportion to the cost of fire, theft, and accident coverage. Where and how this point is reached—and whether it is reached—will depend upon the insurance cost structure in your state at the moment.

3. But don't neglect liability coverage. In an age when juries tend to hand out big damage verdicts, the loss from an accident due to your negligence or the claim of a neighbor who slipped on your uneven sidewalk and broke his collar bone is likely to be big enough to wreck a financial plan for years to come. Without liability coverage you might live worse on less money instead of living better on the same income.

4. Medical, health, and hospitalization coverage is vital. It will be treated in more detail as part of a later chapter on health care costs.

5. Take advantage of group policies where you can. This low (and sometimes no) cost coverage need not be duplicated by having private policies which, together with group coverage, would insure your family beyond a needed amount.

6. Pay premiums annually or semiannually where the payment can be worked into the budget. Longer-spaced payments save you money.

7. Consider the advice of an insurance professional. Conditions vary from state to state and decade to decade, just as needs vary from family to family. The pro with up-to-date knowledge of possible combinations can save many times his fee.

TAX DOLLARS BUY TWICE

"Two long, cold ones—fast," said George, putting his tennis racket on the table and dabbing with a wet handkerchief at perspiration that had sloshed over his brows and into his eyes. "It's a hot day to play three sets, Ronnie. I've been meaning to ask you—as an accountant—what are some of those ideas for tax savings you mentioned to Soph yesterday?"

Ronnie spoke slowly. "You have to start with a concept about tax savings as a part of a money management plan," he said. "A tax-saved dollar buys twice. It is not a dollar on which you have to pay tax again (under most circumstances, at any rate). Say you make $100. Depending upon your tax bracket, that might shrink anywhere from $16 to $50 in federal taxation alone, and then in many states another nick would go into the maw of the state treasury—sometimes cities take their whack at you with a local income levy, too. If you can avoid paying some of this, the saving isn't like that first $100. It does not (again, in most cases) incur new taxation. That is why tax savings are so important to every family seeking a better life on the same income."

Because families' tax setups are no more alike than Edith, Ethelred, and Frederica are identical to other children of the same age and sex, tax-savings plans have to be individually tailored. The advice of a tax lawyer, a certified public accountant, or some other expert pays more than it costs, and expert advice can set up savings for years to come. Free, but less personal, help can sometimes be had from taxing agencies.

"So you see, George," continued Ronnie, "I can't give you more than generalities here. Within that framework, I have listed a number of ways to lessen federal and local taxes. These might not all apply to you. But they should help in setting a strategy of planning for lessened taxes."

Here is Ronnie's list:

■ 1. *If in a high tax bracket, form a trust.* This can put income into the hands of beneficiaries in lower brackets. But the plan has a drawback—it takes ownership away from the grantor. Regarding this, the Northern Trust Company of Chicago, in an advisory booklet, *Ten Reasons Why a Living Trust Makes Living Easier,* points out that "in the area of income taxes, there can be savings by means of the so-called 'ten year' trusts you may have heard about.... Detailed statutory rules must be precisely followed. The gist of these rules is that an inordinate degree of control over the income or principal of the trust cannot be reserved by the grantor; otherwise the income will be taxable to him. Nor can the income defray an obligation he has incurred or which the law imposes on him."

■ 2. *If self-employed, go Keogh.* The law has been operational since 1962. It allows self-employed people to put off certain retirement income, and in doing so it lets John Jones, owner of the corner haberdashery, enjoy deferred tax provisions that were always available to Richard Jones, employee of the big store across the street, which has a sizable payroll and an employee retirement plan and which sometimes furnishes rough competition to the small Jones store. Says *Retirement Plans for Self-Employed Individuals,* a publication of the Treasury Department's Internal Revenue Service:

> The primary purpose of the act is to allow self-employed individuals to be covered by qualified plans and to extend to them some of the favorable tax benefits which have been available to corporate stockholder-employees.

Keogh plans are usually implemented through insurance policies or by purchase of mutual fund shares.

■ 3. *If a home is used to carry on some work, it can sometimes be used to reduce taxation.* The operable instructions that cover this situation can be found in *Your Federal Income Tax*, published by the Treasury Department. According to the 1970 edition:

> If you use a portion of your home for business purposes on a regular basis, the portion of the depreciation and other costs incurred in maintaining the residence that is properly attributable to the space used in business is a question of fact.
>
> However, if circumstances warrant, you may allocate expenses by comparing the number of rooms or square feet of space used for business purposes to the total number of rooms or square feet in the home, and apply the ratio to the total of each expense attributable to your use of part of the home for business purposes.
>
> If you regularly use a portion of the home for business purposes only part of the time, a further allocation must be made on the basis of the ratio of the time you actually use the area for business purposes to the total time it is available for all uses.

■ 4. *Keep up with changing tax-law features.* The new law places a maximum percentage bite on earned income. This makes it advantageous—where possible and where legal—to put income into a year when it might be subject to lower taxation.

■ 5. *Some income isn't "income" at all for tax purposes.* The distinction depends upon a taxpayer's age, the source of the money, and the reason for which it was paid. Sickness and injury benefits may be excludable. If you worked under U.S. civil service and retired on disability, for example, "your annuity is considered sick pay until you reach retirement age," according to *Your Federal Income Tax,* 1970 edition. Moreover, according to the same source, "if you are granted an option to buy stock or other property as payment for your services as an employee or independent contractor, you will ordinarily realize income taxable as compensation. However, if your option is a statutory stock option—a qualified stock option, an employee stock purchase plan option, or a restricted stock option—special rules generally postpone the tax until you sell or exchange your shares of stock."

Federal taxation is only part of the bite on income. Local taxes hurt, as cities, states, and counties participate in programs for the disadvantaged and in efforts to brighten blighted areas. Sometimes, sales and gasoline taxes can be avoided by making larger purchases in a county other than your own—before doing this, make certain it is legal in your locality—and the increasing heavy real property taxes of states and cities can sometimes be lightened by exemptions. In my state, there is a doubled homestead exemption available to veterans. "I was amazed to find that a large number of people for whom we voted in the exemption didn't know about this," a state senator told me recently.

RETIREMENT: PLAN NOW FOR PAYOFF LATER

As with death and taxes, retirement comes to us all unless we happen to step in front of a fast-moving truck during our younger and middle years. Much current literature stresses the troubles of people who have not planned in advance the hobbies, travel, or other postwork occupations that will keep them from staring at four walls of a room and, in the words of one unhappy retiree, "trying to extract some pleasure out of fishing eighteen hours every day because there isn't anything to do except fish."

"Those people don't know what retirement trouble is," snorted a seventy-three-year-oldster with whom I discussed the problems of life in the years after a company president has presented the traditional gold watch. "I planned to retire under a set of conditions that prevailed at the time I was forty. A nickel was more than a sales-tax token then, and even a penny bought something. Now the money won't stretch. I have to fish for money—I haven't pity to spare on people who go fishing only because there is nothing else to do at their age."

Money management must thus include wise retirement planning. That planning has to take into account future as well as present conditions. If it is wisely done, the present dollar can do the work of two.

One way to bring about such a happy result is through Keogh planning, discussed under Ronnie's exposition of income tax tips. Because of the taxation angle, a Keogh plan—if you are self-employed—stretches dollars by deferring taxation on such currency of the realm.

People on wage or salary frequently have an option of how much to contribute to retirement or similar plans. It is a usual practice for company contributions to match the individual's. Thus each dollar you spend can do double work toward a more secure future.

And smart retirement planning should provide for *phases.*

Writing for people about to retire, I noted in an article in the July, 1970, issue of *Dynamic Retirement* that "planning for an affluent retirement breaks into two phases with a slower, smaller transition between them."

In the first phase, we try for growth. Not very rapid growth of the sort exemplified by what were called the go-go stocks in 1968; in 1969 and 1970, those went-went. Say you have $20,000 cash capital. If this should be lost by trying too hard in go-go stocks, or any other way of attempting to make it in a big hurry, then such a stake is not easily replaced. We will look for growth, but not necessarily rapid growth.

Later on, we'll institute good income-producing investments. With those, too, we will try for gradual growth—this time of income itself—so that inflation during your retirement years won't render those years progressively more strapped and less pleasurable.

We'll transition slowly between those two phases. A quick switchover might be unadvisable for the soundest way to get somewhere quickly is not always the fast way. Your capital consists of more than merely cash in the bank. There is the value of your home, for example, perhaps long paid for and worth many times what you paid. You may want to move on retirement to a sun climate. Will you be able to sell that house in a hurry? Do you know what you wish to accomplish with proceeds of such a sale? Will you buy a new home elsewhere? Invest the money? Use part for a condominium purchase, part to produce income? Such decisions should be accomplished slowly.

Now all growth-type investments you can make would be as easily sold as stocks and mutual funds. You should think in terms of one or more of these growth vehicles:

Stocks of good corporations with growth potential.

Mutual funds aimed at capital appreciation (but not necessarily at in-out stock market trading to produce it; such funds tend to be winners one year, losers the next).

Real estate with good, growing rentals.

The remodel-resell property market in which you can sometimes find rundown houses at distress prices, remodel to the level of the neighborhood and resell at a capital gain.

Participation in petroleum drilling and production, in citrus groves, or cattle raising. In these there is tax shelter in addition to growth potential.

You should not spread yourself thinly among all of these. But all should be considered.

HIRE THE EXPERTS WHO WORK FOR LESS

"Here's a way to afford all kinds of small services formerly out of our reach," said Sophie as she placed dinner dishes in the dishwasher and rinsed table scraps into the garbage disposer. "Remember our college days? Today, many students often are looking for outside income just as you and I did when we first met at the state university. Some are pretty expert, too.

"When my mother and father asked for pictures of Edith, Ethelred, and Frederica last month, we couldn't afford the $52 a regular studio wanted. Today I had an idea. I called the job reference bureau on the campus and asked if a student who knew photography wanted a few hours' work. Out came a journalism major who spent the afternoon shooting Edith, Ethelred, and Frederica. Next time we need odd things like that which might be performed by a student, I'm going to call the campus again. Students might need the employment to stretch out their tuition costs, and we will benefit from services many people with our income can't afford."

TO RECAP:

1. Better living can be obtained from the dollar bills that can be stretched to do the work of $1.25 to $2 and sometimes more. Where income can't be stretched out in absolute dollars, the dollars must stretch to buy more.

2. In taxes or in the prices of goods and services, we often pay for things we don't use. An initial step for maximizing the purchasing power of income is to obtain as many of these free, or semifree, things as possible. Federal and state governments provide many services. A first place to look is Social Security, which in today's welfare state covers more than the original old-age assistance for which it was instituted. The Veterans Administration and other bureaus of national and local government offer aids and services that cost nothing and that frequently duplicate budget items outside the cover of the governmental umbrella.

3. Leasing is a way to save tax dollars over the cost of owning the same items, and to free the funds which are tied up in ownership of wheels, bricks, mortar, grass plots, or other assets for the purchase of items which cannot otherwise be afforded. Leasing has drawbacks, too; these must be taken into consideration.

4. Seed packets cost less than fresh vegetables. Families that grow produce say that there is fun as well as saving for those who plow the backyard for radishes, artichokes, corn, or beets.

5. If you know how to do it, clothing in need of replacement because of stains, burns, and rips can often be salvaged—salvaging at the same time the cost of new garments.

6. It is possible to use others' money for short periods of time without payment of interest. This adds to the buying power of fixed income.

7. While insurance is necessary for everyone, many of us overinsure. Study of changing needs for life insurance, fire, casualty, and liability frequently discloses areas for saving.

8. Tax-saved dollars can buy twice, since a dollar not ex-

pended on taxes functions exactly like a dollar of new income but does not incur the shrinkage from taxation to which a new dollar is subject.

9. Proper early planning for retirement puffs up the eventual value of today's income dollar.

10. Frequently, as Sophie discovered, expert services are available at cut rates from such sources as work-hungry college students.

3

How the Smart Shopper Shops

You're reading through the afternoon paper and there it is on page 23—a sale of men's suits advertised at only $35. The quality is promised as comparable to $75 garments, and you are assured that the suits have been made by a nationally known factory whose name the store won't tell in view of the low, low, *low* price. "Hey, Soph," you call to your spouse, who is out in the kitchen making chuck steak look like filet mignon so your new budget can bring you better living on the same income. "Here's a deal down at Lemuel D. Plainfellow's Big Bargain Store. Guess I'd better rush there in the morning before they run out. Two of those bargains should set up my clothing needs for next season and save a lot on what we planned to pay."

Guess again.

Unless you know the source of those suits and just *how* bighearted Lemuel "compared" them to $75 clothes, you might not be buying a bargain at all but only a $35 suit marked at $35. This might be true even if, as advertised, it is made by a hush-hush manufacturer of big-name, more expensive garments. Plymouths are made by Chrysler, yet few can be fooled into thinking that an Imperial is obtainable at a Valiant price tag; clothing manufacturers, like auto makers, turn out products tailored for many price lines.

This chapter is about how to be a smart shopper and, in the process, make the income dollars buy a better standard of living.

SHOPPING DOWNTOWN

Begin with an awareness that there are different sources from which the same kinds of merchandise can be bought, and that one isn't necessarily or always "better" than another —all have advantages, and they shine under different circumstances and at different times.

Take Lemuel D. Plainfellow's Big Bargain Store.

It was founded by Lemuel's grandfather seventy years ago on the same site but not in the same building that presently houses the store, and it has grown since Grandpop Plainfellow's time from a soft goods outlet, selling mainly fabrics that ladies sewed into the dresses of the day, to a full-line department store handling a little of everything on its six floors. The town has grown with the store, but not to an extent that Lemuel cannot still call many of his old customers by name when he stations himself in a ground-floor center aisle every noon, as his father and grandfather had done before him. Lemuel's sons are beginning to share management of the store whose total ownership they will one day inherit, but they recognize very few of the customers, with the exception of personal acquaintances such as George, with whom Lemuel Junior attended two business-administration classes and a language course at the state university.

Prices at the Plainfellow store are not always the cheapest in town. "But you can depend upon one thing in regard to that advertisement for a $35 suit," Sophie called to George from the kitchen. "You are going to get honest value from Plainfellow's. And if you have any trouble with the merchandise, a department store such as this will make good on your complaint, probably far in excess of any legal obligation to do so."

Plainfellow's Big Bargain Store is typical of most of the nation's department stores and the established, old-line clothing and other stores. Its prices will be competitive. They probably won't be as low as the cheapest discounter might charge. But the store will give charge-account service; it will deliver what you buy to your home; it will stand behind its merchandise. ("I'd rather have Plainfellow's store guarantee than the warranties of most manufacturers," noted Sophie. "They will go beyond strictly legalistic obligation when there's a fault in something I buy—and even sometimes when the fault is mine rather than that of the merchandise of the store.")

Good faith, convenience, and wide selections are what stores like Plainfellow's have to offer.

But when such a store puts on a sale, the customer is not certain of finding a bargain. As Sophie pointed out, the $35 suit will be honest value. It may not be the same as a $75 suit.

When buying at store sales, you should know the difference in the phraseology used to describe merchandise offered as a "$75 value" and merchandise which "compares with" clothing usually sold at $75; this is not necessarily worth more than the amount for which it sells unless it carries a brand name which is recognizable as one normally commanding the higher price. But if the store uses words such as "formerly $75" or "regularly $75," chances are that a true, honest-to-God, spit-in-your-eye $75 bargain is being offered at $35. *Especially* if you can see the big brand name described above and if you know a believable reason why the $75 suit should go on sale at $35. (Realistic reasons might include the offering of a last year's style or model or a purchase of distress merchandise. Merchandise is in "distress" when it must be sold. Perhaps Plainfellow bought the suits from a manufacturer whose deep financial troubles produced a need for money in big chunks from any source, and who was willing to sacrifice part of his inventory at a loss in order to alleviate this monetary distress.)

Even "regularly $75" items are not always true bargains, however. Although reputable stores such as Plainfellow's seldom use such a tactic, there are retailers who follow a practice described by the Federal Trade Commission in its advisory booklet *Guide against Deceptive Pricing*:

> The following is an example of a price comparison based on a fictitious former price. John Doe is a retailer of Brand X fountain pens, which cost him $5 each. His usual markup is 50% over cost; that is, his regular retail price is $7.50. In order subsequently to offer an unusual "bargain," Doe begins offering Brand X at $10 per pen. He realizes that he will be able to sell no, or very few, pens at this inflated price. But he doesn't care, for he maintains that price for only a few days. Then he "cuts" the price to its usual level—$7.50—and advertises: "Terrific Bargain: X Pens, Were $10, Now Only $7.50!" This is obviously a false claim. The advertised "bargain" is not genuine.

As a general thing, such outlets as Plainfellow's Big Bargain Store offer wide selections. Occasionally these stores are willing, at no added charge, to order for a customer a special model or size from the factory.

Stiff competition to Plainfellow's Big Bargain Store is furnished by Friendly Frank, the discount house out on the fringe of town. Discount stores are nearly always located in a district of lower rents and lessened accessibility. Often, they offer free parking, and they are usually open six nights a week, occasionally on Sundays as well.

Prices at the discount store tend to be lower than at Plainfellow's. But the store does not as a rule offer free (or any other kind of) delivery. Nor does it accept charge accounts or permit long-term credit buying by its customers. (Many such stores now accept the big bank cards such as Master Charge and BankAmericard; on these you can usually pay over extended periods, although in doing so you incur sizable interest charges—more on this in a moment.) Friendly Frank's probably won't alter the suit, should George buy there rather than at Plainfellow's.

"Cheap! Cheap! My merchandise is cheap—and just as good as Plainfellow's" is the appeal made by Friendly Frank the discounter. He usually *is* lower in price than Plainfellow's, but not always for the same merchandise.

Not long ago, George shopped for a piece of luggage to take on a trip. He found a nationally known name brand in Plainfellow's third-floor luggage department at $43.95 plus sales tax. That evening, he and Sophie drove out to Friendly Frank's to look for similar goods.

"Here's a piece like it for only $28.50," George shouted to Sophie when they reached Frank's luggage section. "The salesman says it's made by the same manufacturer that made Plainfellow's $43.95 two-suiter."

"He may be correct," Sophie pointed out, "but it doesn't bear that manufacturer's name. I wonder whether this one has flaws that would make him ashamed to put the advertised brand name on it. I can see two hinges instead of three; maybe some of the other features are inferior, too. Let's buy the $28.50 item, but let's not think we're getting goods identical to the $43.95 luggage at Plainfellow's Big Bargain Store."

Many of the items at Friendly Frank's are indeed national brands which sell at prices lower than those that established merchants such as Plainfellow can offer, given the department store's higher overhead which results from more customer services. But a great many items on Frank's shelves and on the shelves of discount outlets that are similar to Frank's are almost, but often not quite, identical to the brand-name items with which they are compared. I discussed this matter with the head of a local Better Business Bureau. "People do find bigger values sometimes at Friendly Frank's," he told me. "Often they find a sound value for the money, but no true 'discount' because the 'discount' merchandise is sufficiently different from the item with which it is price-compared that trying to equate the two is something like making a comparison between pecans and walnuts. Both are nuts, both grow on trees, yet they are not the same. You may prefer either one—you may also prefer Frank's offered 'values' to Lemuel Plainfellow's higher-priced merchandise. You should be aware that in either case you are exercising personal preference, not necessarily securing a bargain from either outlet."

The question of brand versus offbrand merchandise is a hard one. But on it can depend the real bargain which smart shoppers seek in order to live better on the same means.

Said President Richard M. Nixon in his message of October 30, 1969, recommending passage of an act to protect consumers:

> . . . I believe the buyer in America has the right to make an intelligent choice among products and services.
>
> The buyer has the right to accurate information on which to make his free choice.
>
> The buyer has the right to expect that his health and safety are taken into account by those who seek his partonage.
>
> The buyer has the right to register his dissatisfaction, and have his complaint heard and weighed, when his interests are badly served. . . .
>
> . . . No matter how alert and resourceful a purchaser may be, he is relatively helpless unless he has adequate, trustworthy information about the product he is considering and *knows what to make of that information.* [Italics are the President's.] The fullest product description is useless if a consumer lacks the understanding or the will to utilize it.

The consumerism movement, and how it can fit into your plans for better living on the same income through effective money management, will be treated in detail in a later chapter. At this point, however, we should understand the matter of comparisons between brand and offbrand merchandise.

■ You may be buying greater satisfaction in a brand name. People appreciate a Cadillac over a Chevrolet, to some degree because it is a lot more car and partly for the fun and prestige of driving a Caddy. If your host hangs up your coat when you visit, you're likely to be understandably prouder, should the lapel turn back to show the name tag of a big brand rather than the house label of Friendly Frank the discounter. Enjoyment is one of the things for which you pay. So if the brand gives it to you in greater degree, then you may be living better by purchasing the known name tag.

■ Facts about the merchandise are frequently revealed by the label or by literature which, often as a legal requirement, accompanies merchandise. Take clothing. On this subject, the Federal Trade Commission said in a booklet, *Look for That Label:*

> Manufacturing and processing skills in the textile and fur industries have reached a point where no amount of narrow-eyed examination or fingering or stroking of their products can give you absolute assurance you know what you are buying. You also would have to have a chemical laboratory, a microscope and months of training to be sure appearances were not deceptive.
>
> Fortunately, reputable producers, manufacturers and sellers wanted the truth about their products known. They did not relish the idea of cheap substitutes being passed off as the real thing. And the public joined them in wanting protection from the spurious seller who would upgrade inferior merchandise by deviously and falsely describing it. The result was that Congress passed laws necessary to assure that purchasers get the kind of textiles and furs they pay for. . . . Occasionally a merchant in his zeal for creating an atmosphere of elegance for his store removes these legally required labels in the belief they insult his reputation for integrity. You might do well to congratulate him on his reputation, but certainly you would do even better to insist upon receiving the protection the law affords you. Incidentally, gyp artists are also too elegant to permit the necessary labels to be attached to their merchandise.

In the realm of furs and fabrics, descriptive labels can tell you a lot, but only about the material. They cannot tell you much about the tailoring or the style sense of the people who put the material together into a garment. Of such values you will have to judge for yourself.

In other areas, you can compare horsepowers, guarantees (and the good faith of those making the guarantees), content, apparent workmanship, and obvious items such as the hinges on the two pieces of luggage which George found at Plainfellow's Big Bargain Store and at Friendly Frank's. All can help in firming a judgment between national brand and offbrand merchandise.

Label information which will assist you to find the items which serve your needs at the best price is not the concern of government and industry groups alone. But a program undertaken by Federated Department Stores indicated that few take fullest advantage of this kind of information. In the company's booklet *Buying Guide Tag Program,* it reported:

> An experiment . . . to develop a Buying Guide Tag System, and to try it for a limited time with customers buying certain products.
>
> The project was undertaken with these conditions: (1) Lazarus would design and place Buying Guide Tags on each item, with the understanding that ultimately such service should be provided by others than retailers. (2) For reasons explained below, the experiment would be limited to three small appliances—steam irons, blenders, and electric percolators—with a high sales volume. (3) The tags would not attempt to evaluate the product since the retailer could not be "judge" of the "goodness" of varying qualities or features of different appliances. Consequently, the tags would simply contain comparative information on performance characteristics, particular features, etc. (4) The experiment would have no unusual demonstrations, promotions or sales efforts beyond the normal context of business operations. (5) After a limited period of time, evaluation of the experiment, necessarily limited and provisional in character, would be made available to all interested parties.

Based upon consumer studies, interviews with salespeople, and department managers' comments, Federated reached certain conclusions:

> 1. Any significant sales effect for specific models was not discernible. The sales pattern continued to be similar to our historic patterns.
> 2. The pattern of customer returns also followed patterns of past years.

3. Customer reaction to the tags was positive, but only mildly so.

4. Sales people benefited from readily accessible point-of-sale information. They were able to give the customer more complete information on the product.

5. For a period during the course of the test, manufacturers' tags were displayed in conjunction with the Buying Guide Tag on the test appliances. (It should be noted that of the 143 models used in the pilot program, only 17 or approximately 12% had manufacturers' tags designed to be attached to the appliance.) Customer observations during this period indicated that, of those customers who did look at appliances containing both tags, there was no specific preference for the Buying Guide Tag.

If you, George, Sophie, and Ronnie find such labeling helpful, your local Plainfellow's might be persuaded to try an experiment like Federated's.

It is a mistake to take quantity prices without checking the unit price to be sure the quantity figure is a true bargain. In one experiment in human behavior, 25-cent merchandise was thrown on a table under a sign "Three for 79¢." The quantity price—higher than the price of the merchandise by the unit—outsold the unit price!

Frequently, industry sources have set up information standards against which you can weigh the merits of competitive merchandise. There are consumer publications which make comparisons between products. "Before we use these, let's make sure in our own minds that we're aware they usually give subjective judgments, not objective comparisons," Sophie noted as she and George examined the luggage in their living room. "Still, they're possibly better than no comparison standard at all, and if we are going to get more for our shopping dollar, we have to use some standard."

There are times when even Friendly Frank and Lemuel Plainfellow, honest merchants both, are led astray in offering bargains. Then they tend to instruct salesmen that the merchandise is "nailed to the floor." That means woe to the salesman who actually sells the advertised $35 suit. He is expected, instead, to point out its flaws once the customer is in the store with his cash or credit card in his hand. Then the salesman is to upgrade the prospect to a more expensive purchase.

"You have every right to buy an advertised special whether the merchant wants to sell it or not," advised my informant at the Better Business Bureau. "If you insist, he'll sell—and you'll probably have a real bargain."

"Bait advertising," said the Federal Trade Commission in an advisory titled *Guides against Bait Advertising*, "is an alluring but insincere offer to sell a product or service which the advertiser in truth does not intend or want to sell. Its purpose is to switch consumers from buying the advertised merchandise, in order to sell something else, usually at a higher price or on a basis more advantageous to the advertiser. The primary aim of a bait advertisement is to obtain leads as to persons interested in buying merchandise of the *type* [italics mine] so advertised."

In addition to Plainfellow's Big Bargain Store and Friendly Frank's out on the skirts of town where parking is plentiful and hours are long, George and Sophie can shop other kinds of retailers for many of their merchandise needs.

Mail-order outlets often feature real bargains. But you have to be careful when ordering by mail. You will seldom be cheated outright. But some (happily a small fringe) refuse refunds, send second-rate merchandise, cash your check but hold your merchandise delivery for weeks and occasionally months.

"However," Sophie remarked as she signed the check to enclose with a mail order and licked the stamp to send it off, "in most cases I find mail-order merchants readier to make refunds than in-town sellers. They cannot sell an unseen item unless you know they'll take it back, and the few times I require an exchange or want a refund, I usually have it by return post. Not everything offered by mail is a bargain. But some things are. When I find them, I have opportunity for squeezing a little more mileage from our budget."

"Bully!" answered George. "See if you can squeeze enough so I can buy two of the suits advertised by Plainfellow's."

But why buy retail at all? Who has no friends able to buy wholesale for him? It's hard to resist such a deal. However, sometimes it pays to stand off and look at the wholesale deal.

"I'm one who believes in extreme skepticism," said Ronnie as the three neighbors discussed their mutual problem of making a set amount of wampum do more than the work for which it was intended by the great wampum manufacturer in Washington. "Not long ago I bought a suit wholesale. A real bargain, it seemed, until I had to pay extra for alterations, go out in my car to pick it up, and miss an hour's work in order to get to the wholesale office before it closed. Finally I had to have a tailor sew on two loose buttons that the retailer, if I'd been smart enough to buy retail, would have sewn for nothing."

Before you buy wholesale—which is sometimes, but not all of the time, a way to save—you should compare the price with the retail price. Wholesalers usually have several price scales, depending upon quantities in which a retailer purchases from them. The price asked by a wholesaler selling single items might therefore be slightly above the retail price at which another outlet, purchasing in carloads, could price the same merchandise for retail sale.

The wholesaler will seldom take back a purchase on any ground. Sometimes the retailer, too, says, "Sorry, no returns." The reason may be that you bought on sale, or purchased on Tuesday, or maybe he's a fellow who doesn't like returns. What then?

"There is always recourse to the company president," said George. "Forcing a return where we're legally and morally entitled to one becomes important if we are to make this money management work so we can indeed live better on the same amount of lettuce. Remember that shirt I bought which came apart at the seams the first time you washed it? The clerk said there were no returns on sale merchandise. I wrapped it up, sent it with a letter to old Lemuel, and sure enough—back came a check in full refund."

Many smart shoppers routinely say "Charge it" for any purchase. They figure, usually correctly, that the merchant will more willingly give credit to an account where the customer still possesses the option of saying, "Nuts—I just won't pay!" than where real bills and real change have to be taken out of the register to make a cash refund.

There is a new movement afoot aimed at obtaining more for less through people's joining together in buying clubs. Farmers form cooperatives to purchase what they need and to sell what they produce. A buying club functions much like a farmer's cooperative. Housewives, plumbers, secretaries, single gals, people with three wives and ten children, doctors, dentists, and Indian chiefs band together in these clubs.

"My group started from the roots of an investment club," one buying co-op leader told me. "We are a bunch of neighbors who, several years ago, got together to invest in the stock market, hoping that our combined ignorance of financial things might be a little better than our individual lack of knowledge. Together, we have learned a lot and had a lot of fun—and we have made some money, too.

"One day, a member asked: 'With all this inflation, why don't we buy household things the way we buy stocks collectively? Stocks seldom sell for less in bigger quantities, but clothing, appliances, and other needs can frequently be purchased at lower individual cost.' We took her up on the idea. Our buying club is an actuality. It has been estimated that members save as much as $400 per year per family through the club, which quantifies their small buys into large orders."

Another group activity that can help you live better on the same income was described as a price posse in my book *How You Can Beat Inflation*. In this book, an enthusiastic housewife explained the plan:

> "We'll begin at the school," Alice said. "All of us have children there. So do 400 other parents. If we start with the families with whom we are in contact, we can later spread out to other school parent groups, then to existing organizations of a different kind, until we cover the city."
>
> At the next monthly PTA meeting she arose. "What I have to say may be outside the regular purpose of a school parents' organization," she began, "but it is important to all parents'

ability to provide for their children. If the suggested action cannot be done by a PTA group, let's form a separate organization, and as soon as routine school business has been concluded, we will adjourn the PTA and re-meet as a price posse. My proposal is this. . . ."

An hour later a quickly organized price posse had formed and determined upon certain steps:

"We will jointly agree to fight every price increase that comes along," Alice said. "Maybe the merchant whose costs are higher has to up his price. But we are hurt should he do so. If the group refuses to sit still for *any* inflationary increases, perhaps the merchant, along with the distributor, manufacturer, union leader, and everyone else, will give thought to cost cutting instead of price increases. Eventually the high cost-spiral might be rolled back." The posse agreed.

"Our posse possesses three weapons," said the housewife. "One is publicity. The second is moral force. The third is a buying strike." Again, the group agreed.

"We will first try moral force when a price goes up," Alice went on. "If three or four of us call as a group upon every passer of higher prices, show the problem both nationally and locally, and explain the necessity for fighting an increase at its birth before it can grow into a big cost-push able to spawn fresh price increases, then a certain percentage of businessmen will join us.

"For those who don't, we'll use the publicity weapon. In the West, where my grandfather still rides a trail, during the old wild and woolly days the practice was to quickly try malefactors who were caught by a posse. If the judgment was guilty, sentence was speedily carried out. For those days and those ways, nothing but such rough and ready justice would have sufficed. We will hold a public 'trial' of every firm and individual who raises prices. The newspapers, radio stations, and television newsmen will be invited. At first they will come for the novelty news value of a mock trial of price offenders. Later, I hope, they will continue to report our vigilante trials because they will see the merit of the method and the absolute need to do something to mitigate inflation before we all end up carrying a wheelbarrow full of big-bill money when we go to shop for necessities. The second step of publicity will be carried out—but only when moral persuasion fails.

"For the worst cases, we reserve the third step. A buyers' strike on many occasions has brought prices down. It is true that prices have usually gone back up. But that has happened because a group, victorious in its buying strike, later disbanded and there was no one to fight the increase when it was quietly reinstituted."

Can such a posse be effective?

"If you doubt it," said an observer, "you should look to the success of pollution control. For many years, thoughtful people were worried about our air and water resources. Nothing happened—until they organized. Now much is being done to clean up the environment, all because there exists organized demand instead of a few individual voices crying in the wilderness of concrete and carbon monoxide."

Whether shopping wholesale or retail, certain habits can save you money. One is to avoid meandering or aimless wandering through a store. "Leads to too much impulse buying," Sophie confided to her friend Florence as the two set out to purchase their families' back-to-school needs one hot August day. "I find that if I have a set list and refuse to add to it, I generally avoid purchase of things I don't need while making sure that the things we do require are obtained. And another thing—don't ever go into a store just to pass the time. Two of my friends do so when they have lunch each week in a downtown restaurant. They see and buy all kinds of things they wouldn't have wanted at all if they hadn't shopped, promising themselves it was an eye exercise and not a purchasing expedition. They invite me along, but I always refuse since the day I did accompany them and came home with a $150 coat 'on advance sale' at $80."

George stormed: "If you make a few more savings like that we'll not only blow our budget, but I'll have to start moonlighting to afford the money you say we are saving!"

Notes the Division of Home Economics, Federal Extension Service, U.S. Department of Agriculture, in an advisory titled *Be a Good Shopper:*

Plan at home. This is where good buying begins. Make decisions before you start your shopping trip. Wise shoppers buy needed things first, then add the extras. Your family's needs will not be the same as those of your friends, neighbors or relatives. As you plan, keep in mind what you have; what you need; how the item will be used; what size, color, quantity, quality you want; the price you want to pay. . . . Organize your list by location of stores and the location of things within the store. This will save back-tracking, prevent forgetting something, and help stop you from buying something you don't need.

Whether you're shopping Lemuel Plainfellow's Big Bargain Store or Friendly Frank's out-of-the-high-rent-district discount emporium, you will run into a bewildering variety of man-made fibers and combinations of these new synthetics with the old staple wools and cottons. You can shop more intelligently and thereby stretch the lettuce if you know what sort of miracle lies behind each of the brand names (synthetics are always "miracles" when the advertising copywriters describe them) and where each finds maximum usefulness. The two tables that follow come from the USDA's *Consumers All* yearbook.

Part of the cost of buying at Plainfellow's—and also at Friendly Frank's—comes about if you give in to the temptation to enjoy easy credit via the BankAmericard or Master Charge you carry in your wallet. There is a sizable cost to this seemingly easy credit. In a later chapter, we will explore the how and why of borrowing. Right here, it is opportune to issue a warning:

Retail credit costs. Depending upon how high the blue sky of your state legally extends, "easy" credit via either Lemuel Plainfellow's time-payment plans or the pay-when-you-will provisions of Master Charge and BankAmericard, you might pay up to 18 percent yearly interest (1½ percent per month, compounded sometimes into even higher real interest) for the privilege of buying now and paying next year. An 18 percent (or greater) addition to the cost of any item is hardly a method of managing money for better living.

In conversation with a local banker recently, I brought up this matter of sizable annual interest charges on purchases not paid for in twenty-five days. "You bet we allow delays in payment," he told me. "From how many other sources can we obtain interest as big as 18 percent a year? Our bank

MAJOR MANMADE FIBERS

Generic name	Manufacturer's trade name	Manufacturer	Fiber type	Major end uses
Acetate ..	Celanese* Estron* Avisco* Acele*	Celanese Fibers Co. Eastman Chemical Products Inc. American Viscose Div. (FMC) E. I. du Pont de Nemours & Co.	Secondary cellulose acetate, filament and staple.	Lingerie, dress goods, drapery, sports and casual wear. Fiberfil.
Triacetate .	Arnel*	Celanese Fibers Co.	Cellulose triacete, filament and staple.	Tricot lingerie and outerwear dress goods, sports and casual wear.
Acrylic ...	Orlon* Acrilan* Creslan*	E. I. du Pont de Nemours & Co. Chemstrand Co. American Cyanamid Co.	Polyacrylonitrile (primarily staple).	Sweaters, knit goods, men's and women's slacks, carpets, blankets.
Nylon 66..	Du Pont* Chemstrand* Celanese Beaunit	E. I. du Pont de Nemours & Co. Chemstrand Co. Celanese Fibers Co. Beaunit Fibers.	Polyamide (primarily continuous filament).	Hosiery and socks, lingerie, dress goods, blouses, upholstery, carpets, knit sports goods, uniforms and work clothing, and industrial yarns.
Nylon 6 ..	Caprolan* Enka* Beaunit Firestone*	Allied Chemical Corp. American Enka Corp. Beaunit Fibers. Firestone Synthetic Fibers Co.	Same as for Nylon 66.	Same as for Nylon 66.
Polyester..	Dacron* Fortrel* Kodel* Vycron*	E. I. du Pont de Nemours & Co. Fiber Industries, Inc. Eastman Chemical Products, Inc. Beaunit Fibers.	Polyester (primarily staple), filament for special applications.	Blends with cotton for shirting, sports clothing, dress goods, slacks. Blends with wool for suitings. Knit goods for shirting and sports wear. Fiberfil.
Rayon ...	Avril* Zantrel* Cuprammonium Fibro*	American Viscose Div. (FMC). American Enka Corp. Beaunit Fibers. Courtaulds North America, Inc.	Regenerated cellulose filament and staple.	Men's and women's slacks and suitings. Women's wear. Linings and drapery. Blankets, carpets, industrial yarns.
Glass	Fiberglas* Beta Fiberglas PPG* Garon* Vitron*	Owens-Corning Fiberglas Corp. Owens-Corning Fiberglas Corp. Pittsburgh Plate Glass Co. Johns-Manville Fiber Glass, Inc. Johns-Manville Fiber Glass, Inc.	Silicon dioxide (sand) plus fluxes to lower melting point.	Nonflammable drapes, curtains, bedspreads, industrial fabrics.

* Registered trademark.

A FEW OF THE IMPORTANT BLENDS AND THEIR APPLICATIONS

End use	Fiber blends	Fabric construction	Important properties
Dress shirts	65/35 polyester/cotton.	Batiste. Broadcloth. Oxford.	Ease of care, fast drying, wrinkle-resistant, durability.
Blouse	65/35 polyester/cotton.	Broadcloth. Crepe. Combinations. Taffetas. Failles.	Ease of care, lightweight, appearance retention, fast drying, durability.
Dress goods .... Printed and plain ..... Dyed	65/35 polyester/cotton. 50/50 polyester/cotton. 50/50 polyester/rayon. 50/50 triacetate/cotton.	Broadcloth. Challis. Checks. Crepes. Twills. Linens.	Washability, ease of care, color styling, shape retention.
Sportswear .... Shirting .... Circular knit goods ..... Slacks	65/35 polyester/cotton. 50/50 polyester/cotton. 55/45 acrylic/wool. 50/50 acrylic/rayon.	Sharkskin. Serge. Twills. Linens. Poplins. Sateens. Oxfords. Flannels.	Ease of care, durability, appearance retention, color styling, pleatability.
Slacks .... Casual .... Dress	65/35 polyester/cotton. 50/50 polyester/cotton. 55/45 polyester/wool. 55/45 acrylic/wool. 70/30 polyester/acrylic. 50/50 triacetate/rayon. 50/50 acetate/rayon.	Gabardine. Twills. Tropicals. Denims. Sharkskin.	Appearance retention, washable or dry-cleanable (wool), ease of care.
Lightweight	55/45 polyester/wool. 50/50 acrylic/wool.	Gabardine. Tropical worsted. Twills. Flannels. Serge.	Durability, shape retention, ease of care.

is delighted when people extend their payments beyond the minimum twenty-five days."

(In the preceding chapter, we considered a way to get terms longer than twenty-five days by making the stretch in advance of the billing date rather than before it. With such a system, you can use this banker's money without paying his stiff 18 percent—or any other rate of interest.)

You can reduce shopping costs if you save the money in advance rather than buy on time. Ronnie explained this as the three talked over a cup of coffee one hot, lazy Sunday afternoon:

"Say you want $1,000 in merchandise but wish to pay over five months. Don't buy on time—instead, accumulate the thou over the same five months. Stash the money in a savings and loan or a bank savings account. Time it so your withdrawal will come up after the quarterly date on which interest is paid. Put the money directly into the account, and when it comes out it will have grown a bit—not too much, I'll admit—and in that way, by doing without for a short time instead of indulging yourself by an immediate purchase, you will make money on the purchase instead of paying stiffly to buy on time."

Sometimes needs are immediate even when cash is not present, and despite Ronnie's advice, it becomes necessary to buy on time. If that happens, follow the advice in a *Consumer's Quick Credit Guide* issued by the Superintendent of Documents in Washington, D.C. "Before you sign," this checklist recommends:

- Read and understand contract. Don't rush.
- Never sign a contract with spaces left blank.
- Be sure the contract tells exactly what you are buying . . . purchase price or amount borrowed . . . interest or service charge in dollars or simple annual rate . . . total amount due and down payment. . . . Amount and number of payments, dates due. . . . Trade-in allowances if any.
- What if you can't pay? Or pay ahead?
- Know whom you make all payments to.
- What are seller's commitments for maintenance, service or replacement?
- Be sure you get a copy of contract to keep.

PASSING THE FOOD BUCK

Just as you can shop at Plainfellow's or Friendly Frank's for clothing and other downtown needs, you have a choice of outlets for purchasing the family's food.

The first is the supermarket in the Plaza Shopping Center in the northeast suburbs. The Plaza is run by Melvin and Salvatore, first cousins whose fathers began a brother act in selling food on a street corner that was once a middle-middle-class residential neighborhood but has now changed into an area of light industry and heavy slum. Long ago, Mel and Sal moved to the suburbs where they could set up a parking lot and a big operation for the change in food retailing they were smart enough to see when families first began moving out of the central city. Now, they own three stores. A fourth is in the plans stage, and a central warehouse handles all purchasing.

The cousins' business began in a middle-middle-income section of town, and their three giant stores still cater to the middle-middle groups who now live on the outskirts rather than the city proper. It is important to understand this about Mel and Sal's Plaza stores. Selections there, and in most middle-middle-slanted superstores, are big, the aisles are wide, the snack bar is clean and inviting. But the prices are likely to be fractionally higher than in a store set up to sell to a lower-income group. The latter store is likely to have fewer selections on its shelves. The aisles are narrower, because when you operate on smaller markup you have to pack more food into the same floor space in order to keep costs down. The low-low-income store won't always cash your check or furnish a uniformed bag boy to tote the supplies back to your station wagon. Its customers seldom have station wagons. Sometimes they don't have cars at all, but trundle groceries home by hand. Prices at the low-low-income store might be lower by 1 to 5 percent than the prices in Mel and Sal's Plaza stores.

There are also superstores that cater to the upper-middle-income and upper-upper-income groups. In the Central Heights Store all kinds of gourmet selections are to be found and prime cuts of meat are routine. Naturally, you pay more to go through the Central Heights checkout counters. After you have shopped there for a few weeks, the employees are likely to greet you by name. They haven't as many faces to remember as do the employees of the Plaza stores, and they have vastly fewer than do the hurried checkers of the in-town store which offers necessities of life to a disadvantaged many whose incomes are low-low.

There is a price bonanza to shopping in town where the disadvantaged buy. But the surroundings are not as pleasant, nor the selections as wide. If the selections and decor matter to you, it would probably be a mistake to take the fractional savings possible in the low-low-income store in preference to the wider aisles, brighter paint, and more abundant choices that Mel and Sal give to their customers. If you are able to afford the extra markups and employee bows found in Central Heights, you may not need to read about money management at all. Or you may be making a mistake, unaware that nearly everything Central Heights offers, except employee deference, can be found at lower prices in the Plaza stores and at vastly lower prices in the downtown store that is set up for those of low-low income.

While most food shopping is done in one of these kinds of supermarkets, the superstores have competition for the food dollar.

One kind of competition offers a convenience. If you are shopping for all or most of your food needs in this kind of store, you should be aware that even the uppity Central Heights Store is likely to offer you better bargains.

"That's very true," said Sophie as George arrived back at the apartment with a bag of groceries bought at a corner convenience store. "It is all right to buy an occasional loaf of bread or half-gallon of milk down at the corner. Stores like that are open until nearly midnight and start the day at 7 A.M. before any of the supermarkets open. But they are expensive. We can't afford to buy from them regularly if we are going to keep within the budget."

Down the block from the apartment pile in which George

and Sophie live next door to Ronnie is an outlet of the Buy-It-Fast chain, whose smallish stores dot the city and its suburbs. It is typical of convenience food stores. Usually, these offer parking facilities that hold six to eight cars. Turnover based upon fast service empties the parking slots fast enough so that a limited number can serve a store's customers. Many customers are like Sophie and George. They live close by and walk. In that way, the convenience store takes the place of the old Mom and Pop corner grocery. Unlike that fast-dying kind of retail outlet, convenience stores offer neither credit nor delivery; their convenience is based upon staying open long hours and offering a selection of many kinds (but seldom brands) of foodstuffs, along with drug staples such as aspirin and toothpaste. Many sell beer, a few sell harder liquor. Usually, these alcoholic beverages are priced slightly higher than a regular package store would charge and considerably higher than prices in the liquor departments of either the low-low-income stores, the middle-middle Plaza outlets, or the tonier Central Heights Store.

Like the convenience store, the delicatessen offers advantages of we-have-it-here-and-now. But you pay handsomely for this when you shop Dave's Deli. Partly restaurant, partly food store, the delicatessen will serve you food to take out or will make up sandwiches, snacks, even full meals to eat at its tables. Deli food is enjoyable. But supermarket food—even food from the convenience store—is likely to cost less.

Lowest in cost of the outlets at which you can purchase is the farmer's market. Many cities and a large number of small towns which serve as rural centers have one. At a typical farmer's market, the municipality provides stalls or loading docks to which farmers pull up their produce-loaded trucks. These open at awful hours of the morning—maybe 4 A.M. Restaurateurs frequently buy at the farmer's markets, and unless consumers shop early, they might find the best selections of truck-farm goods picked over by professional buyers who get up early in the morning to secure top grades at bottom prices.

Bottom prices are frequently a feature of the farmer's

market. However, you must sometimes buy in large quantities to obtain these low prices. Sophie and two of her friends band together, go once a month to the farmer's market, and stock their freezers with food for the weeks ahead.

A farmer's market offers food that is seasonally (or even momentarily) plentiful. Buying plentiful foods is one secret of how to save on the food buck, according to the USDA's useful guide. *Consumers All.*

Consumers All notes:

> You can save up to 6 percent of your weekly food bill by buying meat, poultry, eggs, fruit, and vegetables when your local market has them in good supply and features them as sale items.
>
> That means a sizable saving in a year. It is wise therefore to be flexible with your meal plans and serve the items that are in biggest supply.
>
> Improvements in harvesting methods, packaging, transportation, and storage have extended the traditional season for most foods. But—especially for fresh fruit and vegetables—there is still a major harvest season when they are most plentiful in your locality.
>
> Favorable weather or other crop and marketing conditions can bring about bumper harvests that overstock normal marketing channels. When there is a big supply of fresh produce on the market, prices tend to go down. That is the time to buy fresh fruit and vegetables.
>
> For example, you may be tempted to serve fresh tomatoes and sweet corn in December, but unless they are in plentiful supply you may pay 14 cents a pound more for tomatoes and 29 cents more for six ears of corn in December than in peak harvest periods.
>
> Another advantage is that fresh foods bought at harvest peak may be highest in flavor and nutritive value. A processed food in heavy supply probably was frozen, canned, or packed at the peak of quality.

Many foods serve as substitutes for other foods, frequently at lower prices. In my book *How You Can Beat Inflation,* a housewife told her friends:

> All my life, I believed that epicurean dishes had to be made with meat. Topgrade dining out meant filet mignon or sirloin. Then we took a trip to San Francisco—you can eat well

GUIDE TO REFRIGERATOR STORAGE

FROZEN FOOD	FREEZER AT 0°F

FRESH MEAT, POULTRY, FISH — Loosely wrapped	MILK, CREAM, CHEESE — Tightly covered	COLDEST PART OF REFRIGERATOR
Roasts, steaks, chops — 3 to 5 days	Milk, cream, cottage cheese, cream cheese — 3 to 5 days	
Ground meats, variety meats, poultry, fish — 1 to 2 days	Hard cheese — Several weeks	

BUTTER, MARGARINE — Tightly covered – 2 weeks   EGGS — Covered –1 week

MAYONNAISE AND OTHER SALAD DRESSINGS – Covered — Refrigerate after opening

OPENED CANNED FOODS, FRESH OR RECONSTITUTED JUICE — Tightly covered

NUTS — Tightly covered
PEANUT BUTTER — Refrigerate after opening

FRESH FRUITS, RIPE – Uncovered

Apples – 1 week

Berries } 1 to 2 days
Cherries

Apricots
Grapes
Pears
Peaches } 3 to 5 days
Plums
Rhubarb

SOME FRESH VEGETABLES – Uncovered

Ripe tomatoes   Lima beans } In pods
Corn in husk   Peas

OTHER PARTS OF REFRIGERATOR

MOST FRESH VEGETABLES

Leafy green vegetables	Beets	Cucumbers
Asparagus	Cabbage	Green onions
Brussels sprouts	Carrots	Peppers
Cauliflower	Broccoli	Radishes
Summer squash	Celery	Snap beans

CRISPER AND / OR PLASTIC BAG

Source: "Consumers All," 1965 Yearbook of the U.S. Department of Agriculture

Figure 4   Guide to refrigerator storage. (SOURCE: *Consumers All,* 1965 Yearbook of the U.S. Department of Agriculture.)

there—and learned that its people put seafood higher on the gourmet list than meat. So do many in New Orleans, another stronghold against taste mediocrity.

Cheeses, eggs and other foods that have a lot of protein will fill in for meat. Eggs sardou, eggs soufflé au gratin, or a creole omelet make even my steak-minded husband happy.

Regarding low-cost substitutes for sometimes high-cost meats, D. R. Meldahl, marketing coordinator, Soy Specialties, for Archer Daniels Midland Company of Illinois, wrote me that

> the necessity for a low cost, high quality protein has become imperative for the well-being of all persons. The emergence of vegetable proteins, especially soy proteins, in the last decade has provided the food industry with an excellent protein that can be used in an unlimited number of food products. Soy protein has a very bland taste, making it adaptable to meat flavors, fruit flavors, baked goods, etc. The protein itself is of high quality, containing all the essential amino acids. The cost per unit of protein from soy is about one-tenth compared with animal proteins.

(For ideas on combining good taste and lower cost, write to the Superintendent of Documents, Washington, D.C. 20402, for the booklet *Money-saving Main Dishes*. Enclose 30 cents in payment.)

Whether you buy at the farmer's market or the city housewives' superstore where Sophie buys, it is sometimes a saving step to buy in quantity. Be warned that not all quantity vendors really sell quality or truly charge less than you would pay by the pound in two-pound purchases. Sometimes, according to the Federal Trade Commission, bulk "savings" in meat can be as illusory as the "saving" in clothing or appliances nailed to the door by an unscrupulous retailer. Regarding what it terms "'bargains' for home freezers," the FTC notes:

> Very low prices were advertised for bulk meats. Then, when customers were shown (and told) what poor quality the advertised meat really was, the salesmen persuaded them to buy far more expensive meat. This time-worn trick might

easily plunge a family into spending far more than it intended to spend or than it could afford.

This warning does not mean that all, or even most, advertisers of bulk foods are rascals or that Sophie will do well to have a padlock on her purse when she visits such an establishment. Most are honest businessmen. The warning does give you—and Sophie—notice that bulk buying is not necessarily the cheapest. Make sure your food bargain is indeed one.

A knowledge of food grades can help to determine relative values. U.S. Department of Agriculture grading is applied to dairy products, poultry, fruits and vegetables, and eggs as well as meat. Notes a Department advisory, *How to Use USDA Grades in Buying Foods:*

> The grades are measures of quality. If a food has been graded by a Government grader, it may carry the official grade mark, shaped like a shield. . . . You won't find the USDA grade mark on all foods. *No law requires it.* [Italics mine] It is used on foods only when the packer or processor wants to use it and can meet the requirements for using it.

Whatever the quality level of food you buy, the more "convenience" the food company packs in, the higher your eating costs are likely to be. Only about 39 cents of the consumer's food dollar goes to the farmer. The rest is made up of costs added to the basic food price. Some costs are added for making it present in your store—whether deli, farmer's mart, supermarket, or convenience store—and on a shelf that is easily reachable. Other costs come from convenience. Today, an increasing amount goes for making a food instant, frozen, freeze-dried, canned, or precooked. In other words, these "conveniences" add more to the price.

Aware of this, Sophie proposed a regimen for her household. "While I'm cooking the meat for dinner, I can also prepare the beans or slice the potatoes into french-frying size myself," she noted to George one evening as they sat, the budget spread out for review and the dinner smells coming in from the kitchen. "The more convenience I add instead of buying it from the packer, the lower our food bills will run. The instant I save on instant foods is a big part of our meal cost."

Hopefully, other food chains—perhaps under customer prodding—may follow the lead of Ralph's, a West Coast outfit which recently introduced "Price/per/Measure" as a guide in helping people such as you and Sophie to choose the most advantageous purchase. Here is how the chain described "Price/per/Measure":

> This new consumer service . . . makes price comparison easy on 1,179 grocery items in the 50 important product categories where manufacturers distribute a multiplicity of product sizes and varieties. . . . The basic idea of Price/per/Measure is that products are compared to common units of measure, such as ounces, pounds, quarts, gallons and 'count'. Special price tags show both the retail price of the item and the price per unit of measure.

With or without such a plan, certain habits of shopping can be a factor in keeping food costs down. "It is as easy to pass down the supermarket aisle and pick up a half-dozen things I didn't know I needed until I saw them as it was to buy that $150 coat for $80 from Plainfellow's—the coat we couldn't afford even at $30," Sophie said. "I sometimes suggest to one of my neighbors that she take our shopping list while I buy from her list. That way neither of us is tempted to stock up unneeded items."

Included in Greyhound Corporation's *200 Tricks to Beat Inflation*, these food-shopping ideas might help you to save more money for better living:

> CUT YOUR MILK BILLS considerably by getting the family to drink reconstituted powdered milk instead of fresh whole milk. If they balk at the switch (and they're likely to), try this money-saving compromise: mix half a quart of fresh milk with half a quart of reconstituted powdered milk. The "finished" full quart will look and taste much more like the real thing; your family may stop objecting to this economy.
> ALWAYS BUY bread that comes in a reusable plastic bag—

and be sure to keep the bag. After a while, you won't have to spend as much as you're spending now on sandwich, freezer and refrigerator bags.

MEDIUM EGGS are often a better buy than large eggs of the same grade. To figure out which size is more economical on any given day, use this simple formula: subtract one-eighth from the price of the large eggs; buy medium eggs if they cost less than the resultant figure. For example, if large eggs are 72¢ a dozen, subtract 9¢ (one-eighth of 72¢) and check the price of medium eggs. If they are less than 63¢ a dozen, they are the better buy.

BUY A SMALLER STEAK for the family than you normally do; broil it atop thick crusty pieces of French bread. Cut the meat into individual portions and serve with a slice of bread beneath it. Thanks to the delicious steak-flavored bread, no one is likely to realize that there is less meat on the table than usual!

YOU CAN SAVE as much as 10¢ a pound by purchasing cold cuts in chunks and slicing them at home.

BUY LESS HAMBURGER than usual; make up for the difference by adding grated raw potatoes to the meat before cooking. Tastes good—and the hamburgers will be juicier!

THE COST OF serving pork chops will drop if you buy a pork roast and cut the chops yourself at home.

YOU'RE WASTING MONEY—and energy and time too—if you buy solid- or chunk-pack tuna and then stand breaking it into little pieces for use in salads, casseroles, etc. For these purposes, buy the least expensive "style" of tuna—flakes!

THE COST OF having milk delivered at home is appreciably higher than buying milk in a store. How much higher? Depending on where you live, from 2-12¢ per quart!

IF YOU SERVE butter atop vegetables, you can economize by browning the butter instead of just melting it. Browning greatly heightens the flavor of butter; therefore, you can get away with using about half as much as you're using now.

CUT BACK ON your purchases of prepared salad dressings. For example, 8 ounces of bottled French dressing runs anywhere from 39¢ to 89¢, but made at home—with the best oil and imported wine vinegar—the same 8 ounces will cost less than 25¢. You may not want to attempt a homemade Green Goddess or other "fancy" dressing, but chances are you can make an excellent, money-saving French, Thousand Island, etc.

PLAN YOUR MENUS with a neighbor whose family is about the same size as yours. That way, the two families can trade leftovers!

When shopping the supermarket, remember nonfood departments. Some superstores even sell heavy appliances at prices based upon low food-store markups rather than regulation stores' pricing formulas. "I cut as much as $25 per month by purchasing routine drug items in the supermarket once a month," Sophie remarked as she, George, and Ronnie sipped before-dinner cocktails at a restaurant meal made possible by the previous month's food savings. "Ditto savings on liquor and many housewares items such as brooms and mops. Remember your electric razor last month, George? It was listed at $33, but we paid only $22.95 at the Plaza superstore."

LOWER THE BOOM ON ELECTRICITY

Lemuel Plainfellow runs the department store and Mel and Sal own the supermarket where Sophie shops. The utility which supplies gas and electricity to their community is owned by many people. Its president, and one of the substantial stockholders, is Ernest Electrixec. He grew up in the town and belongs to every civic club. He knows over half the town's citizens by name. Most people call him Ernie. Sometimes they call him other, more profane names when they consider the utility bill too high.

"It's a shame," he confided to George one day when the two were lunching at a local club. "First place, the rates are set by regulatory authorities; *I* don't make 'em. Second place, most customers could save a lot by their own efforts."

"How?" asked George.

Ernest showed him a list, *Hints for Economical and Efficient Use of Utility Service:*

> 1. Install adequate insulation in roofs and walls. In a typical house, just four inches of roof insulation may reduce heating costs one-third.
> 2. Reduce drafts by installing weather-stripping around windows and around outside doors.
> 3. Keep drapes and shades down to reduce heat loss through windows.

4. Close the damper when fireplace is not in use to prevent heat loss up the flue.

5. Keep windows closed when you are heating your home, except perhaps for a little ventilation.

6. Wash a full load of dishes each time you use your dishwasher. It will hold the dishes from two or more meals, depending on the size of the family.

7. Keep furnace air filters clean. Dirty filters slow down circulation and make your furnace work harder.

8. Plan your laundering so you can do a full load in your washer and dryer each time.

9. Frequently clean the lint from your clothes dryer. Lint holds water, obstructs circulation and makes your clothes harder to dry.

10. Close off rooms not in use.

11. Plan meals so you can cook more than one item in your oven.

12. Iron a number of things at a time. It's cheaper than turning your iron off and on through the day.

13. Set your thermostat as low as comfortable. Overheating is expensive. When it is 50 degrees outside, it takes half-again as much heat to warm the average house to 80 degrees as it does to 70 degrees.

Telephone bills can be shaved in some localities by accepting limited-service telephones. Under this plan, a minimum number of calls are included for a fee smaller than full-service charges. Additional calls above this number are billed separately. The advantage is found only if you make few calls per month; inveterate phone chatterers will find the full-service setup more economical.

Long-distance charges can be reduced by calling at night and on weekends when rates are lower, and by direct dialing. Person-to-person calls handled by an operator cost more, but under certain circumstances can still result in a lower bill. If you want to talk only to Aunt Susie out in Los Angeles or Uncle Philip in Binghamton, call station to station only if you are certain that your target is at home and that you won't waste costly time while loquacious Cousin Willie rambles on.

Banks often charge for each check you write. You can save money when paying the bill to Ernest Electrixec's company or to the Blue Bell Tel and Tel by using cash. Many stores such as Mel and Sal's Plaza food center accept payment of utility bills. Sophie pays hers when shopping for food every Thursday. The saving in bank charge and postage isn't large, but it can mount up over the course of a year.

MISCELLANEOUS MONEY-SAVERS

"We gotta have a pet," George insisted one evening as he and Sophie settled down to watch the adventures of dauntless Dick Daredevil in a 1926 movie on television. "Maybe a beagle? Or would you rather buy a boxer?"

"I'd rather not buy at all," Sophie answered. "If you insist that we have a puppy to wet the floors and keep us awake half of every night, let's obtain one from the SPCA. Not all the pets they offer for adoption are strays from the streets. Sometimes people can't house a pup or kitten and turn it in with the hope that the animal shelter will find it a good home. The SPCA will charge us only for veterinarian's shots. We'd have to pay those in any case. And who knows? We might find a beagle or boxer there. Even pedigreed pups are sometimes offered for free."

"Look into it. And call a pest-control operator, Soph. This place is getting overrun."

"Spending money unnecessarily again," Sophie said. "Why a pest-control man? Why not good old George, putting in an hour every other Saturday to kill off the varmints? We'll order a book called *Controlling Household Pests* from the Superintendent of Documents in Washington, D.C. [20402]. For 20 cents, it tells how to use *your* labor instead of that of a specialist to eradicate insect pests."

In Greyhound Corporation's little *200 Tricks to Beat Inflation* are these miscellaneous ideas for managing money by spending less:

IF YOU USE PERFUME every day or very often, switch to the same scent in cologne. Even if you splash on double the amount of cologne, you'll still be saving money—and chances are, no one (including you) will be aware that you've switched.

SAVE YOUR OLD plastic shower curtain to use as a dropcloth when you paint, wash woodwork, etc. Not only will you save the price of a dropcloth, but because the shower curtain is heavier and easier to walk on, it does a better job than most thin, inexpensive cloths!

DON'T DISCARD a window shade that is cracked or soiled beyond cleaning. Instead, prolong the life of the shade by giving it a coat of good rubber-base paint. Note: This is one of the few painting jobs that requires only one coat of paint.

HOW MUCH CAN YOU SAVE by going to a do-it-yourself dry cleaning store? Prices vary somewhat from state to state, but generally you can expect that eight pounds of cleaning will cost about $2 if you do it yourself—and about $8 if the local cleaner does it. Note: Until you're sure of your "talent" at do-it-yourself cleaning, practice on the kids' old sweaters, send your husband's suits to a professional.

DON'T SEND LETTERS, postcards or packages airmail without considering these facts: (1) according to the Post Office Department, most first class mail going to distant points—for example, Newark to Denver—is sent airmail anyway; (2) first class mail will usually arrive just as fast as airmail if the letter, postcard, etc. is sent on a weekend.

YOU'LL GET LONGER USE (and better use) from steel wool scouring pads if you use them "dry." What that means is, wet the pot or pan you're going to scrub; don't run water on the scouring pad.

IF YOU OFTEN WASTE cleansing powder because it pours out too quickly, don't discard the square of adhesive that covers the holes on a new can. Instead, move the adhesive so it covers half the holes.

NEWSPAPERS COST LESS if you buy them in a store or at a stand instead of having them delivered to your door. On the other hand, magazines cost less if you take out subscriptions instead of buying them at a stand or in a store.

TO RECAP:

1. Downtown shopping for clothing and household items can be done in many different types of stores, each offering certain price and service advantages.

2. You should know when real values and lowered prices

are offered and when the additional value is more seeming than real.

3. Items advertised as "bait" are sometimes true bargains. A salesman might be instructed not to sell the merchandise. But if you wish it and believe a true bargain is there, you have the right to demand an advertised special (if still in stock).

4. Credit can be a convenience. It is also a dragging cost if carried longer than the twenty-five to thirty days most stores and banks allow before they begin to assess interest. This interest is often as high as 18 percent yearly.

5. Informative labeling can help you to compare values. Some stores carry out a policy of labeling that goes beyond the demands of law.

6. There are times when offbrand merchandise can be purchased at less than nationally advertised brands, but on many (not all) occasions the "savings" on unbranded merchandise are made possible by shoddy workmanship or material of lower value.

7. When friends can obtain merchandise wholesale, it is well to examine such an offer skeptically. Wholesale prices are sometimes only minimally lower than the retail figure charged by a store which offers return facilities and full service.

8. Buying clubs obtain many things for their members at prices lower than charged in retail stores. A club can be formed in any community.

9. In days of inflation, costs seem to increase daily. Organized consumer pressure on merchants and suppliers can mitigate the effects of cost-push pricing, and on occasion can halt it.

10. Certain habits (for example, shopping from a pre-pared-in-advance list instead of purchasing merchandise which looks good on the shelf) can reduce the downtown bill.

11. Food is purchasable from many different kinds of stores. Generally, supermarkets price closer to the cost bone than do convenience stores and delicatessens. But even among supermarkets, prices vary widely.

12. Frequently, substitute foods cut the food bill without lessening enjoyment of meals on the table.

13. As a usual thing, instant and pre-prepared foods cost more than the same items purchased in a more basic form.

14. High utility bills—seemingly unshavable—can be cut by following procedures recommended by the utility industry itself.

15. Low- or no-cost sources (example: an SPCA as a place to secure a pet) can reduce peripheral costs and allow you to live like the rich without joining their ranks.

4

About the Big Things You Buy

BY PROFESSION, I am a financial analyst. A financial analyst, according to one definition, is a fellow (or gal) who exhaustively studies possible investments and other monetary matters, and who, behind his or her thick spectacles, has a giant computer-type brain that whirs and clicks and totes things up in dollar language. According to another definition current in the profession, a financial analyst is a fellow (or gal) who knows everything about money except what matters. I suspect we're somewhere between those two definitions.

One of the things about money that very much matters and that you will have to master if you're going to manage money efficiently in order to live better on your existing, and possibly unstretchable, income is how to buy, care for, service, love, house, and finally part with those big-time investments such as cars, appliances, furniture, and other things that cost more than merely a nickel or two.

That is what this chapter is about.

CONSIDER THE FAMILY CAR

"The first decision," said George to Sophie as they pondered a sizable estimate for repairs and service to the family's four-year-old station wagon, "is whether we'll have the work done or say to hell with it and buy a new car."

Except for a man whose business calls for extensive automobile travel, it seldom pays to trade a car too frequently. Trading a car every year is a too-rapid turnover except for those whose wheels move 80,000 miles in a year or whose pocketbooks are so well lined that a new car can be purchased with as little thought as most of us would give to ordering a battery or a brake reline. If you have read this far, you are probably not in the latter happy group of people who live better without having to manage their funds.

In its September, 1970, issue, *Changing Times, The Kiplinger Magazine,* produced a table, "What Is Your Car Costing You?" This gave average figures for an average-type automobile likely to be owned by the average sort of people such as George and Sophie, Ronnie, you, or me. (See page 78.) For such a tabulation, it is possible to obtain "average" costs, indicating whether that Plymouth station wagon belonging to the Sophie-and-George family should be traded or whether the service costs for keeping it running should be endured.

"The important thing," George noted as he totaled a column of cost figures, "is how long we can expect trouble-free travel from the old vehicle if we go ahead. Every two years, tires and batteries have to be replaced in most cars used for family driving. The brake linings wear out in about the same length of time. These things are routine and can be calculated. What we can't calculate is whether more major repair work is likely to crop up. I'll allow maybe $100 per year over the average cost of the last four years, to figure in inflation's

WHAT IS YOUR CAR COSTING YOU?

Here's your chance to discover what it costs to own and operate your car—for a year and for every mile you drive—and to compare your car expenses with a national average.

Read the accompanying article first. It will help you get the information you need to fill in the blanks.

The figures in the "average cost" column, based on 10,000 miles a year, were computed by Runzheimer and Co. for a 1969 Chevrolet Impala with 8-cylinder engine, radio, automatic transmission and power steering.

variable charges	your cost (av. per mile)	av. cost
gasoline and oil	_____	2.76¢
maintenance	_____	.68
tires	_____	.51
total	_____	3.95¢

fixed charges	annually	
fire and theft coverage	_____	$ 44
collision insurance	_____	102*
property damage and liability	_____	154†
license and registration	_____	24
depreciation	_____	729
finance charges or interest loss		
total	_____	$1,053

* $100 deductible
† coverage: $100,000/$300,000/$25,000

Now add up the costs. To obtain your total variable charges, multiply the number of miles driven by your average cost per mile. (In the national-average column, the computation is 10,000 miles at 3.95¢ = $395.) For total fixed charges, enter the total obtained above. Add total variable charges and total fixed charges to obtain total cost. Divide by the number of miles driven to obtain your cost per mile.

	your cost	average cost
total variable charges	_____	$ 395
total fixed charges	_____	1,053
total costs	_____	$1,448
cost per mile	_____	14.5¢

SOURCE: *Changing Times,* September, 1970.

increases in service costs and because none of the parts except those just replaced are new any longer."

According to *Changing Times*, "The most economical trade-in time is at the end of three years or 60,000 miles, whichever comes first. Over-all, that's the period when the car will deliver its maximum economy."

For Ford Motor Company, three experts agreed on five questions a car owner should ask himself in deciding the best time to trade. They are:

1. *How Often Do I Want a New Car?* Trading a car every 2½ years lets you enjoy the freshness and value of a car that's new (or close to it) all the time. You'll be able to switch models to meet changing family needs. Trading only once every 10 years means that you'll be missing all of the improvements and styling of nine new models in succession. You'll be amazed when you see how very little more it will cost to have four new cars instead of just one in the next 10 years.

2. *How Much More Will I Spend on Repairs in Longer Periods of Ownership?* Repairs include expenses such as ring-and-valve jobs, transmission repairs, suspension and body work repairs. Maintenance items not included as repairs are items such as spark plugs, tune-ups, batteries, oil filters. (Note that on late model Fords, warranty protects you against defects in all parts except tires for 2 years or 24,000 miles. On all 1967 Ford lines additional warranty covers defects in power train, suspension and steering parts for 5 years or 50,000 miles.)

3. *What Will My Cost of Ownership Be?* Cost of ownership combines the cost of repairs and depreciation. It does not include such fixed cost items as insurance and license fees, or running expenses such as gas and oil. The 10-year trader's ownership costs him $4,204 plus about $1,000 for maintenance. If you finance the purchase of your car, you will need additional cash to complete the down payment, if you wait much longer than three years to trade.

4. *How Many Miles Do I Want to Put on a Single Car?* If you trade your car every 2½ years, the 30,000 miles you'll probably drive will be pleasurable, top-performance mileage. After 5 years and 60,000 miles, performance declines, while driving 120,000 miles brings on clear signs and sounds of old age. You will have to concern yourself with a good deal of maintenance as well as batteries and tires between 75,-000 and 100,000 miles. After 80,000 or 90,000 miles and 8 or 9 years it becomes increasingly difficult to maintain appearance and performance levels.

5. What Will My Trade-in Value Be? Those who trade every 2½ years may get a new car without either a cash down payment or (quite probably) an increase in monthly payments. A 5-year trader will have lost about 80% of his car's value. After 10 years there's so little equity that buying a new car means starting from scratch. If you finance your car, you should consider the additional problem (and expense) of raising the funds for almost the full amount of the down payment.

The United States Department of Transportation recently (February, 1970) published a study called *The Cost of Operating an Automobile*. Regarding optimum trade-in times, this study noted:

> If we consider only the money costs of owning and operating a car, it would be cheapest, in most cases, to keep a car for its entire 10 years. But dependability, comfort, and appearance are important to most car owners, and weigh heavily in their automobile decisions.
>
> The person who trades every year might be surprised by the fact that over a 10-year period, depreciation alone costs him about $9,550 (10 times the first-year depreciation). If he trades his car in every second year, the 10-year depreciation cost is lowered to $7,565 (5 times the depreciation of the first 2 years). The longer he keeps the car, the greater are his savings in depreciation. But after the first two years, he begins to face a series of outlays for tire and battery replacements, repairs, and incidentals that more than offset his savings in depreciation.
>
> Assuming a normal amount of driving, keeping a car after it is two years old does save some money, but not very much. Therefore, except in States where there is a substantial property tax on the value of a car, and for financing charges, the decision to trade in a car or to keep it a while longer should be based on the owner's tastes and circumstances, rather than on any thought of increasing or decreasing his cents-per-mile owning and operating costs. As far as economy is concerned, he can make the decision with a clear conscience.

"Hard" versus "easy" driving habits can rack and wreck an automobile, wearing it out in less time than it should take to give up its mechanical ghost. Better ways behind the wheel are thus a factor in effective money management.

Tires last longer if kept properly inflated; they wear out less often and are not as frequently a factor in that shall-we-buy-or-shall-we-trade decision. Check the recommendations of the manufacturer whose tires you now have. He's likely to suggest different pressures for city and highway driving. Inflate for the kind of driving you do most. But *inflate*. Under-inflated tires seem to give you a smoother ride. However, you pay for it; the tread wears off and the sidewalls weaken. Check pressures when the car is cool. And do it every two or three weeks.

Many service stations recommend rotation of tires. This is a good idea if you do it yourself. But if you have to pay $5 per tire every 5,000 miles, it is cheaper to let them wear unevenly. At $20 per 5,000 miles, you will probably pay $100 over the 25,000 miles that the tires might be expected to wear. That is close to replacement cost.

You can't govern the cost of gasoline in your locality, or the extent of local and state taxes. On a recent trip, I noticed that gallonage went up as much as 40 percent when we crossed a state line. Nor can you do much, except by talking to state senators and representatives, about the registration, license, safety inspection, and other fees which vary from area to area. But you *can* do things which will help your car to burn less gasoline for the mileage you use it.

■ *Item:* Your car's condition is important. Check mileage from time to time. If the old wagon starts to burn appreciably more gas, any of several malfunctions might be occurring. Consult a good mechanic.

■ *Item:* Don't race. Jackrabbit starts burn up gas (and rubber from the tires as well). Sudden variations in speed cause gasoline consumption to mount and wear and tear in general.

■ *Item:* Despite what many believe, it does not pay to keep the engine idling for longer than the short stops occasioned by traffic lights. One minute of idling, experts say, uses more gas than you'd consume restarting the car.

■ *Item:* Depending upon the make of your car and the kind of tune-up you had, you might find greater long-run economy in higher-test gasoline. Ask the friendly mechanic at Amicable Arthur's repair shop for an opinion. Then back it with a couple of weeks' careful tests of cost and mileage.

■ *Item:* High road speeds use more gas than reasonable ones. Usually, state speed limits (most range from 60 to 70 mph) are around the level at which good road mileage comes. If you can hold the speed down to 50, you'll do best of all.

■ *Item:* Frequent lubrication and oil-change services, as recommended, cost but are likely to pay in the long run. Ditto tune-ups and carburetor checks.

The make, model, and body style of the car you drive should suit your family's needs as well as its purse. The less expensive car is not always the cheapest to own in the long run. I discussed this with a manufacturer's representative whose regular driving has averaged about 150,000 miles per year over the last half-decade and who has kept close records on his vehicular costs.

"I buy a heavy car in the medium-price range," he says. "True, the gasoline consumption of such a car is higher than I'd have from a lighter, cheaper car. But the automobile handles road conditions better and stands up longer."

Said the USDA's *Consumers All* report:

> The car you choose should fit your own needs and purse. At the same time, the selection of a car that buyers of used cars will want when you are ready to trade is one way to cut the high cost of depreciation and protect your investment.
>
> If your family is small or you need a second car to drive to work, a low-priced compact may be the one for you. If you have several children, a standard-sized car may be better for you and worth the higher cost. If you cannot decide between these two sizes, consider one in the intermediate size—between compact and standard models in size, price, and operating costs.
>
> As for body styles, the four-door sedan is a good investment because it is the most popular. If you prefer a two-door, the hardtop generally is considered a better buy than the regular sedan. You will get back most, if not all, of the extra cost

when you trade in the hardtop. Station wagons (the four-door models) are always in demand among big suburban families.

The extras can add several hundred dollars to the cost of a new car without adding much to trade-in value later. Judge them on their worth to you.

Radio, heater, automatic transmission, and power steering are among the accessories most likely to offer a fair return. An automatic transmission will add to the cost of running the car, because it takes more gasoline than a standard transmission. All-vinyl upholstery looks good and is easy to care for.

Some accessories are nice to have but do not add much to the usefulness of the car. In general, you get back only a small part of their original cost. Among them are whitewall tires, tilt-type steering wheels, and power seats and windows.

The manufacturer's representative who was quoted earlier has a plan for providing a second (and, now that his oldest son is in college, a third) automobile for family use. "Each year, I put a lot of hard miles on a car," he told me. "The car is in good condition, but needs some replacements and some services. Those services are cheaper than a new car—even a compact—for family use. So my wife takes over the year-old automobile and passes on the two-year-old car to our son in college. Everybody has a car in good shape, the cost per car is minimum, and I'm provided with needed new transportation for my business." His plan is worth consideration if, like him, you are the owner of a business or a professional practice in which an auto is a factor.

New car? Used car? That question arises for many families which, unlike my friend's, do not base their car purchases upon the exigencies of business wheels. Writing in *Dynamic Maturity*, September, 1970, Raymond Schuessler suggested some tips on how to buy a used car:

> First of all, if you can, buy during the fall or winter season; cars are cheaper then when the brand-new models are coming out and many are giving up their old cars.
>
> The most important thing is to find a reliable dealer. Some judgment of a dealer might be formed by studying his advertising. A dealer who exaggerates in his advertising is also likely to mislead in his selling. Such statements as "the

greatest value," "best deal in town," "we undersell" are all signals for you to be on guard against.

Find out from your friends where they bought their cars. In some places local licensing authorities of used car dealers can advise whether complaints have been filed. Better Business Bureaus have information regarding dealers in their cities.

Sometimes a good deal on a used car can be had from a new car dealer who must constantly take in used cars in trade and must keep them moving. But this is no hard rule.

Remember that the better make and model car you buy the better value you will receive. If the previous owner paid a great deal for a luxury car he probably took good care of it. You can therefore expect less upkeep on such cars if you buy them.

Beware of "highball" and "lowball" dealers. An unscrupulous salesman may offer you a high trade-in and then at signing time he will say he made a mistake and lower his trade-in price. Or his price for such a car is lower than anyone else's, but at contract time he raises the figure claiming he made a mistake, or his boss won't let him sell at that figure. Walk out. These are crooks, and you may not be able to trust anything about the car.

When you purchase a suit or a skirt you can brag: "I paid X dollars—and isn't it a beauty for the money?" But you can't do that with an automobile. The system of pricing is inexact. Sometimes things that don't crop up until later govern cost more than the items on the window sticker or the payments to finance the car. When George and Sophie went shopping for a new car recently, they discovered that there are trade tricks in the new as well as the used car field. There was, for example—

The Case of the Bargain That Wasn't

"Tell you what," said the dealer as Sophie and George turned to leave his showroom. "This wagon lists for $4,438.50 with factory air, power steering and brakes, radio, whitewalls, and heater. You're nice folks. I'll take that four-year old jalopy of yours in trade and give you $1,000 for it. I'm losing money. The old car won't bring $200 on the lot, but we need volume and I like you."

A bargain?

George checked further. The next dealer offered him a similar car similarly equipped for $3,000. "You mean that old auto of mine is worth $1,438.50?" asked George in amazement.

"Shucks, no," said the salesman. "We'd be lucky to get a hundred for it. Even without trade we'd sell you the car for $3,100.

Moral: The window sticker doesn't mean much, and quotations for trade-in based on it mean less. Currently, the system of window-sticker prices is under governmental investigation. The way to shop is to ask: "How much plus my old car do you want for that wagon over by the wall?" *Net* outlay is the only cost determinant.

The Case of the Tire Trap

George and Sophie were in a showroom. The dealer's salesman quoted a price which seemed competitive with other dealers' offerings. "Before I take this car," George asked, "what kind of tires come with it?"

New cars sit in dealer showrooms with deeply grooved, wide-track tires that aren't as good as they look. Most are two-ply with four-ply rating. Original-equipment tires frequently wear out in 10,000 to 15,000 miles. Good replacement tires will give around 20,000 to 25,000 miles' service. Thus the cost of a car with two-ply tires is higher because the big-ticket item of new-tire replacement comes around faster.

Moral: Ask the dealer to substitute four-ply replacement-type tires. If one dealer will do this without jacking up price, his car is cheaper in the end than that of a competitor who gives you run-of-mill new-car tires.

The Case of the Worrisome Warranty

George was unhappy. His shiny new station wagon was back in the dealer's shop—for the fifth time in a month.

"I don't believe they do a thing to it," he complained to Ronnie. "When I show up in the evening, the service manager smiles and says, 'Yes, sir, we got it corrected this time.' But it isn't corrected and we are not only losing full use of our car, but I'm losing my reason over the thing."

It pays to talk to the man who has been there, as George discovered when he discussed the problem with an acquaintance who had earlier bought from the same dealer. "There are lots of good dealer service operations," said his informant, "but that shop has a philosophy that if it ignores things, the problems will go away. You might complain to the manufacturer, or take your car to an independent shop—but you're not going to get much from *that* dealer."

Moral: Part of a car's ultimate cost is the time it is out of operation. Look into a dealer's reputation for postsale service before signing to buy. And be aware that warranties on 1971 cars are not the same as they have been previously.

The Case of the Competitive Spread

"A Ford is a Ford is a Ford," said Sophie in a Gertrude Steinish mood as George insisted that they shop competing dealers. "The price must be the same."

But it wasn't.

For an identical car, quotes ranged as much as $450 apart.

"Goody, we'll take the low bidder," Sophie declared.

"No, we'll also shop for a Chevrolet," George replied. "Maybe that spread can be made even wider."

Moral: On the same day in the same town for the same car, the amount of net money a dealer wants to go with trade-in toward purchase of your car might vary 25 percent. Shop around. It further pays to shop surrounding towns because sometimes the dealers there will give extra consideration to a buyer from another community. Chances are his competitor in your home town will have to carry out the warranty service.

THE FAMILY CAR'S PERIPHERAL COSTS

You can count upon certain things wearing out at regular intervals. Brakes need relining after a year or two, depending upon how hard and long the car has been driven. The battery will die beyond revival, the tires will wear smooth and become dangerous. These replacement parts and services are a car's peripheral costs. They offer you worthwhile, wide areas for saving by smart money management.

Today, price alone is not the only thing to consider. Tire ads claim advantages for new concepts in construction. It helps to understand these in choosing the right tire for the expected need. The Tire Industry Safety Council, in its *Consumer Tire Guide,* tells us:

> Today, tires with new designations are accounting for a rapidly increasing share of the market. Also, new cord materials such as polyester and fiberglass cords have been introduced, in addition to rayon and nylon cord.
>
> In order for the motorist to select tires intelligently, he should be familiar with current designations and materials. The more widely used constructions are as follows:
>
> *Bias Tires*—May have 2, 4 or more body plies, made of rayon, nylon, polyester or other material which crisscross at an angle of approximately 35 degrees with the center line of tire, giving rigidity to both sidewall and tread. This construction is the most common in use today.
>
> *Belted Bias Tires*—Have a body similar to that of bias tires, plus two or more layers of fabric, or "belts," under the tread.
>
> *Radial Tires*—Have body cords which extend from bead to bead at an angle of about 90 degrees "radial" to the tire circumferential center line, plus two or more layers of fabric, or "belts," under the tread.

Tips on how to determine whether you need new tires at all, or whether the old rubber can safely hit the road for a while longer, are offered by the Louisiana Division of the American Automobile Association. In the July–August, 1970, issue of *Louisiana Motorist,* it suggested:

> Take a penny, and with Lincoln's head upside down, insert it in the tire groove that appears shallowest. If you can see any part of the coin over Lincoln's head, replacement of the tire is overdue. This means you only have $\frac{1}{16}$ of an inch or less tread left on the tire. In fact, you'd be well advised to replace your tires before they reach this minimum acceptable tread.

Though you might obtain more mileage out of worn tires —you also are pushing your luck.

Check your tires for spotty wear. Tread wear in the middle of the tire indicates over-inflation; on the edges it means under-inflation. Usually, uneven tire wear indicates faulty wheel alignment.

Did you know—few people are aware of this—that when you buy new tires, you will get better eventual wear from them if you break them in gently? The Tire Safety Council recommends that speeds no higher than 60 for the first fifty miles "enable the many complex elements of a tire to adjust gradually to each other and function as an integral unit." Wheel balance and alignment with every tire purchase are small additional costs which pay off in longer, as well as safer, eventual wear.

It sometimes pays to make other small purchases when equipment is bought for the car. One manufacturer recommends, for example, that every new battery needs new cables. "The average life of battery cables is about two years," a company advisory points out. "They may look all right from the outside, but there is a lot of hidden deterioration which can rob a new battery of its power and efficiency."

Other steps to keep that new battery grinding are these:

1. Check the water in the battery every time you stop at a service station. Make certain that the attendant uses distilled, not tap, water.

2. From time to time, have a mechanic make a routine check of your alternator. This is the dingus that charges up the battery, and if it isn't functioning, your battery will soon work its way to at least temporary death.

3. Watch for signs of an undercharged battery and have Amicable Arthur's service emporium throw a charge into it before you find yourself some cold morning with a car which, if not dead, sleepeth when you're unsleepy and raring to get roaring. One sign is a slow "rrrrrr" instead of a fast turnover when you start. If the engine is turned over satisfactorily but the lights dim and the radio volume drops, that's another hint that it is time for Amicable Arthur to check on things.

4. Don't buy a bigger battery than your car needs (see the auto manufacturer's specifications), but if in doubt remember that you are better off in the long run with over- rather than under-capacity.

THOSE BIG-TICKET HOME PURCHASES

"We need a new washing machine, but I can't decide on the conflicting manufacturers' claims," Sophie said. "Which, George? G.E. or Westinghouse? Maytag or Whirlpool?"

"You're confusing carts and horses," George replied. "Look first at the *place* from which we'll buy. Friendly Frank or the Plainfellow store? A big national chain such as Sears or Montgomery Ward? Or Old Bill's Appliances three blocks away? Except for gimmicks and gadgets, appliances tend to have pretty much the same features. You'll deal more with the retailer than with the manufacturer. Consider him first."

This is true for appliances which bear national brand names or the house brands of big retailers. The store from which you buy makes a difference. Offbrand appliances are often less desirable than offbrand clothing or other soft goods unless you are very knowledgeable about points of wear, construction, and probable workmanship; few of us are. In the other big-ticket item of furniture, it is even more important to know with whom you deal. (Many furniture brand names are nationally advertised and their quality—sometimes their lack of it—becomes known and is "rated" by consumer services. As with soft goods, you should be aware of the usually high degree of subjective judgment in these ratings.)

Strong and weak points of Plainfellow-type stores and of Friendly Frank's discount outlets are much the same in big-ticket, hard goods sales as when you purchase soft goods and small-ticket items. As with the soft goods we considered in the previous chapter, you can often realize savings by banding with neighbors to purchase through a buying club. Your friends can on occasion find wholesale items for you. The advantages and drawbacks of buying a washing machine, freezer, or bedroom set wholesale rather than at retail are much the same in the big-ticket hard goods area. A rereading of the discussion in Chapter Three can help you, George, and Sophie in determining the best place to buy.

Before deciding whether Old Bill in the neighborhood might have advantages over any of these outlets, it is helpful to look at ideas and criteria proposed by Jane Day in an article that appeared in *The National Observer*. Her advice was concerned specifically with small appliances. Its pointers apply also to the big things such as refrigerators or washer-dryers.

> It's a good idea to consider ease of repair before buying any ... appliance [Miss Day wrote]. Here are some tips on appliance buying gathered from repairmen.
>
> Buy name brands. Repair parts are more readily available. Repairmen are more familiar with the brand appliances so chances of getting the appliance fixed are better and the job may be finished sooner.
>
> Check on local repair shops. You can avoid frustration if you buy a product that you know you can get repaired locally. The appliance might be first-rate and trouble-free for months, but when repairs are needed or even the smallest part has to be replaced, it will be costly if you must travel to the next town to get what you need for necessary repairs.
>
> Ask salesmen if their store services the appliances they sell. Many dealers sell a number of brands and refer customers to factory-trained shops for service. Be sure such service is available in your area.
>
> Warranties are the tags many persons put in safe places and can't find when they're needed. Even if the warranty is at hand, repairmen warn that just as important is the sales slip showing date of purchase. This is the best evidence of whether the warranty or guarantee is still in effect. So keep the sales slip and the warranty together.

Pointers-to-look-for on specific appliances can be obtained by writing to manufacturers, to trade associations, and to the USDA and the Federal Trade Commission, which have put out such informative booklets as *Washing Machines, Selec-*

tion and Use (USDA Home and Garden Bulletin No. 32, price 15 cents), *Buying Your Home Sewing Machine* (USDA Home and Garden Bulletin No. 38, price 10 cents), *Equipment for Cooling Your Home* (USDA Home and Garden Bulletin No. 100, price 10 cents), and *Color Television and the X-Ray Problem* (Federal Trade Commission, free).

Mindful of Miss Day's advice on the availability of service as a factor in deciding where to buy an appliance, you should also consider whether to say "yes" or "no" when the salesman at Friendly Frank's, Plainfellow's, or Old Bill's Appliance Store puts a service contract before you as part of the purchase. Most appliances are sold with a warranty on the parts, generally for a year. But they are sold sans the serviceman's labor. Purchasers find—usually with surprise and often with anger—that a charge is tacked on for the repairman's time. This can run higher than the cost of the part he replaces. There is, therefore, reason for a service contract on a new appliance even though it may have manufacturer warranty.

But not all service contracts are worthwhile. "You can say that five times more," Ronnie swore as he and George discussed Sophie's new washer purchase. "I had a manufacturer's service contract on a TV set. Old Bill in the neighborhood would have sent one of his people over at two hours' notice if I had called on him. But not the manufacturer. It took his genius five days to arrive. Then he forgot to bring a part on his truck. Five more days were spent scheduling his return. Believe me, George, you had better check what you're getting, and how fast you're likely to get it, before you sign one of those service contracts."

Speed is indeed a factor. If Sophie must be without her washer for many days, the family clothes will have to go to a coin-op launderette at considerably higher cost than running a machine at home. "And not only that," Ronnie fumed. "I was paying on the contract for an estimated five calls which weren't likely to happen on a new appliance. It would have been cheaper to pay Old Bill by the individual call."

Sometimes service contracts pay. But sometimes they merely cost.

When buying furniture it is not as easy to obtain known value as when buying appliances. There are certain things you can do:

1. Check the grain on parts of the wood that must bear weight. Arms and leg of chairs, bedposts, and table legs should have a straight grain.

2. Likewise drawer fronts, table tops, and other places where the appearance of the furniture—a main reason for buying it—is affected. Lack of straight grain may mean future warps as humidity changes affect the piece.

3. Beware protruding corners. Who enjoys knocking a shin or tearing a blouse?

4. Do all four legs meet the ground evenly? While this seems basic, the lack of it is a sometimes, although not frequent, fault of furniture.

5. Stand off and look from an angle under strong light. This will throw into shadow small defects you might otherwise miss.

6. How are the woods jointed? There is no "best" way to build a joint. Jointing methods are designed for different purposes. Drawer corners, for example, are commonly made to dovetail. This method is effective where used properly, but it would fold under stress in the wrong place. Thus, a rabbeted joint or a butt joint is out of place where weight and stress must be borne. Chair arms, posts, and legs should be connected with doweled or mortise-and-tenon joints.

BEWARE THE ADDED COSTS

"Easy" long-term credit offered by your friendly bank, car dealer, tire retailer, Old Bill, and Lemuel Plainfellow is part of the cost of a big-ticket item. Says the USDA's booklet *A Guide to Budgeting for the Family:*

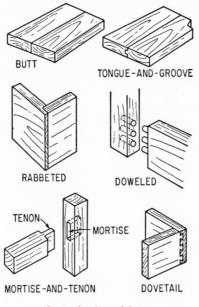

BUTT

TONGUE-AND-GROOVE

RABBETED

DOWELED

TENON

MORTISE

MORTISE-AND-TENON

DOVETAIL

Basic furniture joints

Figure 5   Basic   furniture   joints.
(SOURCE: *Consumers All,* 1965
Yearbook of the U.S. Department
of Agriculture.)

If you want to use credit, it is a good idea to compare costs
of various plans available.

The cost of credit varies:

—From dealer to dealer.

—With the size of the purchase.

—With the length of the loan period.

—With the credit reputation of the borrower.

Credit charges may be given:

—As a percentage rate.

—In dollars and cents.

The extra cost . . . of buying on the installment plan is not
listed on the price tag. But you can figure this by comparing
the credit price with the cash price of the washing machine,
TV set, car, or other item you want to buy. To get the dollar

cost of credit, you need the following information: the trade-in allowance, if any; the amount of the downpayment; the amount of the regular payments; the number of payments; and the cash price. When you have the information—

Add all costs—trade-in allowance, downpayment, and regular payments multiplied by the number of payments required—to get the total price you will pay.

Subtract the cash price. The difference is the dollar cost of buying on the installment plan.

TO RECAP:

1. Before you buy a new car, consider the condition of the old one. There is a point—financial as well as mechanical—at which it no longer pays to make repairs, and smart money management calls for a chariot with that fresh new-car odor.

2. Car operation as trouble-free as the lot of mortals in these imperfect times can be is the result of careful steps taken during an automobile's useful lifetime. Such things as proper tire inflation affect the whole automobile, not merely the rubber tread.

3. A new car should be chosen by need and purse. Certain styles and add-on items enhance the eventual trade-in value of a car; others, while pleasing to have and often economical and useful to own, should not be considered as investments but rather as conveniences.

4. Many factors other than the dollar total on the window sticker go into the immediate and eventual cost of the car; these should be taken into account.

5. When buying tires, it is important to know the new varieties and to buy the right tire for the car, driving need, and length of time you expect to keep the vehicle before trading it in.

6. Sometimes small peripheral purchases (example: a battery cable) add to the expected life of a replacement item such as the car battery. While an immediate cost, wheel alignment and balancing put off the day when a new tire purchase will wear out.

True Annual Interest Rate of Consumer Installment Credit

Item (1)	Price of merchandise or stated amount of loan (2)	Downpayment or amount discounted (3)	Credit extended or cash advanced (2) − (3) (4)	Repayment schedule Monthly payment[1] (5)	Months (6)	Total amount paid in installments (5) × (6) (7)	Total financing cost (7) − (4) (8)	Approximate annual TRUE interest rate (9)	Plan offered by— (10)
	Dollars	Dollars	Dollars	Dollars	Number	Dollars	Dollars	Percent	
1. Automobile loan	1,500.00	......	1,500.00	55.00	30	1,650.00	150.00	7.7	Bank.
2. Modernizing loan	1,500.00	......	1,500.00	55.17	30	1,655.00	155.00	8.0	Do.
3. Unsecured personal loan	1,500.00	131.25	1,368.75	100.00	15	1,500.00	131.25	14.4	Do.
4. Modernizing materials	350.00	......	350.00	11.74	36	422.50	72.50	13.4	Mail-order house.
5. Furniture or major appliance	360.00	10.00	350.00	16.92	24	406.00	56.00	15.4	Do.
6. Revolving charge account	......	Varied..	......	......	......	......	......	18.0	Do.
7. Unsecured personal loan	100.00	......	100.00	6.72	20	134.40	34.40	39.3	Consumer finance company.
8. Unsecured personal loan	500.00	......	500.00	28.88	20	577.60	77.60	17.7	Do.
9. Unsecured personal loan	1,000.00	......	1,000.00	56.81	20	1,136.20	136.20	15.6	Do.
10. Holiday tour	290.66	29.66	261.00	15.66	20	313.20	52.20	22.9	Airline.
11. Holiday tour	909.00	91.00	818.00	48.02	20	960.40	142.40	19.9	Do.
12. Holiday tour	2,763.05	277.05	2,486.00	142.53	20	2,850.60	364.60	16.8	Do.
13. Automobile loan	2,000.00	......	2,000.00	173.53	12	2,082.36	82.36	7.6	Bank.
14. Automobile loan	2,000.00	......	2,000.00	64.53	36	2,322.08	323.08	10.5	Do.
15. Automobile loan[2]	3,126.15	1,042.05	[3]2,250.90	81.60	30	2,447.85	196.95	6.8	Do.
16. Automobile purchase[2]	3,126.15	1,042.05	[4]2,266.60	86.89	30	2,606.59	339.99	11.6	Sales finance company.

[1] Final payment is rounded, when necessary, so (7) = (4) + (8).

[2] *Administered Prices-Automobiles*—Report of the Subcommittee on Antitrust and Monopoly of the Committee on the Judiciary, U.S. Senate, p. 164, November 1, 1958.

[3] Includes $162.80 premium for fire, theft, comprehensive, and $50 deductible insurance for 30 months, and $9 initial membership fee (excluded if previously had policy with same company); also includes $4 filing and notary fees.

[4] Includes $182.50 fire, theft, comprehensive, and $50 deductible insurance, 30 months.

SOURCE: McIntosh, M. B. *Why Installment Credit Costs Vary.* Presented at the 37th Annual National Agricultural Outlook Conference, Washington, D.C., November 1959.

7. Dealer reputation, location, and service are as important as brand choice in picking a new appliance.

8. Some service contracts are useful; others merely add to your costs. Examine an offered contract carefully.

9. In looking over furnture, check the design, quality of wood, and, with an eye to long life, the type of jointing used.

10. Credit is an added cost. If you buy on "easy" terms, be sure to add it in when deciding whether the budget should include a big-ticket purchase.

5

Home Sweet Savings Area

CAN GEORGE OUTWIT SELLER SAM? Would Sophie be happy
in a condominium? Will bachelor Ronnie find contentment
padding around a suburban garden with a trowel in one
hand and a can of insecticide in the other?

Tune in, folks, because we are going to discuss the largest
single investment (and greatest area of continuing expense)
the average family has. That's the home, a place to be considered reverently—however so humble, says the song—and
to be taken as a pregnant area for spawning ideas that can
shave your costs and contribute toward better living through
money management, whether home is a shaded shanty on
the outskirts, a suburban ranch-style split level, an inner-
city condominium, or quarters rented from a money-grubbing
landlord (in folklore and song, all landlords are money-
snatchers).

Over a year, a decade, and a lifetime, you will pour more

money into the rooms you inhabit than you are likely to spend on anything else. Where so much money is spent, there is correspondingly large opportunity for saving.

YOUR HOME—WHERE?

"Who cares?" asked George. "Where we live hardly affects any plan to save money."

"You *say*," replied Ronnie as the two walked up to the first tee on a hot summer afternoon. "Where a home is located is a definite, big factor in what it costs you to live. And it is an even bigger factor in how well you live."

From an accountant's point of view, Ronnie spelled out the angles to be considered:

"Basically, it's city or suburb," he said. "There is a lot to be said for each. In making the decision, you and Soph have to take cognizance of factors which are esthetic as well as financial. Take transportation, for example.

"As long as you continue in your present job, you'll face commuting if you move out to the suburbs. Commuting is a frustrating, maddening experience for many. And for all, it can be a costly business. When you go by mass transit, you have to worry about breakdowns, slow service, late arrivals at both ends of the line. Sophie won't like your coming home late for dinner. Your office won't function if you're late to work. It all can breed unhappiness.

"Living better calls for contentment as well as cash. So count in transportation—and don't forget that it costs to garage your car when you arrive if you go by freeway, in addition to the gas the thing burns in traffic both ways. Regular public transportation is not always available. In one suburb the buses run only until 10 A.M. and resume at 4 P.M. Nights, Sundays, and Saturdays you drive or hoof it, brother. That's the price for all that green grass. If the price seems good after counting in transportation, however, buy it. Your home will cost less to purchase and maintain in Smalltown-

ville, and that balances some of the cost and sweat of transportation back to concrete country five days a week."

Another cost to consider in deciding whether to live in city
or suburb surrounded by greensward is the matter of taxes.
These are nearly always cheaper out where trees shade the
streets. "But don't think taxes are no factor to city fellers
such as you and me," Ronnie cautioned. "Sure, we pay rent
and the owner of our apartment building pays taxes. His
costs are increased by those taxes and his rents have to re-
flect the fact."

"Nonsense," George answered. "Metro is coming. Anyone
who opts for the suburb should be aware of it. The political
trend is to unite all those nice, low-tax suburbs into which
people move, sometimes to get away from in-city taxes, into
'metropolitan areas' which are taxed equally to support old
cities which would die without such help. *That* fact has to be
considered before you believe that suburban taxes will always
and inevitably be lower than city taxes. Metro has arrived in
some localities already. It is a trend and I believe it will
spread over the country. Program that into your computer
when you ramble on about lower taxes on the city fringes.
Lower today. But who knows about tomorrow?"

"Those taxes buy things, George. Less tax, less service is a
rule of thumb. You'll pay to escape taxes, so don't look only
at the low-tax areas," Ronnie said as he watched a ball slice
off into the rough. "Take that patch beside the fairway. It's
full of poison ivy. A little more tax paid in this community
and the grounds people might be able to afford some weed-
killer."

Taxes buy more schools as well as local services to kill the
poison-ivy growth on golf courses. Where public schools are
weak, concerned parents frequently have to pay—often
heavily—in tuition to private schools. That is a cost item
Sophie, George, and you must consider when choosing where
the family roof will be located.

Writing in the USDA's advisory *Consumers All,* Richard
D. Cramer pointed out:

When you attempt to estimate the fiscal soundness of a city or county or your future tax costs as an owner of real property within its jurisdiction, do not oversimplify the problem.

An example: Nothing is more important than excellent public schools. They are not easy to develop. They are built by the efforts of dedicated people over long periods. Your children of school age get no benefit from long-range improvements. They need good schools now.

Good schools are expensive. Usually they coexist with high real property taxes, but differences in tax rates in communities with good schools and those with poor schools are seldom great enough to influence one's choice.... Communities with good schools usually are stimulating in other ways, too. So, when you are looking for a place to live, look into opportunities for intellectual activity, libraries, museums, theaters, concerts, a little-theater group, an amateur symphony. Mutual interests foster friendships more than geography does.

Anything which contributes to the quality of life should be weighed along with the factors which can be measured in dollar bills. Another example is the availability of commercial services.

"Face it," Sophie said. "Our family has to eat. And we need medicines and other things we find so easily in the city. When we move—*if* we move—we have to balance the advantages of being in an area where nothing commercial is permitted against the inconvenience of being unable to buy without a car trip. There will be no sending Edith or Ethelred out to the corner convenience store for a pound of sugar if we run out between supermarket days. The cost of sugar will include gas and time to get it. So let's look, again *if* we move, for commercial facilities within easy distance even though we don't want them on the same block."

Your search for the right area in which to live should focus on the future value of your roof and your rooms, as affected by the possibility of your area being downgraded by the zoning board. There are other zoning angles. What if you wish to add on to a house and find you can't do it legally? Suppose George becomes a free-lance toiler and wants to work out of a room in the house or the apartment, and the zoning rules say "no"? Advises Richard D. Cramer of the USDA:

> After you have made a ... selection of neighborhood, find out how it is designated on the master plan: Is it to be permanently residential and free from highways or overhead transmission lines? What will be its relationship to future developments—schools, libraries, transportation, recreation, and shopping and services facilities?
>
> Look up the zoning regulations. Find out what you can and cannot do there, the restrictions on the house itself, and the kinds of activities that can take place in it. Can you have a separate house for your guests? Rent out a room? Practice a part-time profession or occupation? Build a swimming pool in the backyard?

Eventual cost and inconvenience can be caused by the wrong kind of community and neighborhood wiring. If, like Sophie and George, you are thinking about a move to new quarters, sound money management demands you be aware that underground wiring is safer and can add to ultimate value as well as convenience. In my home city of New Orleans, hurricanes are a regular danger. I have lived through five of them. But it doesn't take a hurricane to blow down overhead lines; any strong wind, sometimes an ordinary rainstorm, might leave a section without service. When you wish to sell the house you buy now, people willing to invest in a neighborhood of potential power failure could be hard folks to find.

Insurance companies frequently charge for home coverage by the distance from fire and similar protection. This, too, is a matter worth considering for sound dollar management.

OWN OR LEASE?

Partly, this will be dictated by the kind of living you enjoy. In an apartment building such as that inhabited by Sophie, George, and Ronnie, you once had to lease; no one owned his apartment. Now things are different. The condominium and cooperative have come into being.

The Cooperative League of the U.S.A. defines a housing cooperative this way: ". . . families work together to own and control their environment. Members buy shares in the cooperative corporation which holds legal title to the entire development and signs the mortgage that provides part of the financing. Members also sign an occupancy agreement that establishes each family's right to occupy a specific dwelling and spells out occupancy rules."

Thus in a cooperative, George and Sophie would be part owners of a corporation which operated, subscribed to a mortgage for, held title to, and made rules for the ten-story human anthill in which they lived.

A condominium is a different thing. Each occupant of an apartment owns his particular part of the building, just as he would have title to (and pay taxes on) a set-back, ranch-style split level with its surrounding land in the suburban greenery belt. A condominium has been called a "subdivision in the sky." The condominium owner can sell his interest as he would sell a suburban split level. He undertakes to share certain common costs he would not share in suburbia. These costs include elevator service, the sweeping, painting, and upkeep of hallways, building entrances, hedges, and shrubs outside the common building, etc. The condominium idea which so many North Americans think to be a new thing is not new at all; references are found in medieval monks' manuscripts and in legal records of ancient Rome and Egypt.

Should George and Sophie plump for condominium, cooperative, or split level out at the end of the freeway in what city cynics call "the sticks"? Or should they continue renting their quarters at the anthill where their apartment now abuts that of bachelor Ronnie?

It boils down to personal preference and to taxation, zoning, and convenience conditions in their (and your) community. Advantages which would accrue to suburban living in Indianapolis are not the same as those in Ithaca or Ittabena. Nor are other families—yours included—identical to the five members of the ménage over which George and Sophie preside. The things to look into are the same; the decision whether to lease, own outright, or own through a cooperative must be made by *you*. Better living is an individual thing, and money advantages are both local and ever-changing.

"Keep one thing in mind when you and Sophie decide," Ronnie cautioned. "As an accountant, I'm concerned with figures. The figures for inflation have been big ones in late years. In an inflationary economy with rising market prices, there are financial advantages to ownership over leasing. You at least keep pace with inflation's inroads as your owned living quarters hopefully rise in value over the years."

WHEN YOU'RE BUYING A NEW HOUSE

The first think to look for is clear title to the land. Real estate experts say this should never be taken for granted. Money loss and personal headache are the accompaniments of a faulty land title. In some states, land titles go back hundreds, not dozens, of years, and an imperfection in transfer long ago can boil into a lawsuit which is expensive if you win it and disastrous if you lose.

Let's listen to an expert. The quotation below comes from an article, "Sherlock Holmes of Real Estate," which appeared in the June 5, 1970, issue of *Financial Trend:*

> The developers had spotted a perfect piece of raw land in Denton County for a large, regional shopping center. The land was for sale, and planning went full steam ahead.
>
> Late in the game, a little before the closing transaction was to take place, the title insurance company discovered one small but crucial detail:
>
> Many years before, in 1913, an Oklahoma company had bought a narrow easement across the property for an oil pipeline. Technically and legally, the pipeline company could have owned the center aisle of a department store and anything else in the shopping center that was built over the easement.
>
> The situation was resolved, a nasty hassle was avoided, and title insurance companies gained more believers.
>
> That vignette is just one of several that Robert P. Stewart

Jr. likes to relate. He is president of Southwest Title Insurance Co. . . . Anyone who's bought a piece of property has heard the term, "title search." A search is exactly what the title company conducts . . . even courthouse records can be inadequate. A title search locally for strings attached to development around Lake Dallas would fail to turn up one important restriction. It was filed in the Federal Register— not at the courthouse. The restriction says there will be no human habitation below a certain elevation around the lake.

Because an entry in the Federal Register has the effect of federal statute, it would take an Act of Congress to change the restriction—if or when developers feel that urban sprawl calls for more intensive development around the lake.

Litigation is one way an apparent owner can lose legal possession of land, but there is one other important way. In the profession it's called easement by prescription.

In Dallas' early days, Stewart explains, the lower end of Live Oak was a diagonal short-cut across a block of property. Because the public used the shortcut often and for a considerable length of time, it subsequently became public property.

Unless you want to find an easement across the spanking new property where your builder is beginning to put down the concrete slab, it will pay to consult a title searcher such as Mr. Stewart. "Don't think that applies only to land out in the suburbs," Ronnie cautioned. "Faulty titles crop up to plague owners of old homes as well as new."

Now you have the land and the title is clear. You're going to build—what? One way (not the lowest in immediate cost) is to hire the services of an architect. In many areas, building codes demand this if the value of the structure to be put up exceeds a certain minimum amount (varying with the locality). In that case you have no choice. You hire an architect. It often pays you to do so because he is familiar with building restrictions and requirements, knows shortcuts you wouldn't be likely to have in your own bag of tricks, and, under most circumstances, casts his professional eye over the workmanship of the contractor and the way the builder follows plans you have approved.

But you can do it without the architect for less money.

Start with a booklet from the Forest Service of the USDA, *Designs for Low-Cost Wood Homes*. This free broadside lists eleven house plans which you can order for $1.50 each. Other sources of low-cost, detailed building plans include lumber-yards and building-material companies.

Sophie and George pored over one such set of plans which they spread out on the table of their apartment kitchen. "It's what we need—almost," Sophie said. "We should modify this, however." Most people who follow canned, cost-cutting house plans do this. Some hire architects only for the modification of preplanned specifications.

According to *Consumers All*, "Features you want to plan for include adequate size of rooms and closets; a good traffic pattern; adequate natural and artificial light; convenient kitchens and other workplaces; sound and economical construction practices and materials; pleasing views; good ventilation and an adequate and economical system of environmental control; an efficient and effective plumbing layout; and interiors and exteriors that are pleasing to the eye yet durable and economical to maintain."

"If someone recently built a house in the same area of about the same size you propose, it might be a good idea to ask how much everything cost, what snags arose, and which features proved usable and which merely costly," advised a building-supply dealer with whom George discussed possible construction ideas and costs. "Costs are not identical everywhere you might build. If the land is low and soggy, a basement might seem a good idea on the plans, but prove only a mildew factory in actual usage. That's one example. There are others where conditions affect costs and the eventual livability of a new home."

WHEN YOU BUY AN OLDER HOME

In my earlier book *Nine Roads to Wealth* (which shows ways to make funds grow; this volume is devoted to obtaining maximum livability from the money you already have), some criteria were listed for picking an older neighborhood in which home repair-and-resale could be profitable. These criteria are applicable to choosing a new home location with an eye to its eventual value:

1. *Has the Section High Marketability?* There are older areas that tend to keep their faces scrubbed and their limbs and bones in good shape because a staid, settled group lives within. But sometimes the look is only superficial. If there is not high marketability, you will do better giving such a section the go-by.

One frequent cause of low marketability is that the children who grow up within an area move to newer sections when their families begin to grow up. A large number of older inhabitants, few children at play, and low enrollment in schools of the neighborhood are bad signs. Marketability might be low. The people within meticulously maintain their property, but no new families move in.

Watch For Sale signs within such an area. If these stay overlong on the houses that are offered, the section has low marketability.

2. *Are Values on the Upgrade?* Marketability isn't enough. You want your section to be one whose values are increasing. Records of real estate transfers are usually public documents. Consult these. Nothing can give you as close a feel of the trend of values as a look at the prices for which houses actually went to new owners.

3. *What Is the Trend of Recent Zoning Board Rules?* You do not want a section that zoning authorities are beginning to open to commercial or industrial usage. Real estate people say that the *trends* of zoning rulings are as important to know as the current rulings themselves.

4. *What Is the State of Repair of Surrounding Structures?* If the neighboring houses are themselves rundown—even if they are only beginning to be so—your chances for this particular repair and resell gambit go glimmering. A friend whose profession is the rebuilding of inner-city property says: "I take a car window survey. That is, I drive by and examine other houses up and down the street and around the corners. If it appears that they may reach a state of disrepair and peeling paint about the same time my proposed acquisition is spruced up, then the potential house bargain isn't any bargain at all. But I am always impressed when I see work underway at other houses. That indicates that the property

which surrounds my proposed acquisition is itself on the up-grade."

5. *Does the Price Represent Real Undervaluation?* Two years ago, I watched a pro go about evaluating a bargain home. The buyer was an architect schooled in structural values. He lived in the area, an older city section of very good homes.

"The house was pretty shabby," my architect friend told me when we discussed it one morning. "No one has lived in it for a couple of years, and no one has kept it up for a lot longer time than that. However, the changes do not need to be structural. A lot can be done with landscaping. Inside the plumbing is so old it has museum value. There are wash basins in the bedrooms that no one wants today. All those old touches will have to go. But again, the thing is structurally sound and what makes me want the house is the asking price: $40,000. Homes right on that block go for twice as much. I would judge that the lot with nothing on it is worth the asking price all by itself."

That was his criterion of a bargain: A house, sound but in need of repair, situated on a lot which, even without the house, appeared to be worth the price.

6. *Is the House Close to Schools, Churches, and Public Transportation?* The advantage of close public facilities is seldom found in an outlying area. It is the reason why many people willingly pay high prices for older central city homes.

7. *How Close Are the In-city Universities?* "University section" was a valued real estate phrase some years ago. But there appears to be a trend for the big-attendance schools such as universities to deteriorate rather than add value to surrounding property. Students now come in automobiles and sprawl these cars over the surrounding blocks, since older campuses in the midst of cities seldom have off-street parking for any except a few faculty members. Neighbors find the parking spaces in front of their houses taken away. Students who do not live in dormitories seek rooms or small apartments near the campus, and this, too, lowers real estate values. Crowds brought to football and basketball games are not always considerate of the grass and gardens of the homes where they park their cars.

The condition of the house is as important as the condition of the neighborhood in establishing a worthwhile value for that old home in the well-kept section on Moose Street which Sophie and George are considering as a new habitation for their family of five. George talked this over with an experienced builder.

"You can't buy a house by just looking at its rooms," he told George. "First, go outside and examine the walls. The foundation wall should extend at least 6 inches above the ground. Watch out for vertical cracks, too. These might indicate settling and a need for expensive shoring work. See if the concrete is smooth and even. Uneven, honeycombed concrete means that it might have been carelessly put into forms when the house was built—poor workmanship. Check the jointing in block or stone walls; if the mortar crumbles easily when you pick at it with a pocketknife, there could have been too much sand in the mix. If the house has crawl space—an open area between floor and ground—get underneath and check for dampness. This could indicate poor ventilation. If there is a concerte slab, be sure a slope allows rain to run off.

"Then, sidewalls. Whether covered with brick veneer, shingles, stucco or whatever, there's a frame of studs behind it, usually two-by-fours. If the siding has been painted, what is the condition of the paint? It may indicate a possible need for repainting, and the condition of the construction underneath. Do the sills have proper pitch for good drainage?

"Next, inside. Are there waterstains in the basement? Are the holes which carry pipes through wall and floor properly finished? If wood posts are used for support, have they concrete supports? Wood joists should be spaced evenly, about 16 inches apart. Are they warping or sagging? To lower heat loss, areas between the foundation and sill should be filled. This also prevents the entry of vermin. Do floors squeak? This shouldn't happen where floors are properly laid. However, don't condemn the flooring in an old home because it is cracked; this is a cosmetic matter and can be easily redone.

"Check doors for easy swinging and easy closing. Will they clear the rugs or carpeting? Do they latch smoothly? Check roof shingles and make sure there is the right shape for snow and other local conditions. Look at the flashing in valleys and around a chimney. Examine, if you can, the condition of the felts under the roof shingles. By all means, check for the existence of termites. If you are uncertain, ask for professional advice. It will be cheaper in the long run."

IMPROVEMENTS AND REPAIRS

"We must establish how much we'll pay to put that house over on Moose Street into the shape we want," George pointed out to Sophie after the real estate salesman had driven them back to the apartment. "Whether we look at things as reasons for buying a house or whether we later consider improvements and repairs on a house, the operational words will be 'cosmetic' and 'structural.'"

Cosmetic repairs are things such as paint, floor refinishing, landscaping, etc. These add to the looks of a house. Structural changes add to its strength. Cosmetic repairs and improvements contribute toward the livability of a structure, and frequently to its resale value. Structural changes are not as easy to spot as cosmetic changes, but they make the structure stronger, help it to last longer.

Structural changes tend to cost more than cosmetic changes, and some structural defects are reasons for avoiding a particular purchase or for putting a house on the sale block if you already own it. An example is shoring which, in addition to being a costly item in its own right, brings other costly changes in its wake. Where foundations have cracked or sunk, a house has to be jacked up just like an automobile whose tire is being changed, and new foundations are put in place or reinforcing is added to the old. Your bill for shoring only begins with job itself. Shoring is almost certain to crack some interior walls as the house is lifted and jostled. It puts door frames out of whack, splits ceilings, makes things cease to function, and brings about the need for a host of cosmetic repairs as well as minor structural jobs.

Some kinds of change add eventual value to a house—a prime consideration to astute money managers—while others do not. Take a kitchen. Sophie will cook more easily and the hours will go more smoothly in a remodeled kitchen, should she and George decide to become owners of the Moose Street residence. And the remodeling will add value to the home.

"When you are ready to sell it," the real estate man told George, "women prospects will be interested in a modern kitchen. Likewise bathrooms. Those are the first things women examine when they look at a house. It's the woman's word that will sway the purchase of a home most times."

In *Nine Roads to Wealth* it was pointed out:

> Nearly any remodeling of an older house will involve plumbing. Where this can be kept to a minimum, go ahead. People who have done this sort of thing warn that it is a good idea to keep plumbing additions close to existing plumbing. If you plan to add a bath, put it atop one which is on a lower floor. Or directly below the upper bathroom, even beside it. Carrying plumbing long distances through an old house can make the bills grow big without adding conpensating value to the investment.

Some people are weekend plumbers, carpenters, and handymen who can do work like this themselves. The savings are considerable if you happen to have skill and available time. Most of us have neither and must call upon the services of a contractor. You can be awfully gypped if you aren't careful about the people who repair and improve your home sweet home.

In 1969, Hurricane Camille, a concentrated wingdinger of a blow and the worst natural disaster ever to hit the continental United States, came in from the Gulf of Mexico and wiped most of the Gulf Coast of Mississippi clean of houses, stores, buildings, and some unwary people as well. Its hardest blows were struck at the towns of Pass Christian, Bay St. Louis, Waveland, and Long Beach.

Disasters such as Camille bring out the best in people. The cooperation and mutual aid that come in the wake of such an awesome event would cheer any believer in the perfectibility of man. His belief would not be reinforced, however, if he watched the con games, cheating, and scrambling for relief goodies that come after a hurricane or other catastrophe has

passed on. Writing about practices in the building business—typical also of a fringe of operators in more peaceful surroundings than the post-Camille Coast—Ronny Caire, publisher of *The Owl,* a widely circulated community newspaper, told in his August 25, 1970, issue about contractors fleecing Coast residents:

> Unscrupulous contractors are fleecing coast residents of thousands of dollars in Long Beach, Pass Christian, Bay St. Louis, Waveland and surrounding areas, investigation by The Owl revealed. Contractors have taken money and not performed work on funds provided by the Red Cross, the S.B.A., and other sources of funding.
>
> "I wound up paying twice for my home repairs," reported one well-known sports figure in the area. "The first contractor collected in advance, and I foolishly paid him because contractors were hard to find. He left and didn't do any work. Now, I have had to scrape up money to get the work done by a reputable contractor. Both costs came out of me."
>
> In some cases, the unscrupulous contractors preyed on the lack of education on the part of homeowners. On investigation, it was found that the homeowners had signed a certificate of completion before any work was done, and were subsequently bilked out of the entire amount of money. In other cases, builders' liens are being filed against property when the contractors collected for building materials and failed to pay the supply houses.

Doing business with a contractor of known probity is the only way to avoid being suckered into such deals as beset Coast Mississipians in the hard months following Camille. Beware the "firm" just in from out of town. How such fast-moving, fast-buck artists can rob homeowners on repairs was detailed by William Mathewson, staff reporter, in the *Wall Street Journal's* June 4, 1970, issue:

> The Williamson family, as usual, wintered in Florida. With the coming of spring, they headed north. Awaiting their arrival were many of their long-time acquaintances: Better Business Bureaus, the police and a number of local agencies specializing in consumer fraud.
>
> "We call them the Terrible Williamsons," says Louis

Sisapel, chief investigator for the Better Business Bureau of Metropolitan New York. For the Williamsons, according to Mr. Sisapel, are an itinerant band of men, women and children whose specialty is bilking homeowners with a variety of "home improvement" offers and phony sales pitches.

You say your roof leaks? Or maybe your driveway is cracked or your paint is peeling? Never fear. For a trifling sum, the Williamsons will reseal the roof, resurface the driveway or spray on a new coat of paint. Then they'll take your money and disappear. And before long your roof will leak, your driveway will crack and your paint will peel. "The slickest and most successful clan of bunco, flim-flam confidence artists in the U.S." is the way New York City's Department of Consumer Affairs describes the Williamsons.

. . . The Williamsons may rake in as much as $500 a day from a single truck, the BBB estimates. They have generally left an area by the time complaints to the BBB start flooding in, and arrests hold little terror for them in any case. That's because few of their activities can be defined as felonies. "When arrested, as they often are, gang members usually jump bail," says an inspector in New York's Department of Consumer Affairs. "They regard such disbursement as normal operating expenses."

POINTS TO WATCH IN A MORTGAGE

"Don't sign!" Ronnie shouted as George's pen was poised above a mortgage form.

"Interest rates are high today. Don't tie yourself to big interest for twenty years to come. There will probably be periods when interest rates go down. Make sure there is an adjustment clause in the mortgage."

You and George should settle this important question before signing a mortgage to buy the home on Moose Street or the ranch-style split level in suburbia. Recently Paul S. Anderson and J. Philip Hinson of the Federal Reserve Bank of Boston reported on "Variable Rates on Mortgages" in the bank's *New England Economic Review* (March/April, 1970):

To find out the extent to which variable rates are being included in mortgage loans, the Federal Reserve Bank of Boston undertook a survey of New England mutual savings banks, savings and loan associations, and commercial banks in late 1969, . . . then examined some problems that arise with variable rates. In brief, the survey shows that the incorporation of variable provisions in mortgage contracts is quite widespread, and is by no means an entirely new development. About half of the 532 survey respondents now have some provision for adjusting rates in their outstanding mortgage loan contracts. Further, variability clauses appear with nearly equal frequency in mortgage loans on single family residences, apartment buildings and commercial property.

Although writing from the viewpoint of the lender, Hinson and Anderson described a method interesting to you as a potential borrower. They called this "Tied Rates":

The second most common method for achieving rate variability is to tie the mortgage rate to some other indicator so the rate moves when the indicator does. This procedure imparts an automaticity to the rate change unlike the case with short-term or demand notes, where rate changes are at the initiative of the lender. All 38 respondents using this method were found to tie their mortgage rate to the prime rate. A common method is to set the mortgage rate one percent . . . above the prime rate.

Mortgage "points" seldom vary. These are to the advantage of the lender, not you or George. Their use is so widespread that you can hope only to shop for a low-point contract, not achieve a mortgage without them. Points work this way:

Say George decides to buy the Moose Street property. Usury laws in his state prohibit lending above 7 percent. This proved an unreasonably low rate during the late sixties when all interest rates soared. Explaining this, the mortgage company representative told George, "Okay, we'll make it 7 percent. But my company will need nine points." A point is 1 percent of the mortgage amount. The lender holds this out of the mortgage payment, decreasing the amount actually received and increasing his real return. At that time, George's recourse was to bargain and haggle for lower points—possibly shopping other lenders. His hope of avoiding loss of the points was in vain.

George has three other hopes for lowering mortgage interest and thus setting aside money for better living through money management. Sometimes, collateral other than real estate will result in lessened interest. A loan on a portfolio of stocks, for example, might be made at lower interest and without the sometimes-staggering legal cost of developing a mortgage acceptable to both lender and borrower. "You can always switch to a regulation mortgage later if you choose to do so," a bank officer told George. "Meanwhile, a loan on securities can be made in minutes and at our lowest interest charges."

George's other hope is a lease with option to buy. Often leases are available on which payments may accrue toward eventual purchase of the land or buildings involved. In some cases this is a neat way of having your cake and eating it too. But it pays to first check with an attorney and with a tax man where income tax provisions apply (example: when the home is also used for business) because the terms would have to be carefully tailored so that the Bureau of Internal Revenue would not consider the lease a disguised selling contract.

Every well-negotiated mortgage should contain allowance for the borrower to prepay principal. Often there is stipulation as to the minimum amount the lender will receive, and sometimes such payments can only be made at set times, as, for example, each anniversary of the mortgage contract. Often the clause permits prepayment only in multiples of a predetermined number.

A sizable amount paid down shrinks the mortgage cost by lessening the amount borrowed on which interest can be charged. In some cases that is a consideration of importance. The sizable downpayment might come from excess capital funds accumulated. It could come from liquidation of part of an outside portfolio of stocks or bonds. Sometimes, a seller will accept a package of bonds or common stocks outright as downpayment without the necessity of the borrower's selling them (and paying commission).

However, there are other angles to downpayment than the

immediate one of shrinking interest payments. You have to decide whether the funds might be needed in other directions.

POINTS TO WATCH IN A LEASE

"Nuts," said George. "We don't want the headaches of being homeowners. Let's sign a lease to stay another year in this apartment."

In signing such a lease, there are many money management angles. The standard apartment or home lease is on a printed form. This form strongly favors the lessor over the lessee (that's you if, like George, you decide to live in rented quarters). Here are some things to examine before inking the bottom line of a lease for living quarters, whether it is printed or prepared to order:

1. *Is the Rent Stipulated and Does the Lease Specify How It Is to Be Paid?*   Some leases call for a tenant to sign rent notes, due in different months and carrying interest charges if not paid on the due date. Such a practice is not itself bad. But you should make sure how much interest and on what date the note is considered overdue.

"When I was away on vacation no one else remembered to pay the rent," a friend told George. "On my return I was told that I was 'delinquent' and the lessor wanted 15 percent interest!"

2. *Who Pays Utility Bills?*   Gas, water, and electricity are furnished with some leases, while with others the tenant must pay for what he uses. If the bills belong to you, make sure that you have a separate meter for such service.

3. *Are Things in Good Order When You Enter?*   The standard lease says that they are. "But you should have seen the mess a previous tenant left in our place," one apartment dweller told me. "It was not the landlord's fault and he wasn't even aware of the state of things until I pointed them out. But 'good order' called for in the lease was actually a mess of broken plaster, unhinged doors, and general filth. When he was shown this, the landlord readily agreed to put it into shape. If I hadn't looked first, however, my real rental costs would have been increased by the amount needed to put things in livable order."

4. Does Your Lease Describe the Place to Be Rented?   It is unlikely that a landlord might force a substitute property on you—but this *has* happened, more through misunderstanding than chicanery, in a few cases where lessees have examined one place and found themselves occupants of another.

5. Does the Lease Fully Describe the Furnishings?   Even an unfurnished place often contains several items which are the landlord's property and on which he can demand accounting. One of George's friends found this out to his cost when he made a recent move.

"Where are the hat racks I left in the place?" demanded the landlord. "How about my awnings? I see you have worn out the floor tile, too. Let's have an accounting." Regretfully, the tenant remembered that he had discarded the hat racks as junk—which they had been until they suddenly acquired antique value on the lease expiration—and he had no idea what had become of the ancient awnings. Except for the floor tile, which a judge considered had had only normal wear and tear, he had to pay top dollar prices for unnoticed pieces of junk.

Some people take Polaroid pictures of each room and have them made part of the contract. "That way," a real estate man advised, "nobody loses and there is no room for misunderstanding between lessee and landlord."

6. Who Handles Repairs?   The following wordage is found in a typical standard, preprinted lease:

The said premises and appurtenances, including the locks, keys and other fastenings, are delivered in good order *and the lessee obligates himself to keep the same in good order during the term of this lease* [italics are the author's] and to comply with all city ordinances at his own expense. No repairs shall be due to lessee except such as needed to the roof or rendered necessary by fire or other casualty not occasioned by lessee's fault or negligence. . . . The water pipe and plumbing are delivered in good order and the lessor will not be responsible for damage resulting from bursting pipes or plumbing and lessee agrees to repair and keep said pipes and plumbing in good condition at his own expense.

No one has to sign a lease with such a clause as this. It can be stricken out of the agreement.

7. What of Storm Damage? After Hurricane Betsy of 1965 had destroyed much property in New Orleans, there were instances—mercifully few—in which landlords and tenants wrangled as to who was to repair gaping holes in the roofs and sides of business structures into which each fresh rain poured further water and through which each new wind blew.

Responsibility such as this should be made clear by the lease agreement.

8. What If the Building Is Destroyed or Condemned? A new interstate superhighway was scheduled to go through the area in which one apartment structure was located. The courts condemned the property and the landlord was paid. "Fortunately, he was a fair man and arranged to obtain similar quarters for us elsewhere in the city," a tenant said later. "But our lease did not say he had to do this—didn't even contain provision for canceling the lease when there was no longer a building for it to cover!"

9. Suppose Insurance Rates Go Up? Read a clause on this subject from one standard printed lease:

If business carried on by the lessee, or anything which he brings into or maintains on the premises shall cause an increase on the premium of insurance, the lessee shall be re-

> sponsible therefore and shall pay the difference in premium; and in the event he fails to do so, the lessor shall pay the same and shall be entitled to claim the same as part of the rent and shall have therefore the same lien and privilege accorded by law to the rent.

Today's insurance rates seem to go up as often as prices at the supermarket. Such a clause needs to be defined more clearly.

10. *Who Judges Whether You Have "Defaulted" on Terms of the Lease?* I talked recently to one man who retained his rented quarters only after a bitter legal battle. His lease had a clause which read:

> If the lessee should in any way violate the provisions of this lease, the lessor hereby expressly reserves to himself the right of cancelling this lease without notice to the lessee.

The perturbed tenant told me: "The landlord interpreted that as permitting him to throw us out—even though the rent was paid—when we had a dispute. It was over one of those small matters which can be settled in a minute if both parties grin and give a bit. Neither of us did so. I was as much at fault as he was. The trouble would still have been minor, however, if the lease had not contained that confusing clause.

11. *Who Has to Comply with Fire and Building Codes?* It could be the tenant's responsibility if his lease contains the following wording, taken from a typical lease form:

> The tenant shall comply in every respect at his own expense with the rules and regulations of what is known as the Fire Prevention Bureau, or those of any similar association in existence at the time, and in such manner as not to increase the rate of insurance on building or contents.

TO RECAP:

1. Your home location affects living costs. Suburbia and in-city locations alike have advantages, and the satisfaction

of living where you like is as much a factor as the saving of dollars.

2. Taxes and some other costs are usually lower in suburban communities. This might be balanced by the high transportation cost and annoyance of commuting by car or mass transit. Again, preferences are as important as immediate cash cost.

3. In judging a community, look at the excellence—or lack—of its services such as schools. These govern how much added cost you might incur for things which should be covered by the tax dollar but are not.

4. Both ownership and leasing have advantages. Today, you can own an apartment as well as a detached dwelling, and, if your liking is for residence in a tall human antheap, you can look into pointers and drawbacks of a condominium or cooperative.

5. In buying a house, first check the land title. The saving of a few dollars in fees here can cost thousands if title faults later develop.

6. If you build, consult an architect—often a legal prerequisite. You can also use, adapt, or extend plans from ready-made building designs available at low cost.

7. In buying an older home, the first requirement is a good neighborhood, preferably well maintained and on the way up.

8. Next, look at the condition of the house. Hours or dollars skimped in checking this out frequently turn into years and big sums spent in heartache and pocketbook losses.

9. Improvements and repairs can be structural or cosmetic. The former are likely to be costly but might add little to the value because they don't show on the surface. Cosmetic repairs cost less; paradoxically, they add more to eventual salability of a property.

10. Whether cosmetic or structural, remodeling and renewing a home can cost twice as much as they should if you deal with shoddy contractors and material suppliers.

11. A mortgage is the largest single indebtedness most of us incur in our lives. Be careful about its provisions. A recent Federal Reserve computation showed that a change from 6 percent interest to 8½ percent on a $20,000 mortgage over

a twenty-five-year term resulted in payment of an added $10,000.

12. In times of high interest rates, variable interest mortgages can be negotiated. These protect the borrower from paying 8½ percent interest charges should going rates drop back to 6 percent.

13. Mortgage costs can sometimes be reduced by use of a lease with option to buy, a clause allowing prepayment of principal, or payment of an extra-large downpayment to reduce the amount on which interest is charged.

14. Lessors of apartments and single houses should beware of traps written into many printed contracts. These leases usually favor the landlord.

_6_

Cures for the High Cost of Health

"WHAT DO THEY WANT TO DO—live forever?" growled one commentator as he looked at the staggering and growing amounts Americans pay each year for medical care, health and disability insurance, and hospital and nursing-home stays. "With all that money going to the health industry, you'd think it had discovered a way to keep us breathing ad infinitum and was peddling forever pills."

Whether you believe that proper care will help you to live forever or merely make more pleasant and active the years that have been allotted you to stay aboveground, chances are that your health bills are among the largest you pay. Sophie noted this recently. "A healthy family like ours should pay almost nothing. But our expenditures to insurance companies, doctors, dentists, and pathological laboratories are enormous. Still, I suppose there is nothing to do about it," she told George as she closed the family checkbook.

In this, Sophie was wrong. There is a great deal that you, she, George, Ronnie, or anyone else can do to lower the cost *and still maintain a high level of health care.*

The health industry is as concerned as you are. The American Medical Association has a Department of Health Care Financing. Maynard L. Heacox, staff associate, wrote recently to me:

> There is a differentiation between "health care" costs and "medical care" costs. In the area of money management . . . there is not much that the individual can do to save money *after* he has become sick. At this point it becomes necessary to see a doctor and/or go to the hospital and there isn't much to be gained in shopping around, even if you are still ambulatory. The really big gains are to be made in preventive health care. Diet, smoking, drinking, physical and emotional strain, and other areas of care that might prevent disability and medical care expenses offer opportunities for potential individual savings that can be very substantial over a period of years. Unfortunately, a lot of people want to indulge their minor discretions and then try to find a way to save money if it becomes necessary to go to the doctor.
>
> Assuming that it is not possible to avoid medical care costs entirely, good money management would presume adequate insurance (the same as you would have in order to protect the investment on your home or car) and regular checkups to discover conditions that, if left unattended, might develop into situations requiring costly treatment.

This chapter will consider the steps proposed by Mr. Heacox, along with others which can prove helpful in reducing the high cost of health care. But first, let's examine just how high health costs are.

They are staggering.

The paragraph below was written not to scare but to inform. It comes from *The Size and Shape of the Medical Care Dollar,* a study published by the U.S. Department of Health, Education, and Welfare:

The medical care dollar today is a large one, amounting to $60.3 billion in fiscal 1969. Its growth has been at a rapid pace—faster than that of the economy in general. In fiscal 1950, medical care expenditures amounted to $12.1 billion and represented 4.6 percent of the Gross National Product (the total market value of the Nation's annual output of goods and services). By fiscal 1960, its share of GNP had reached 5.3 percent and today it is up to 6.7 percent. Part of the increasing share of GNP is the result of the higher prices for medical care compared with other items.

What has caused this tremendous increase that threatens to make us poorer despite higher wages? According to HEW, half the rise in health costs is attributed to increases in prices. These increases are found all down the line, from the bottle of aspirin you buy at the drug store (if you are money-management-minded you probably buy at the supermarket's discount department) to the doctor's and dentist's bills. Largest among the price increases are the charges made for hospital beds and services.

Another 10 percent of added cost is due, said HEW, to population growth.

The remaining 31 percent of our whopping medical-health-hospital-drug-insurance bill is due, the study noted, "to increased use of services such as seeing the doctor and dentist more often or going to the hospital more, and having access to many miracle drugs not available in 1950, and life-saving but expensive new techniques such as open heart surgery or kidney dialysis." (See Figure 6, p. 124.)

Thus, health care costs are getting bigger all the time. The rate of cost increase is itself increasing. In June, 1970, for example, the government's consumer cost index indicated that medical care costs were up *in a single month* from 163.6 percent of a 1957–1958 base (1957–1958 figures represent 100) to 164.7 percent. "That annualizes at approximately 8.05 percent," accountant Ronnie pointed out to his friends.

"But will they continue to get worse? Maybe things are stabilizing," suggested Sophie.

Higher prices caused half the 19-year growth

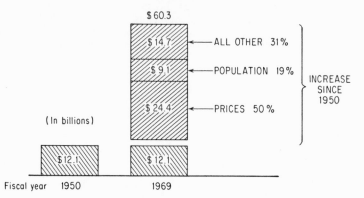

Figure 6 **Higher prices caused half the 19-year growth.** (SOURCE: "The Size and Shape of the Medical Dollar," U.S. Department of Health, Education, and Welfare.)

To answer that, I'll quote from a projection, made in my recent book *How You Can Beat Inflation,* based upon current rate-of-increase data extended ten years into the future:

> An assumption is necessary before anyone can project figures or trends because none of us possesses a crystal ball or a mess of tea leaves capable of infallibly foretelling future events. Our assumption—a very conservative one—will say that inflation won't abate. It might accelerate its pace still further in the next ten years. Acceleration of inflation, automobiles, snowslides, and other such things usually picks up ever faster. . . . We will say that the rate doubles in the next ten years as it did in the last decade. The assumption further says that the rate of every two years' increase will stay at 8.2 percent for the next four years. For the four years that follow them, it will be at 1.5 times that rate (12.3 percent), and for the final two-year period it will be at double the 1967–1969 rate.
>
> That would raise the Consumer Price Index to a lofty 213.4. At that level, the dollar would have depreciated in purchasing power by a further 72 percent.

A further 72 percent increase in costs looks bad enough. It becomes worse when we recall that health care expenses have increased at a more rapid rate than other price rises. If they continue to go up faster than apples, oranges, park benches, or applejack brandy, then you could possibly find yourself saddled with health care costs, a decade from now, that are three times today's high figures!

"We gotta do something!" George said. He was right. Here are some of the things you can do. They won't make the nation's health bill any less, but they hopefully will lighten *your* out-of-pocket expenditures to doctor, dentist, hospital, nursing home, etc. That's what matters.

THE KEY IS THE M.D. (AND D.D.S.)

George had a nagging backache.

"Trouble is, you have been so disgustingly healthy for a long time that you don't have a regular doctor. Until now, an M.D. could have grown old in poverty if he depended upon income from your illnesses," Sophie told him. "It's an age of specialists. I have a gynecologist. The children go to a pediatrician. In which specialist's ballpark do aching backs belong? Shall we ship you to an orthopedist? A neurologist? Physical medicine specialist? Internist? Or good old general practitioner?"

Faced with such a problem, people sometimes consult one specialist, go through elaborate tests, and then discover all the time and money were in vain. "Not in my area," the orthopedist might say. "Try an internist. Or maybe a urologist; it could be your kidneys."

Happily, there is a better, faster, less expensive way to light upon the right choice. The American Medical Association offers this advice on choosing a doctor:

> Start by calling your local medical society for the names of several physicians in your neighborhood or within convenient traveling distance. Membership in the local medical society indicates that a doctor is a qualified physician who meets the high standards of those who know him best—his fellow physicians.

If there is no society office in your community, call your nearby hospital, ask trusted friends for their recommendations, or check the pharmacist for his suggestions.

But this is just the start. The American Medical Directory, published by the American Medical Association, is an excellent source of background information. Available in most public libraries and hospitals, this volume will give you the age, professional education, date of licensure, type of practice, teaching affiliation and medical organization membership for all physicians.

Once you've established the credentials of the doctors on your recommended list, match them to the anticipated needs of your family. Is his address convenient? What are his office hours? Do you prefer an older or younger physician? Will he make house calls? Do any of your family members have physical handicaps or disabilities which might require special care?

Also, you may prefer a physician who has staff privileges at a specific hospital with close proximity to your home. Once you've established your preferences, select one physician who seems to meet them. Then, make an appointment with him for a physical examination (everyone needs one periodically as suggested by the attending physician), and get acquainted with him during your visit, explaining that you are seeking a family physician.

Does he impress you favorably? No one personality type is appealing to all, of course, but if you are "comfortable" with him and sense a quality of competence, he has already begun to win your confidence.

In discussing your family's health needs, keep in mind your budget. Ask the doctor about his fees; not all charge the same. Only through a frank discussion can you determine whether you can afford his services. Rather than being embarrassed by this inquiry, he will welcome it as a basis for future understanding and a good doctor-patient relationship.

He may not be able to give you an exact price for every kind of service but he can and will gladly tell you approximately what his basic fees are and outline an approximate guideline for special services, hospital expenses, and the cost of a good protective health insurance program.

House calls are, of course, more expensive and they are, more often than not, unnecessary. In fact, some physicians do not make them—ever.

Once you have found the "right doctor" be completely open with him. If you have any special problems, anxieties, or family difficulties, tell him. Not all illnesses signal themselves with an ache or pain. Many emotional problems can be overcome or controlled if you "talk them out," but your family physician is not all-knowing. You have to cooperate with him by not withholding information. Unresolved problems may become detrimental to your health and well-being.

I am told that, until recently, the laws of one Dixie state specified all teaching texts about the Civil War should be "fair, impartial and from the Southern point of view." The AMA advice above is fair, impartial, and from the medical point of view. *It is extremely valuable advice.* However, while nearly all physicians are trained professionals who take their work and responsibilities with such great seriousness that the North American continent enjoys a high standard of longevity and physical well-being not found in earlier periods of history, you, George, Sophie, and Ronald will not necessarily find yourselves having a point of view which at every minute coincides with that of these sturdy guardians of muscle and bone vitality. You might also consider the following questions when choosing a physician (or dentist) to fit your purse and your physical fitness requirements:

1. *Begin with a Good General Practitioner or Internist.* A G.P. is a fellow who, figuratively, takes all medical knowledge for his province. He treats colds or cancer, saws bones, and studies electrocardiograms. He has had the regular medical-college training and has served time in a good hospital.

An internist is a specialist in the internal organs and their treatment. In addition to the basic medical knowledge, he has studied, usually three years or longer, to become proficient in his narrower field.

Many people start with the general practitioner or internist, either of whom will recommend specialists, such as the urologist, physical medicine specialist, or orthopedist, who should take over the treatment of George's hurting back. The advantage is that the G.P.'s or internist's tests will develop *which* field of special work should be consulted if the care of those aching vertabrae is not within his immediate ken. In that way, you save money and time—and, not least, cut short continuance of a situation which requires treatment.

Change the words "G.P." and "internist" to "generalist" in dentistry, and the recommendation goes for care of the family's mouth problems as well as for George's throbbing back. A good dental generalist will call in the dental surgeon or orthodontists as and if needed, saving you the expense of making rounds of specialists.

2. What Do a Doctor's Colleagues Think of Him?   His standing in the professional community helps to tell you what fellow pros think of him. Their opinion is likely to be better informed than yours. His membership in a professional society does not prove competence. But it proves his colleagues' stiff professional tests have not been too tough for him to pass.

But don't go only by a prominent name. In my community, one M.D. who has not practiced his profession for years is known to almost every newspaper reader because of effective work in civic causes. He is a good citizen and a light of his city—but not necessarily the man to be consulted when George's back hurts or Ethelred has fallen from a roof and broken an arm.

3. Pay Attention to Hospital Affiliation.   Five years ago I had to undergo an operation. "Do you have a surgeon in mind?" asked my internist. "No? Then let me suggest this: First choose which hospital you prefer. Then I will give you the names of three good surgeons attached to the staff of each." Since one nearby hospital equates, in my mind, with the Black Hole of Calcutta and another, located only blocks away, is clean, fresh, cheerful, well served, and, incidentally, lower in per-day room costs, I considered this a good base for choice. So might you.

4. Will He Go Out on Night Calls?   The American Medical Association looks on this as an unimportant consideration. I have presented its fair, impartial, Southern point of view. From mine—and yours as well—it can be a good thing to have a man willing to take night calls should Ethelred run a 103-degree fever or Sophie need help in the middle of the night; not all home illnesses require expensive hospitalization. It is not amiss to inquire what he charges for this convenience; some doctors' house-call rates go up after certain hours just as do plumbers' and TV technicians' prices.

HOW ABOUT THE HOSPITAL?

Other than observing the cleanliness or the relative surliness of harried help in one sickness dungeon over another, most nonprofessional people are not able to judge whether they want to go to the Asclepius Sick Bay or Hippocrates Haven when they are moaning ill and the emergency call has gone out to Doctor Galen Goodguy to do something about that stomachache which just might be acute appendicitis and require 1 A.M. surgery.

However, there is one area of institutional incarceration which you can consider at leisure and whose charges sometimes loom big in the family budget designed for better living on George's salary. This is the choice of a nursing home.

People live longer and inevitably, it seems, find themselves in one of these homes as they recover from operations or illnesses which do not require the more concentrated care of a hospital such as Hippocrates Haven or Asclepius Sick Bay.

Sophie's mother is one of the postretirement people who, according to a study made by the U.S. Department of Health, Education, and Welfare, require more care, at greater cost, than people in the younger years. Said HEW's study, *The Size and Shape of the Medical Care Dollar:*

> The personal health care bill for the average person in the United States was $233 in fiscal year 1968. *The bill for the average aged person is about three times that of the younger person—$590, compared with $195* [italics mine].
> The differential between the aged and nonaged varies considerably by type of expenditure. Per capita hospital care

expenditures for the aged—$282 in fiscal year 1968—are more than three and a half times that of persons under age 65 ($77), but per capita expenditures for physicians' services for the aged ($97) are only about twice those for the younger age group ($50).

Nursing-home care represents a sizable portion of those figures. On the subject of institutional care in nursing homes, doctors' views are fair and impartial and, in this situation, you're a Southerner too. So it is doubly worthwhile to ask certain questions on choice of a nursing home for Sophie's mother—or yours—that are recommended by the American Medical Association in a copyrighted (1966) booklet, *What to Look For in a Nursing Home:*

> *What type of patients does the nursing home accept? Is the home licensed by the state or local licensing agency?*
>
> *Does the institution require a physical examination and a physician's orders for treatment prior to or immediately after admitting the patient?*
>
> *Are there staff physicians who actually spend time in the nursing home with the patients and nursing home staff? Does the nursing home report periodically on the patient's conditions to his personal physician?*
>
> *What level of nursing supervision is provided? What is the total number of nursing staff?*
>
> *What provision does the home have for dental care of patients?*
>
> *Are facilities available for patient rehabilitation? Are they used regularly?*
>
> *Is the nursing staff trained in basic rehabilitation techniques?*
>
> *Are there adequate safety precautions in the nursing home?*
>
> *Does the nursing home maintain high standards in its food service? Are the menus planned at least one or two weeks in advance, and do they include nutritional foods in a variety of combinations?*
>
> *Does the nursing home prepare therapeutic diets when needed?*
>
> *Does the general atmosphere have a home-like quality?*

Are the floors clean, the lawn and landscaping attractively maintained? What arrangements are there for housekeeping service? Is there sufficient space for each patient? (This is particularly important in homes with ward or "dormitory-type" accommodations.)

What is the attitude of the staff and patients?

Are adequate recreational services available?

Find out what the nursing home rate covers in addition to nursing care, room and board. Is the fee on a monthly or weekly basis? Will charges paid in advance be refunded if the patient leaves the home? Are extra charges made for drugs, special diets, extra nursing care, and such personal services as spoon-feeding, tray service, personal laundry, shampoos, haircuts, shaving and the like? How much? The number of patients in a room is another factor determining the cost.

A prime question not suggested by the AMA is this: "Will Medicare and insurance companies approve?" In this world of high (and often covered) costs, *who pays* is the biggest one of all from the budget, if not from the medical, point of view.

HEALTH AND OTHER INSURANCE

It isn't only with a nursing home that insurance enters the health care picture for the Georges and Sophies who are concerned with curing the high cost of staying healthy. As Maynard L. Heacox of the AMA pointed out, you can't do much about the cost of care after you're sick. That should properly begin before George's back begins to ache or prior to Ethelred's fall from the roof with a resulting broken arm.

In Chapter Two, we looked over the shoulders of Sophie, George, and Ronnie as they huddled to work out ways of saving on insurance. Health insurance was brought in only as part of the family's complete package of insurance. Now let's take out that important portion and look at it in detail. Knowledge can reduce costs and up the payoff should a member of the family be sick enough to become covered.

First, the types of health insurance: Policies generally break down into three groups. There are straight hospitalization policies which pay a stated amount for stated hospital services. These sometimes include payments for physician or surgeon. There are disability policies which pay a weekly stipend during the time you are laid up. And there are major medical policies which usually leave the first $500 payment to you, but are designed to protect policyholders from the big blow that can bring financial ruin by providing coverage up to $10,000 thereafter. Many people carry variations and combinations of the basic three.

It pays to ask some questions before you sign to take on any health care policy. In *How You Can Beat Inflation,* these were suggested:

1. Should I Buy a Group Policy or an Individualized One?   Group policies usually cost less. But their provisions may not be the ones which you require. An individual policy can be custom-designed, but like anything else custom-made, it is likely to be higher in cost. Some people compromise by taking the group policy, then adding outside, individualized coverage for protections they require.

No coverage is better than the company offering it. Choose a sound, well-known company. Keep in mind the example of the admittedly far-out, but still real, case of a mail-order life insurance company—now itself happily defunct—whose policies provided that benefits could only be paid if the deceased appeared in person to make a claim five days after death.

2. Is Maternity Covered?   Some health care policies specifically exclude maternity care, or else put such a low dollar limit on the payments that it might as well be excluded. Yet maternity confinement is the hospitalization most likely to be needed by a young family.

3. Do Benefits Apply Immediately?   Several years ago, George had an automobile accident only three days after being accepted for a health care policy. Prolonged, painful surgery was needed. "At least," he said to his wife, "the family's bank account won't be crippled. Even surgeons' fees are taken care of by the new policy." He was shocked when the agent apologetically pointed out that his policy excluded coverage until thirty days after it was issued.

Such an exclusion is not necessarily evidence of chicanery. It is a kind of "deductible," and before you take on health care coverage you should be aware whether a clause of this type has been written into the contract. You don't *have* to buy from that company.

4. Does the Policy Cover Follow-up Treatment?   When a patient comes out of the hospital there sometimes remains long and expensive treatment in the physician's office or hospital clinic. Health care policies differ on this point. Some provide for follow-up treatment. Others exclude it. As a general thing you will have to pay a higher premium to secure the coverage; whether to do so is a personal decision based on your own plans for better living by money management.

5. Are Surgical-Medical Fees Part of the Policy?   Here, too, you will pay more to get the fee coverage. If you buy such coverage, read the fine print carefully. Discover whether the fees to be paid out are realistic or are based upon those charged by doctors when Galen was the medical light of ancient times. Is fee coverage purely surgical, or is your regular doctor's attendance also to be reimbursed by the company? Learn whether nursing care—outside of as well as in the hospital—is covered.

One young woman learned the painful way to look for such extras. When a smashup broke both of her arms, she suffered additional facial damage for which a dental specialist had to be called.

"Nope," said the claim adjuster when she presented the bill. "Your policy calls for payment to medical doctors. The dentist has to be on you."

6. If You have Disability Coverage, Is It enough?   It is not many years since a convalescent could live adequately on $75 per week. The progress of inflation has been steady since then. As I pointed out in *How You Can Beat Inflation*, there is no reason to believe that inflation will not continue even if momentarily arrested.

7. Are Premium Payments Suspended upon Disability? "No use giving it out to a policyholder with one hand while taking it partially back with the other," an insurance agent explained to me. "Unless a policy calls for suspension of payments to the company during the disability period, a policyholder's payments are lessened by the amount he has to continue giving to the company."

8. How Many Exclusions?   Many policies will not pay for treatment of certain diseases or disabilities and will limit the amounts to be paid on others. Generally, you should look for a policy with the fewest exclusions and the widest latitude because you don't want to gamble on what *kind* of disease you might have.

9. Is Your Policy Acceptable to Hospitals?   One man I know had an expensive policy with a soundly rated company. But the hospital clerk shook her head when the policy was presented. "We take only certain companies," the attendant said sweetly. "Yours isn't one. You will have to pay us yourself, then collect from your company. That will be $100 advance deposit, please."

Nonacceptability at the hospital cashier's desk is no proof that a policy is with an inferior company. But it does mean some annoyance and delay in obtaining reimbursement while bills go through the auditing mills.

10. Is Renewability Guaranteed?   There are companies which will pay off promptly on any legitimate claim, but refuse to cover the same policyholder for another year. A clause of guaranteed renewability can be a comforting thing.

It's important to know how the provisions of a policy dove-

tail or clash with such public programs as Medicare. I have seen policies which state that payments made by Medicare are excluded from the expenses they will reimburse. Other companies' policies pay off without regard to the coverage from additional sources.

THE PUBLIC PROGRAMS

An old man in my neighborhood died recently. His last years were not happy. "All my life, Dorothy and I saved," he told me. "Income from our savings was expected to add to social security and the company pension to provide a pretty good life after retirement. Then Dorothy became sick. All those life savings went to the doctors and the hospitals in twelve months."

My neighbor's story unfolded before Medicare became a part of our national life. It and other public health programs cover much of the older population. "For God's sake, tell Uncle Paul to look into that," George urged Sophie. "Here we are, fairly young, paying medical costs of an oldster because the oldster didn't acquaint himself with the public programs."

As George pointed out, these can save money for you even where you aren't eligible for Medicare. It can do so in more cases than merely that of an aged uncle.

"And there are programs for people other than the aged," he pointed out. "Some are mainly for disadvantaged families, but many apply to all of us. Some of us *are* disadvantaged."

In a U.S. Department of Health, Education, and Welfare booklet, *Social Security Information for YOUNG Families,* it was pointed out in regard to disability payments that "a worker 31 or older . . . must have credit for five years of work in the ten year period ending when he becomes disabled. If you become disabled between 24 and 31, you need credit for only half the time between age 21 and the time you become unable to work." Social security benefits vary as changes are made in the law. If you, or a member of the family you're money-managing for a better life, should become disabled, good old SS might have a package to help you overcome the high cost of being unhealthy.

The biggest package is Medicare. This, too, changes as Congress and HEW, in their collective wisdom and under pressures of election-year tactics, might liberalize or tighten up the law. As things stand now (and are likely to continue with minor variations), the setup was explained in the advisory pamphlet, *Your Social Security:*

> Generally, your medical insurance will pay 80 percent of the reasonable charges for the following services after the first $50 in each calendar year:
>
> ■ Physicians' and surgeons' services, no matter where you receive the services—in the doctor's office, in a clinic, in a hospital, or at home. (You do not have to meet the $50 deductible before your medical insurance will pay for X-ray or laboratory services of physicians when you are a bed patient in a hospital. The full reasonable charge will be paid, instead of 80 percent.)
>
> ■ Home health services even if you have not been in a hospital—up to 100 visits during a calendar year.
>
> ■ A number of other medical and health services, such as diagnostic tests, surgical dressings and splints, and rental or purchase of durable medical equipment.
>
> ■ Outpatient physical therapy services—whether or not you are homebound—furnished under supervision of a participating hospital, extended care facility, home health agency, approved clinic, rehabilitation agency, or public health agency.
>
> ■ All outpatient services of a participating hospital, including diagnostic tests or treatment.
>
> ■ Certain services by podiatrists (but not routine foot care or treatment of flat feet or partial dislocations of the feet).

Low-cost and no-cost services are rendered those who have served in America's wars by the Veterans Administration. A prominent VA physician told me:

"Probably not more than 60 percent of veterans know all the care we offer and the ways VA medical service can save money. We're not here merely to treat the wounded or disabled of war, but all veterans in many ways."

In addition to direct hospitalization, veterans can receive

outpatient services, even dental treatment. The things for which VA offers treatment need not be service-connected in every case. Consider these benefits available to all with active military service (quotations are from *Federal Benefits for Veterans and Dependents*, a VA Information Service booklet):

> Veterans needing hospitalization because of injuries or disease incurred or aggravated in line of duty in active service have top priority for admission for treatment of the service-incurred or service-aggravated disability.
>
> Veterans who were discharged or retired for disability incurred or aggravated in line of duty or who are receiving compensation, or would be eligible to receive compensation, except for receipt of retirement pay, who need treatment for some ailment not connected with their service, will be admitted as beds are available.
>
> Veterans with service during any war or the Korean Conflict period and the post-Korean Conflict period and the Vietnam Era (or veterans with peacetime service awarded the Medal of Honor) who were not discharged or retired for disability and who apply for treatment of a *non-service-connected disability* [italics mine] may be admitted to VA hospitals if all three of the following conditions are met: (1) hospitalization is deemed necessary, (2) they state under oath they are financially unable to defray the cost of the necessary hospital charges elsewhere, and (3) if beds are available.

In addition, outpatient treatment is available and domiciliary care, dental treatment, and prosthetic appliances can be obtained through VA. If you or anyone dependent upon you served Uncle, look into his avuncular medical purse before undertaking private care.

Many community services exist, sometimes on a free-to-all basis, sometimes under restrictions. Where they're available, they can cut your out-of-pocket medical payments. In its July, 1970, issue, *Modern Hospital* described one plan operating in New York City:

> CATCH is one of 60 programs financed by federal grants through the U.S. Children's Bureau, an agency of the Department of Health, Education and Welfare, under Title 5 of

the 1965 amendments to the Social Security Act. Programs similar to CATCH include seven others in New York City, several in Pennsylvania and Maryland, comprehensive care programs designed to help Indians in Montana and Mexican-Americans in the Southwest. . . . Under the program, children are cared for when they are sick as well as when they are healthy. Through proper immunization, they are protected against disease. Physicians see them regularly to make certain they are growing and developing properly. Medical specialists are made available to work with physicians to help diagnose and treat physical and emotional problems. Every child receives complete dental care.

Some communities' public programs are privately run. Largest of these is the Kaiser setup. George read about it in a copyrighted article, "Better Care at Less Cost without Miracles," which appeared in the January, 1970, issue of *Fortune*. Describing what it called "Henry J's New Model," *Fortune* reported:

The Kaiser Foundation program is by far the largest of the prepaid systems. It has two million members and its own network of hospitals and outpatient clinics in California, Oregon, and Hawaii. The program began in the late 1930's when the late Henry J. Kaiser, then building hydroelectric dams in remote locations, felt obliged to provide medical services for construction workers and their families. After a conventional, fee-for-service payment system proved unpopular, Kaiser substituted a single fee covering all needed services, and the plan was enthusiastically accepted. In response to requests from hundreds of former shipyard workers, Kaiser kept the program going on the West Coast after 1945, *and opened it to the general public. Today, employees of the various Kaiser companies and their families constitute only about 3 percent of the membership.* [Italics mine.]

The Kaiser plan has made some notable improvements over the orthodox means of distributing medical care. To begin with, access is easy. Physicians of all major specialties are housed in large clinics in each of the regions covered by the plan. A middle-aged man with an abdominal pain can see his internist and can be referred within minutes to another specialist in the same building, which has its own x-ray and laboratories. If the patient requires hospitalization, he is sent to one of the Kaiser Foundation's nineteen hospitals, many of which adjoin the outpatient clinics.

Unlike ordinary private "health insurance," which is really sickness insurance designed to reimburse selected medical expenses under the fee-for-service system, the Kaiser program assumes broad responsibility for keeping its members sound of body. The range of services varies according to the employer group of individual member, but a fairly typical plan offered in the San Francisco-Sacramento area currently costs a total of $35.40 a month for a subscriber with two or more dependents, including the employer's contribution. This covers all professional services in the hospital, in the doctor's office, and in the home, including surgery; all x-ray and laboratory services; all preventive care, including physical examinations; and hospital care for up to 111 days per person in a calendar year. Some nominal charges are made for drugs and for doctors' visits ($1 per office visit, and up to $5 for house calls after 5:00 P.M.), and there is a $60 charge for maternity care. Some items are excluded, notably dental care, psychiatry, and nursing-home care (though some Kaiser plans offer psychiatric and convalescent care, too). For an additional monthly payment of 15 cents, hospitalization can be extended all the way to 365 days.

CALL ON THE COMPANY

"You mean that your firm has a health plan and you want to consult a private physician for your back?" asked Ronnie. "George, you're missing out on one of the major fringe benefits available to you. You're about to spend a lot of money unnecessarily."

While few plans are as ambitious as the Kaiser plan, and almost none extend beyond employees of the company, nearly every sizable firm cares for the health of its employees. A company's plan might cover nothing more than an informal arrangement with Galen Goodguy, the good general practitioner down the block, to check workers' sniffles during the cold and flu season. It might, as many health plans do, give you company-furnished Blue Cross, Blue Shield, or other insurance to supply varying amounts toward the large cost of being sick. The granddaddy of corporate plan is that of

Kaiser Steel, described above. Whatever your company furnishes, take fullest advantage of it if you want to tap an important source of free or low-cost health attention.

To determine what is being done in representative companies, I queried scores of firms across the country. Most asked to be identified only as "a leading corporation." So with respect for their wishes and for the happy leading view taken of themselves, these are reports on the kinds of health care which might be available if you or George were to report to the company health office instead of calling on your own private orthopedist, urologist, internist, or G.P. to treat that nagging backache:

> . . . Our employees have coverage under the plans of the Blue Cross–Blue Shield organizations in communities where they work. After an employee has a full year's service the company pays the premium for him and his family.

> . . . Benefits of our plan are as follows: 80 percent of covered expenses for room, board and other services in a hospital. 80 percent of covered medical expenses outside a hospital and covered doctors' fees in or out of the hospital in excess of $50 deductible in one calendar year. Separate maternity benefits up to a maximum of $200. Overall maximum payment for employee and each dependent: $20,000.

> . . . Major Medical expense benefits covering each hourly employee and dependents with a $50 all-cause deductible. ["Try buying *that* small deductible from a private source," Ronnie pointed out.] Semi-private in-patient care, use of operating and delivery room, dressings, plaster casts, splints, etc. Out-patient service.

> . . . Hospital expenses, generally up to 31 days. Out-patient benefits. Surgical expenses.

> . . . Life and medical insurance for hourly employees. Basic and major medical insurance for salaried employees.

> . . . We offer a comprehensive medical insurance plan for employees at no cost to them. Employees may also insure their eligible dependents by paying the applicable premium for such coverage. However, there is no provision for preventive medical services.

> . . . 100 percent of the first $1,000 for hospital room and board (semi-private) in any calendar year. 80 percent thereafter. 80 percent of other hospital expenses.

TO RECAP:

1. Your bills for medical, health, preventive, and routine care need not be as high as they are for most families. You can take positive steps to manage medical money without sacrificing the quality of care your family receives.

2. The American Medical Association points out that the greatest opportunities for reducing the bill come before sickness strikes, not afterward.

3. According to government figures, health care costs have grown from $12.1 billion in 1950 to $60.3 billion in fiscal 1969. Some of this rise is due to population growth. But much comes from increased costs and increased usage of health care services. A reasonable expectation is that continuing inflation will make additional increases inevitable in years to come.

4. Money management to reduce these costs begins with the doctor and dentist in whose hands the family's health is placed.

5. You can't always choose between hospitals since a patient must go where his doctor practices. But nursing homes—a growing part of the health picture, particularly for our expanding older population—can be chosen with both satisfaction and fee economy in mind.

6. Health insurance comes in several packages. No one type of policy is "best"—that depends upon your setup and needs and upon whether you wish to dovetail with existing company or community health coverage.

7. Local and federal public programs help with health care. Knowing the programs available to you is a starter in obtaining lowest-cost service.

8. Workers for most corporations and for many public bodies are assisted by company doctors and company-furnished insurance programs. If you have one of these programs available, use its aid at no or low cost.

7

Lower the Cost of Learning

"COLLEGE MAY PAY, but it sure costs a lot," observed Sophie.

She and George sat on their living room couch. Catalogs of eleven universities were spread across the coffee table. Three spilled to the carpet. "The hallowed halls of ivy or red brick, as her choice and our circumstances may dictate, aren't so far away for Edith, now she is getting along in high school. We should begin thinking about where we'll find the money to pay for all that learning," she said.

"We'll begin by thinking about the sources of *other* people's money for her university education," George snorted. "It's all perfectly legitimate and aboveboard. There are many ways to make that $3,000-per-year education cost in the area of $300 for people who understand money management."

Can Edith—or your child or mine, or you or I—*really* pull off a feat like this? Quite probably. The purpose of Chapter

Seven on which we're embarking now is to explore some of the ways to do it.

Without use of those ways, high college costs might make advanced education impossible for many of us. Or they might make a sufficiently large dent in the budget to preclude expenditure for anything else not vitally needed. But with knowledge of the moneys available, you can shave this section of budget costs and free money for the better living that this book is all about.

In its copyrighted "Personal Business" section, June 6, 1970, *Business Week* noted that "student tempers aren't the only things that are volatile on campus. Costs have been booming, too, from Cambridge to Berkeley." A broad survey of leading colleges shows the trend: In five years private coeducational colleges jumped their charges an average 30 percent and public colleges 24 percent.

> For both classes, the jump from 1969–70 to 1970–71 is 8%. This means—assuming that your son or daughter goes to one of the "name" colleges—that next year you'll pay a total tab that will often go above $5,000.
>
> Costs are at an all-time high at such colleges as Yale ($3,900 for tuition, fees, room and board), Northwestern ($3,600), and Stanford ($3,600). You won't find much of a break at small, quality colleges in the hinterlands.
>
> For example, at Kenyon in Ohio, the costs add up to $3,715 for 1970–71—and this doesn't allow for spending money or transportation.
>
> State universities, too, will cost more than you might imagine. A BUSINESS WEEK check shows that many state colleges have been making a concerted effort to hit out-of-staters in the pocketbook. For instance, at the University of Wisconsin, tuition fees and room and board for in-staters come to $1,595 for next year. Anyone from out of state pays an extra $1,276.

Happily, ways exist to borrow, gain grants, and finagle funds for educating Edith, Ethelred, and Frederica and for paying the tab when George or Sophie—or you—want to add to education. The biggest giver of financial assistance is Uncle Sugar.

FEDERAL FUNDS—FRONT AND CENTER

Federal aid to higher education dates back to 1958, when the National Defense Education Act was passed. A lengthy study of effects of this and other federal programs was undertaken by J. Philip Hinson, monetary economist of the Federal Reserve Bank of Boston. In the June and July, 1970, issues of the bank's *New England Business Review,* he reported:

> To help ease the burden of higher education on lower income families the Federal Government began to participate in student loans with the passage of the National Defense Education Act of 1958 (NDEA). Title II authorized Federal funds for low interest loans to students who established financial need. Under this plan, which is still operating, funds are distributed to each state which, in turn, allocates them among colleges and universities willing to provide additional matching funds equal to ⅑ of their Federal receipts. Students are permitted to borrow up to $1,000 per year, with college financial officers determining the amount for which each applicant qualified. *The loans are interest free while the student remains in school.* [Italics mine.] Upon graduation, interest is charged at a simple annual rate of 3 percent on the unpaid balance. Repayment may be stretched out for 10 years, with extensions allowed for postgraduate education or duty in the armed services. Further, up to one-half of the principal is forgiven those entering elementary or secondary teaching as a career.

That adds up to quite a package. No money down while Edith attends the university (provided university officials decide that she qualifies), with 3 percent interest afterward and up to half the whole ball of wax forgotten if she should go later into teaching. "Seems we oughta borrow just because it's so cheap," George commented. "No-interest and low-interest loans are a bargain you don't see none of, nohow, nowadays."

The Fed of Boston study described other federal assistance:

> Under the Higher Education Act (HEA) of 1965 the Federal Government established a new student loan program with entirely different administrative procedures. This program

relies on private financial institutions to extend the loans directly to students and permits the lenders to secure guarantees on funds advanced for this purpose. While the old and new plans are now operating simultaneously, many supporters of the HEA program believe that it should ultimately replace the older NDEA plan. . . . Although any student, regardless of his family income, may borrow under this program, an element of subsidy is provided for the great majority of American families with college-aged children. If the net taxable income of the student's family is less than $15,000, the Federal government will pay the entire percent interest bill while the student is in school and one-half of it during the years of repayment. As an example of the liberality of these provisions, a family of four with a gross income of $19,333 or less would be eligible for the interest benefit.

The programs described above lend money. There is another federal program that gives it outright, and still another federal program makes work opportunities available for Edith, Ethelred, Frederica, George, or Sophie to work out tuition costs.

The Educational Opportunity Grants Program "is for students of exceptional financial need who without this grant would be unable to continue their educations. Grants of up to $1,000 a year are available for four years of undergraduate study; and if you are selected for an EOG, you will also receive additional financial aid at least equal to the EOG amount," according to *More Education . . . More Opportunity,* a publication of the Department of Health, Education and Welfare. "The financial officer at your school selects those who will receive grants and determines the amount you will need."

Describing ways to work for your book learning, the same HEW advisory states: "The College Work-Study Program may assist you by providing a job opportunity for the college itself or for a public or private nonprofit agency—such as a school, a social agency, or a hospital—working in cooperation with your school. You may work an average of 15 hours weekly while classes are in session and 40 hours per week during the summer or other vacation periods. In general, the salary paid is at least equal to the current minimum wage, although it is frequently higher. The financial aid officer is responsible for determining the students to be employed, selecting suitable jobs for them, handling the payroll, and the general administration of the program."

That doesn't end the list of educational goodies dispensed by Uncle Sugar to those who want learning at low cost. The GI bill—familiar to old grads of World War II and the Korean dingdong—is alive and well and ready to provide educational assistance today to all who served in the Army, Navy, Marine Corps, or Air Force after January 31, 1955. Generally, if you were in uniform for eighteen months, you can secure thirty-six months of educational aid. This applies to technical and trade training as well as matriculation in a Joe College institution. "Full time institutional training" is ticketed for a veteran at $130 per month. If he has dependents, the vet is allowed $25 for the first, $20 for the second, and $10 each for others. Veterans Administration offices have the details.

Aid to educate war orphans, defined as "children of servicemen whose death was incurred or injuries aggravated as a result of their active service during wartime or peacetime periods after Sept. 16, 1940," is offered by their generous Washington uncle.

If Ethelred, on reaching college age, should decide to become a reserve officer via training at a university's ROTC unit—and if present rules and laws are still operative when he trots with his high school diploma to the college registrar's office—scholarship assistance will be available to provide $50 per month for tuition, lab fees, and books. Information can be had from the professors of military (or naval or air) science at universities that have Reserve Officers Training Corps.

Special assistance is offered to dependents of active, retired, and deceased Naval and Air Force personnel. (Write Bureau of Naval Personnel, Department of the Navy, Washington, D.C. 20370, or Commandant, Headquarters, AFROTC, Maxwell Air Force Base, Alabama 36112.)

The Air Force Aid Society sponsors a General Henry H.

Arnold Educational Fund to lend money at no interest to eligible students pursuing certain undergraduate or technical courses. (Write Air Force Aid Society, National Headquarters, Washington, D.C. or ask the personnel officer at any Air Force base.)

Federal nursing scholarships at $1,500 a year are offered through the Division of Nursing, National Health Service, Bethesda, Maryland. Ask about them only if you feel you qualify under the Division's standard of "exceptional" financial need. Other low-interest loans for nursing education are available through degree-awarding institutions and you don't have to be downright broke to qualify for these. They lend up to $1,500 a year, repayable over ten years. Write the same Division of Nursing in Bethesda.

"Bully," said Sophie. "That may be great for us when Edith reaches college age. But how about me? I'd like to go back for a master's degree so that in a few years, when the children are less underfoot, I can obtain a job teaching. Does the federal government offer grants for graduate work?"

It does.

The Committee on Education and Labor of the U.S. House of Representatives has printed *A Guide to Student Assistance* (cost is 60 cents from the Superintendent of Documents in Washington—or your congressman may send it free). It lists the following federal graduate aids:

■ A two-year City Planning Fellowship at $3,000 per year, plus $500 for each dependent up to two, is available through Urban Studies Fellowship Program, Housing and Urban Development Department, Washington, D.C. 20410. Before applying, you have to be enrolled or accepted for enrollment in an institution offering city planning courses, and you must intend to pursue this urban Big Brother act as a permanent career.

■ Fulbright-Hays Fellowships enable "qualified individuals to visit another country to study, teach, lecture or conduct research." Grants are usually issued for six to twelve months. Full grants provide round-trip transportation, language or orientation courses, tuition, books, and maintenance for a year. Accident and health insurance is included, so if you secure one of these grants you can reduce health insurance costs described in the previous chapter. A travel grant provides transportation to the country where you will study and is "intended to supplement ... scholarships ... granted to American students by universities, private donors and foreign governments."

■ Under the Higher Education Personnel Graduate Training Program (friends of the family on first-name terms call it EPDA), fellowships for one to two years are granted for cramming learning below the doctoral level into heads of people who are interested in higher education careers and have experience at this bag. They are given $2,400 for the first year of study and $2,600 for the second, with an allowance of $500 for dependents such as Edith, Ethelred, and Frederica. To get abroad, Sophie—or you—should apply to the graduate school at your favorite hall of ivy or red brick. (A list of schools participating in EPDA is available from the EDPA Part E Fellowship Program, Bureau of Higher Education, U.S. Office of Education, Washington, D.C. 20202.)

■ The National Defense Education Program, active in undergraduate assistance, can be counted on by those seeking postgraduate training. The NDEA Graduate Fellowships Program seeks to "increase the number of well-qualified college and university teachers by assisting doctoral students to prepare for academic careers; encourage development and full utilization of the capacity of graduate programs leading to the doctorate; and promote a wider geographic distribution of such programs in the nation." These are normally three-year awards for work toward a Ph.D. or an equivalent degree. In the 1969–1970 academic year, stipends were $2,400 for the first academic year, $2,600 for the second, and $2,800 toward the third lap of the doctoral grind. For your dependents, $500 each would be provided. If you do summer study, special hot-weather allowances apply. Application forms are available at graduate schools.

■ Federal Library Training Fellowships help those seeking a master's degree. These provide $2,200 for the academic year with $450 for summer study. People toiling in the Ph.D. vineyard under this program draw an allotment of $5,000 for the academic year with a maximum of $1,020 for summer research. Graduate schools which offer library programs can provide forms. Or write Division of Library Programs, U.S. Office of Education, Washington, D.C. 20202.

■ NDEA Graduate Foreign Language Fellowships are for the encouragement of students specializing in foreign language and related areas. They provide payment of $2,250 per academic year and $600 per dependent, with a summer allowance of $450, plus $120 per dependent ($120 each for Edith, Ethelred, and Frederica, if Sophie extends her studies into the summer). A list of institutions participating in this program will be provided by the Division of Foreign Studies, U.S. Office of Education, whose address is at Washington, D.C. 20202.

■ National Science Foundation Fellowships come in a size providing $2,400 the first year, $2,600 the second, and $2,800 the third, with the usual dependent fringe benefits. At time of application, the ambitious scientist should "have demonstrated ability and special aptitude for advanced training in the sciences and have been accepted or plan to be accepted at an accredited graduate school." The National Science Foundation Division of Graduate Education in Science holds forth in Washington, D.C. 20550, and will furnish application forms.

■ A Nurse Science Graduate Training Program is for the advanced nursing and health-related studies that Florence Nightingales undertake toward doctoral degrees. Fellowships are for four and five years and students "receive a stipend comparable to other Federal programs." For a list of participating graduate mills, write Research Grants Branch, Division of Nursing, National Institute of Health, 900 Rockville Pike, Bethesda, Maryland 20014.

■ Under the Public Health Service Trainee Program, also

administered by the National Institute of Health in Bethesda, "traineeships are granted initially for a one-year period ... for research at predoctoral, postdoctoral and prebaccalaureate (for dental hygienists and registered nurses) level. ... Stipends ranging from $2,400 to $3,600." Predoctoral fellowships are also offered.

■ Research Fellowships in the Field of Vocational Rehabilitation come from the Social and Rehabilitation Service, Department of Health, Education, and Welfare, Washington, D.C. 20201. Applicants must have at least a master's degree and be accepted at an approved institution. The usual graduated federal scale of stipend is provided.

■ NASA's Predoctoral Sustaining University Program is planned "to increase the supply of highly trained scientists and engineers in space-related sciences, engineering, engineering design and public administration." One-year, renewable fellowships are offered if you're aiming at the Ph.D. level. Fellows receive $2,400 per year and a dependent allowance not exceeding $1,000 for all dependents. The participating university decides how much you receive. Details from the Office of University Affairs, National Aeronautics and Space Administration, Washington, D.C. 20546.

■ The Teacher Corps Program "combines practical teaching experience with advanced graduate work in order to achieve two objectives—(1) encourage able college graduates to enter a career in teaching poverty-stricken children; and (2) in this manner help alleviate poverty by improving educational opportunities for disadvantaged students." If this should prove to be Sophie's thing, she can secure, if qualified as a "teacher intern," a stipend of $75 a week with $15 each for Edith, Ethelred, and Frederica. Details available from Teacher Corps, Washington, D.C. 20202.

■ Sophie might also apply to the Teacher Fellowship Program, "designed to meet the growing need in the United States for more and better elementary and secondary school teachers." Two-year graduate study is available, at $4,000 per year stipend plus $600 for each dependent, to those planning to teach or teaching in elementary and secondary

schools. Applications available from Basic Studies Program, P.O. Box 1600, City Post Office, Washington, D.C. 20013.

■ If Sophie's teaching plan revolves around the handicapped, she should look into Training of Teachers in the Education of Handicapped Children. This program with the extended handle offers one-year fellowships, renewable for four years. While Sophie works toward a master's, she can receive $2,200 plus $600 for dependents. Those seeking the honorable initials Ph.D. receive $3,200 plus the same dependent allowance. Details will be sent by the Bureau of Education for the Handicapped, U.S. Office of Education, Washington, D.C. 20202.

■ Everybody wants into the antipollution act. Water Pollution Control Research Fellowships are granted for graduate work leading to the master's or doctorate degree. Fellows aiming at a master's receive $2,400 per year plus $500 per dependent. The candidates for the Ph.D. receive $2,600, increased to $2,800 in the last year of study, with the same dependent payout. Applications are issued by the Training Grants Branch, Division of Manpower and Training, U.S. Department of the Interior, Washington, D.C. 20242.

"Keep in mind," Ronnie warned his friends, "that the federal figures we're discussing now are subject to change by Congress or the agencies involved."

NON-FEDERAL GRANT GIVERS

■ The Tuition Plan allows you to spread out those high costs of higher education instead of plumping down a lump sum when Edith enters the doors of Faraway U. Available, its sponsors say, at more than 1,100 degree dispensaries, it has wide flexibility and can be coupled with insurance so that if George and Sophie should both shuffle from this mortal sphere before Edith has emerged from the graduating end of Faraway U's educational assembly line, the tab will still be picked up. (Cynical observers point out that this is designed more to assure Faraway and other universities of a steady flow of fee funds than to free the Sophie-George family from worry about Edith's degree completion.)

Says a Tuition Plan brochure:

> Since 1938, more than a quarter of a million families have used the convenient monthly payment programs of the Tuition Plan. . . . Many of these families chose the Plan even though they could well have met college costs out of funds on hand. The interest charges are reasonable and are income tax deductible. They are less than the usual amount charged for personal instalment loans or unsecured loans. . . .
>
> The Tuition Plan is both sound and flexible. You may include not only tuition costs, but also room, board, music and laboratory fees, health fees, books, transportation, fraternity or sorority expenses . . . even incidentals. Furthermore, you may increase or decrease your program to reflect changes in expenses. For instance, if your child changes his status from day student to boarding student, you can increase your program to include these additional expenses. . . . Tuition Plan is designed to pay all costs of a college education, not just tuition fees alone.

Faraway U and other degree grantors can furnish Tuition Plan details.

■ Education Funds, Inc., also lends money. This Rhode Island setup (Box 4, Providence, Rhode Island 02903) charges a sizable interest which it correctly calls "less than most bank card or similar credit" (less by ½ of 1 percent a month). Charges are 1¼ percent monthly on amounts less than $500 and ¾ of 1 percent each twelfth of a year on amounts over that. "That's 15 percent on the first half-thou and 9 percent on amounts over $500—hardly the generous gift of a philanthropist," Ronnie sniffed as he, Sophie, and George shuffled papers relating to college costs. "If you borrow $1,000 under these terms, current in 1970, you pay $75 plus $45 interest in a year. That's a total of $120 or 12 percent. A friendly usurer might be more advantageous."

■ United Student Aid is something different. It is described by J. Philip Hinson in the Federal Reserve study, "Student Loan Programs for Higher Education," as beginning with "the earlier attempts of a number of individual states to pro-

vide loan aid for higher education to their own residents."
He noted:

> The earliest of these plans dates back to 1956 when the
> private nonprofit Massachusetts Higher Education Assistance
> Corporation was founded. Under the plan, students borrowed
> directly from private lending institutions, and the latter then
> registered the loan with this agency to secure a partial guar-
> antee of the principal against default.
>
> By 1965 a total of 17 states had developed their own vari-
> ants of the Massachusetts program, and a private nonprofit
> corporation (United Student Aid Fund, Inc.) had been
> established to offer its version of the plan on a nationwide
> basis. These organizations pioneered in developing methods
> for operating loan funds and enabled many students from
> low income families to acquire a higher education.

Interest charges under United Student Aid are low by today's
money-rental standards. A brochure explains that

> no borrower under this plan may be charged more than 7%
> simple interest. This is less than customary bank rates for
> instalment loans and is offered by participating banks as a
> public service. Interest charges run from the date the loan is
> advanced until repayment is completed.
>
> For a student who qualifies under Federal law, the Federal
> Government will pay the 7% interest while he is in school
> and during authorized periods where repayment is not re-
> quired.

■ State aid varies with the state. Louisiana's plan provides state-guaranteed loans to the student. Private lenders
make the loans and may not charge above 7 percent. Terms
are available to residents and other U.S. citizens who enroll
at a Louisiana university or technical school, and to residents attending out-of-state colleges (under some circumstances).

Other states' laws may be different from the Louisiana
example.

■ National Merit Scholarships are planned to "provide
academically gifted students with four-year scholarships to
help finance their undergraduate studies." Merit scholars

receive scholarships ranging from an honorary $100 (where there is no financial need) to a maximum of $1,500 per year.

"Precious little merit there," snorted George. "I'm expected to prove at least partial poverty if Edith is to get anything but an 'honorary' amount."

Whether the award is honorary, or full, or somewhere between—an astonishing number of middle-income families do qualify for some aid when their children make the coveted National Merit—Edith will have to possess a high ranking to be considered. National Merit scholars are generally in the top one percentile of their areas.

▪ It also takes above-average school work to qualify for National Honor Society scholarships. As do the National Merit awards, these look at the parents' financial position in addition to the achievements of pupils. To be eligible, Edith will have to belong to the National Honor Society while in high school.

▪ Union awards and scholarships come in varying amounts for children of members. If you belong to a union, ask your local officers for particulars or write the Department of Education, AFL-CIO, 816 16th St., N.W., Washington, D.C. 20006.

▪ For outstanding black students, National Achievement Scholarship Programs are administered by the National Merit Scholarship Corporation, using funds provided by Ford Foundation. Secondary school officials can furnish details, or write National Achievement Scholarship Program, 990 Grove St., Evanston, Illinois 60201.

▪ American Indian Youth Scholarships are offered through many universities to students of Indian descent. For a list of participating colleges, contact Scholarship Officer, Bureau of Indian Affairs, U.S. Department of the Interior, Washington, D.C. 20242.

▪ Many companies give corporate scholarships. Sometimes, they are for children of officers and employees. Sometimes, they are given to students who will agree to work after graduation for the donating company. Many scholarships are for study in certain fields. In other cases, there are no strings at all. Corporate scholarships are so numerous and varied that description would take up a book in itself. The Director of Student Aid at Faraway U (and other schools) can furnish details.

■ Most older universities have alumni scholarships. My alma mater, Louisiana State University, offers over a hundred through annual Alumni Fund drives. Since many of these have no requirement that an applicant swear perpetual and grinding poverty, they should be investigated by people of average income who are unwilling to range themselves among the disadvantaged in order to obtain help with the high cost of putting university-level education into the heads of their Ediths, Ethelreds, and Fredericas.

■ Private and trade-group scholarships cover many areas. Some are bequeathed to universities in memory of a loved one. Some are trusts established by the living. A few come from associations (example, a scholarship for one Purdue freshman to study entomology is given by the National Pest Control Association) or from campus fraternities (example from the same Purdue catalog: Tau Beta Pi scholarship of $300 for an engineering student, given by this honorary group, and a smaller $50 award by Alpha Zeta to the student having the highest graduation index). In many cases, scholarships are available to those from specific localities and counties. Find out about these from the registrar or director of Faraway U's student aid program.

The nature of a university will frequently dictate the kind of scholarship aid it offers. At Fort Worth's Texas Christian University, for example, funds from the Christian Churches of Texas, New Mexico, and Louisiana provide help for those in Divinity School. If you are on the faculty or staff of a university, discounts from established tuition fees are frequently offered. Some give 100 percent, others less; nearly every university provides some cost cuts for offspring of its faithful retainers.

■ While there are jobs in addition to employment provided under federal programs, many parents believe work time will reduce study time and make Edith a dull girl. The University of Chicago says otherwise. It advises:

> Parents and candidates often wonder if it is prudent for a student to work during his freshman year. The answer, of course, depends upon the ability and study habits of the particular student. Experience at Chicago has revealed, however, that the discipline required for a job often carries over into a student's study habits, and that students who hold a part-time job for a modest number of hours each week often have records of better academic performance than those who do not. The advantages of term-time employment, however, vary with the individual, and all entering freshmen are cautioned against planning to work more than 12 hours a week.
>
> Concerning summer earnings, the following might be said: as desirable as summer academic work might be, or educational travel, or even just plain "loafing," the Committee is more favorably disposed toward the scholarship candidate who has sacrificed these experiences and has demonstrated his willingness to work and to help himself.

THE PAY-BEFORE-YOU-GO PLAN

"It's all very well to borrow when Edith reaches a campus," George pondered. "Maybe we should consider ways to receive interest on the money by funding it in advance since we have time before she gets out of high school."

Advance funding of matriculation costs has the advantage of taking some money out of the (possibly) higher tax bracket of Edith's parents and putting it onto the tax return of a child, with lessened tax consequences.

"See what I mean?" George said to Sophie as she examined the figures. "We pay a 35 percent tax on my top earnings. Now if I give the money to Edith through the Gifts to Minors Act, it will be irretrievably hers, but it will come out of our taxable income for the year. By using the Gifts to Minors Act, uniform in nearly every state, we can invest it for her without the folderol of court orders. The investments should grow as inflation proceeds. Income from this invested money will be in her name. Unless it reaches taxable minimum amounts, there is nothing to pay on it. Even if it becomes in part taxable, it will be taxed at lower rates than our 35 percent bite."

Writing about advance funding by means of a trust rather than the Gifts to Minors Act, *Business Week,* in its copyrighted "Personal Business" section of August 8, 1970, reported:

The revised tax law has a built-in break for the parent who's serious about setting up a college financing plan for a child. With 1970–71 private college costs pushing $5,000, this may be well worth a look.

The basic idea is to split off some of your income and put it into a temporary trust, with the child as income beneficiary. You can pick up the tax windfall for the family, and in the bargain set up the trust with a minimum of technicalities— even acting as trustee yourself.

Before the tax law was changed, you could give enough principal to a child to pay him up to $1,000 a year tax-free. (This was actually $900 of any income, or $1,000 if in the form of stock dividends.)

Now, in 1970, your child can receive $1,725 tax-free, and allowing for some interim changes, this goes to $1,750 in 1973.

You set up a short-term trust for the child—minimum term 10 years—and put in enough securities or other property to pay him, say, $1,700 a year. Not only will the child pay no yearly income tax on the $1,700, but you get back the income-producing property when the trust ends.

Here's a simplified example of how it works: Say that you have a child who will enter college in 1980. Your taxable income is $35,000, which puts you in the 42% top tax bracket. You set up the 10-year trust for the child, and put in, say, $25,000 worth of property which produces $1,700 in income. The income can be in interest, dividends, even rents.

In 1980, the child—with his $1,700 a year placed most conservatively in a 5% savings account—will have more than $22,000 after taxes. This will be his kitty for four years of college. In addition, he will have interest earned on his funds during the four years he's in college—roughly another $2,500.

Since you are in the 42% tax bracket, you save $714 a year in cash by having the $1,700 split away from your income. You can also count the fact that—considering your bracket—it would have taken about double the amount of income-producing property for you to save the $22,000.

The added touch is, of course, returning the trust property to yourself.

HOW ABOUT THE PREP SCHOOLS?

In many areas of the United States, public schools, while fulfilling a need, are below the quality of good private schools and, say their critics, far from the quality they themselves possessed only a few years ago. Yet good private prep schools aren't available for cheap.

Today, many prep school administrations are conscious of the need not to restrict their instruction to the advantaged. I recently queried a coast-to-coast cross section on scholarship aids.

- A Florida school replied: "For academically qualified students whose parents cannot afford tuition, we offer opportunity for mothers to work on a part-time basis at the school in return for their children's educational benefits. The only qualification is that children meet our normal admission requirements."

- The principal of a Laredo, Texas, girls' academy said: "Because we raised teachers' salaries this year there will be a deficit and tuition must go up next year. There are some parents who even now cannot afford to pay for the schooling of their children. We try to find a way to help defray student expenses. The most common is student service after hours and on school weekends. Our neighboring school has all boys and can offer more ways to cut down tuition such as mowing lawns, painting the school in the summer and doing other odd jobs I could not ask girls to do."

(What will Women's Lib say to this discrimination?)

- A Catholic prep school principal in Bethel Park, Pennsylvania, pointed to "full and partial scholarships every year for students who do well on a scholastic entrance test and whose families need financial assistance to send them to the Academy.... The diocese 'has recently inaugurated a program of grants-in-aid."

■ A prestigious Delaware school replied: "This year, we have moved into a program making more financial aid available to incoming freshmen so that, hopefully, about 20-plus percent of the students of each class can be helped. The amount of aid given is determined after parents complete the confidential financial form of the School Scholarship Service."

■ From the headmaster of a Philadelphia prep school: "We use School Scholarship Program as an outside agency to establish relative need.... A normal rule of thumb we follow regardless of the need is not to exceed a 50 percent allowance for tuition.... Total amount expended last year for financial aid amounted to $56,000 or approximately 10 percent of our tuition income."

■ A Los Angeles nun asked me to "put this in your book! Our school is for boys and girls of Japanese origin, mostly third generation. The school doesn't need a program of financial aid because the Japanese people work hard and support their own school."

TO RECAP:

1. College education pays off in higher earning power during a lifetime. But it costs heavily in immediate outlay. This important part of better living can often be obtained with the aid of grants, low-cost loans, and work-for-your-education programs.

2. Finding such help becomes more important as years go on, since tuitions and fees tend to increase faster than the average rate of inflationary cost rises.

3. The federal government offers wide-ranging aid. Many of its programs apply to graduate work. Some are for people planning to help the handicapped and disadvantaged, as well as for handicapped and disadvantaged folk themselves.

4. Private grants and loans for higher education are available through many universities. Grants and aids come from alumni, from campus fraternities, a few from trade associations, and many from corporations. Under some, even people who by current standards are better off than their neighbors can qualify for assistance.

5. Advance funding of college needs brings tax savings, sheltered future income, and, at least hopefully, a sum sufficient to assure four years' matriculation when a youngster reaches entrance age to join the jeans-suited crowd on Faraway's campus.

6. In an age when standards of public schools seem to drop alarmingly in some localities, prestigious private prep schools are opening the gates of monetary mercy to those unable to pay their charges *in toto*.

8

Budget Fun and Travel

TRAVEL EXPANDS THE VIEW, broadens the mind, and lets George, Sophie, you, or me relax from the cares and travail of the daily grind. But travel and fun cost. Few of us with moderate incomes can afford the extensive travel or the long seaside vacations taken by members of the Plainfellow family and others who are at least seemingly rich.

Right?

Wrong.

Travel and vacation fun *are* available on a budget if you're money-management-minded. Steps indicated in other chapters should have helped you to free money from regular uses. For what? For fun, perhaps. And for travel.

This chapter will explore ways to make that money stretch once more to provide the kind of vacation pleasure that can constitute better living. The secret, as always, is management of money. Here are some ways to do it.

WHEN AIR TRAVEL IS CHEAPEST

Recently, I discussed this with Sydney J. Albright, travel information manager of Los Angeles' Western Air Lines. Mr. Albright suggested:

> Perhaps the easiest way for a person to seek out travel bargains is to go to a travel agent. Many people are under the mistaken notion that a travel agent charges them for his services. This is not so, of course. He gets his commission from the airline, shipping company or hotel he books with.
>
> There are many travel bargains. Airlines, for example, have many discount fares: group fares, package plans that include hotels, etc., at rates far below those available to persons making their own arrangements, Discover America fares, youth fares, military standby fares and so on. Most of these are listed on any airline timetable.
>
> In addition, airlines work closely with ground tour operators to put travel packages together that are described in printed brochures. Western has about 350 of them at present, covering virtually every point of the company's system.
>
> Triangle trips are available in conjunction with other airlines. With Eastern, for example, a person flying roundtrip between the East Coast and West Coast may fly in one direction via Mexico City or Acapulco at little or no extra fare.
>
> Western has its own triangle fare in which a person flying roundtrip between Los Angeles and Anchorage can fly one leg of the trip via Hawaii at no extra fare.
>
> These are some general thoughts on what's available in the way of travel bargains for the public.
>
> Even cheaper air fares are available from charter or supplemental airlines, but eligibility for these discounts restricts the traveler."

One of the wealthiest men I know travels extensively by air, always tourist class. Tourist might typically run from 15 to 20 percent less than fares in the first-class cabin.

"If this man can go tourist, so can we," insisted Sophie as she packed to accompany George on a short business trip. "What's good for Lemuel Plainfellow's family is certainly not too lowly for our *ménage à cinq*."

The figures that follow give a rough idea of comparative

costs if you tell the ticket agent, "First class, bub, none of that thar cheap travel for me." Between Los Angeles and Alaska, you might pay $404 for the front cabin where stewardesses patrol more regularly and the alcohol flows freely. Tourist class would be $322. If you travel from a mid-south city to New York, tourist could be $165 versus first class at $206. The differential in percentage is sufficiently large to warrant some effort to save it—*if* you don't have to pay too highly for the privilege. (Fares are as of late 1970.)

"After all," George complained to Ronnie when he suggested that the business/pleasure trip might be undertaken in a rear cabin where *turistas* crowd, "I don't want to be towed in a kite behind the plane. And neither my stomach muscles nor my inclinations, and certainly not my time schedule, would stand a cow-pasture run where the plane lands every time Farmer Brown waves a shirt from his cornfield below to indicate that his mother-in-law wants to be ferried to visit Mrs. Glotz in Dismal County a few miles away. How high is the price I pay for that money saving, friend Ronnie?"

"Not very much," Ronnie replied.

"In the first-class cabin, four people usually sit across the plane, two seats on either side of the aisle. They have more foot room and seat room than the people back in tourist, who sit five or even six across the aisle, depending upon the type of plane and to some extent upon what the particular airline feels it can get away with. When you enter an airplane, the first seats are roomy ones where the top-paying passengers sit. Tourist-class fares have to walk through to their area. When in flight, fewer stewardesses serve tourist class compared to the shapely gals who wait on a favored few up front. Drinks up front are usually on the house. In tourist, you'll pay for your scotch and water.

"All that hardly adds up to a case of poor-relation travel. In both areas meals are served, in both magazines, playing cards, and other amenities of the good life aloft may be had for asking. You walk a few extra feet—*that's* flying the kite out back? Or you have to pay a dollar for your drink and another for Sophie's? Stack those two dollars against the many dollars' extra cost for a front cabin."

Ronnie's case for tourist travel was well made. If you want to save dollars while you scoot through the sky, consider the second cabin, whether a particular airline calls it "tourist," "coach," or "economy."

In addition, there are special family rates on many days of the week, when Sophie might travel at half-fare, with Edith, Ethelred, and Frederica going at an even bigger discount.

"Another thing," George exclaimed as he studied figures on airline costs which Ronnie had laid before him. "When Edith goes to college, she'll be able to procure a student-rate ticket. That allows her to shuttle back and forth at a very wide discount."

Businessmen, too, can shuttle back and forth at wide discounts to certain smaller airlines. One regional line advertises, "Rent a week's wings from us." For a set price, the customer buys a ticket enabling him to fly anywhere during the five-day workweek, provided he restricts his travel to cities served by the airline without interconnections.

"For most travel inside this area, I leave my car home and 'rent wings' for a week," one manufacturer told me. "It's lower in cost and a lot quicker than driving the clogged freeways. Less fatiguing, too. And I can sleep at home every night by utilizing rented wings. That makes a saving in motel/hotel bills on short-radius business trips."

CUT THE CAR COSTS

It isn't every regional airline that offers to rent wings to you or George, whether by the week, minute, or solar year. Many of us find car travel necessary, especially for shorter distances. This is particularly true for people whose travel routines take them up the rural roads and down the lanes to meet customers, suppliers, or business acquaintances with whom they have a regular coffee-break appointment on Tuesdays when the sun reaches over the pole of Sam's Barber Shop.

And it is true for many—the author included—who find that much of the fun of vacation travels is to watch the changing scenery of the North American continent whir past the car windows.

The interstate highway system, damned by many and joked about by others, has made car travel quicker than ever. From my home city of New Orleans, a small, treetop-type airline makes it to Dallas, Texas, in eight hours after stopping in many places. Using highways that are only in part first class (Louisiana could win any competition for the nation's worst roads), it is possible to drive to Dallas in nine.

Commenting upon the shrinkage of distances which makes car travel more practicable for the money-management-minded, Federal Highway Administrator F. C. Turner recently said that many trips which were avoided not too long ago because of the distances involved are now practicable since they require less time when interstate routes are used.

"A 2,830-mile journey from New York to Los Angeles, which took seventy-nine hours of travel in 1956 when interstate mileage was negligible, can now be made in sixty-two hours by using interstate routes in the same general corridor," said Mr. Turner. "The seventeen-hour reduction permits a motorist who drives eight or nine hours a day to cross the country in two fewer days."

The savings in travel time are not limited to long trips but are reflected in trips of varying distances over the interstate system, Mr. Turner stated. An average 10 percent cut in travel time has been achieved between cities because of the interstate routes already opened to traffic. His report points out that

> speed, which determines travel time, has increased from an average of 36 miles per hour in selected corridors in 1956 to 46 miles per hour today in the same corridors that included portions of completed Interstate. When the Interstate is fully completed within these corridors, the average speed, exclud-

ing any stops, will increase to between 50 and 60 mph, cutting travel time still further.

If a value were placed on the time saved by auto drivers and passengers, the benefits would climb substantially. Assuming their time is worth an average of $1.50 an hour, the total saved would increase to $212 billion. At $3 an hour, which is close to the nation-wide average wage, the time saving benefits would climb to $337 billion.

However, you can't put "saved" theoretical wages like these in your pocket. Such "savings" apply in a real sense when George travels on business, but less so when he and Sophie are meandering through the countryside with Edith, Ethelred, and Frederica on the back seat during a Sunday pleasure excursion.

Sometimes auto travel is less expensive than travel by the conveyance that some observers have called "that big, crowded slum up there in the sky." But there are occasions when you get there not only faster but at less expense on Jet Jockey Airlines. If Sophie and George go on a long vacation with the children, gas fed into the same auto engine will carry five people as readily as one. "So it should be a lot cheaper by highway," mused George.

"Think again," insisted Ronnie. "By car, you'll need three days from your bedroom at home to your bedroom in a hotel at your destination. You will need motels along the way unless you plan to drive without stop. And you may find that although five travel over the interstate on the same gas, they eat enough meals along the way and sleep in enough hired beds en route to cancel any saving. Point is, George, that you shouldn't *assume* a saving either way. If reduction of travel cost is your aim, put the numbers down on a piece of paper to make sure a seeming saving is going to be real."

How about auto clubs? Whether, in your case and for your needs, travel plans, and personality, auto club fees will be a saving or just an expense is something to determine after examining what is offered by the American Automobile Association and its twin, Canadian Automobile Association,

Sears Allstate Motor Club, or American Oil Company's Torch program. Among their services are bail bonds ("But I don't plan to be put in jail," said Sophie when a salesman explained this point to her); publications giving travel hints and tips; routine services along faraway, as well as nearby, ribbons of macadam and concrete; tips about speed traps that might save Sophie from needing a bail bond to release her from the toils of Dismal County's rural lockup; reservation services at distant hostelries; and advice regarding prices and excellence or poorness of accommodations at places you might want to go.

HOW ABOUT THAT OTHER HIGHWAY VEHICLE?

". . . I mean the big one that passes with a whoosh when you're driving on the interstates or the country lanes," said George. "The bus, man, the bus. Doesn't it offer some economies?"

George was right. Buses do offer economies. They offer discomfort, too, and the slowness of bus travel for any but short hops is almost as proverbial as the fact that you spend time going to and from airports equal to the hours the jet jockeys need to whisk you back and forth between airports.

"But on short distances, you can't beat the bus," Ronnie remarked. "I have to go up to the state capital several times a week, especially when the legislature is in session. Used to drive the car those eighty miles, hunt for a place to park it, then pile back into the car to return home at the end of the day. By the time I arrived back in the pad, three stiff scotch-and-waters were a minimum to get my nerves in shape. Now I leave the driving to that pro we hear about on TV. He gets me there about as fast as I'd arrive on my own, clogged highways being equal, and it is a short taxi ride from the bus terminal to the halls where our elected wise men practice their wisdom when the legislature is going through its annual antics. Ditto the ride back and the taxi hop home. I still take the three scotch-and-waters home in the pad, but what the hell—a poor bachelor accountant should have some pleasures."

"How about the dollars?" asked George.

"Look only at gasoline and it's cheaper to drive. But count in wear and tear on the old Buick, and how much more quickly it reaches retirement age by shuttling back and forth on our highway. Then I think the bus comes out best for a short-distance shuffle. On a long haul, however, the bus may not be everybody's dish of what our British relatives call 'tay.' "

"That it isn't," George said. "Rode one of the things recently for 300 miles. It was the cheapest in price but the slowest in arrival. That stretch must have included fifty stops. We pulled to the side to pick up children going to visit other children on the next farm, and we dawdled to bus stations in small towns not even on a map."

There is a way to avoid George's unhappy trip and still enjoy the low cost. "Express" buses might make a whole 300-mile stretch in one hop.

Frequent departures are an advantage of bus travel. Likewise the possibility of renting bus-company wheels in the manner that some businessmen rent regional airlines' wings. Count in layover privileges which permit you to stay in a town that takes your fancy, resuming travel when you're ready; lack of driving fatigue and its attendant dangers— bus drivers are changed at frequent time and distance intervals; the view of the countryside which, to some travelers, is as important as fun and dining when the vacation destination has been reached. Also—

The bus is cheap.

That is its largest single attraction to most families intent on money management for better living.

The bus is cheap.

THE STONEWALL JACKSON RAIL EXPRESS

This uncomplimentary term has been applied to rail travel by critics who say that little about the iron horse and its following cars has changed since the day when Stonewall Jackson and other heroes of the war between North and South flagged down the choochoo if they wanted to be someplace other than where they were. The rails have deliberately uncoupled many passenger runs because they found freight more profitable to haul than people. Runs not discontinued have been disconnected from any semblance of comfort, cleanliness, or promptitude.

But things are changing.

Rail managements are gingerly putting passenger runs back on, and efforts are being made to institute fast service able to whisk commuters out of crowded cities more quickly than autos can do it. Amtrack may soon change things.

Many of the advantages and most of the drawbacks listed for bus travel apply to riding the rails as well. With one exception.

The train is rarely cheap.

TOGETHERNESS TRAVEL

Trains, buses, ships, and planes are all utilized by that ubiquitous American form of travel and togetherness, the tour. It frequently presents the lowest-cost way to vacation. On many occasions and in many cases, it's the mode with greatest satisfaction. This is especially true in traveling to lands where your customary ways won't always work and where your customary English is not always understood—or acknowledged, even if understood, should the local citizenry be in a surly mood.

Recently a friend just back from six European weeks on tour reported as we sat over lunch:

"It was great," he enthused. "Flew to London, then went by bus from place to place. How would *I* know where to stop for good local wine in France, or the best scenery in Switzerland? The tour was less expensive than trying to do things on our own. And more pleasure, too."

This was true for my friend, a gregarious man who enjoys being with people and is able to make fast friends. Not all of us are like that. If the idea of close proximity to anywhere from three to three dozen fellow humans seems not to fit your notion of a pleasurable holiday, then the relative cheapness of a tour will be purchased at a cost of taking all the fun out of funtime.

Even for those who like togetherness when they travel, there are traps to be found on tour. A leading national newspaper recently ran an exposé of faked write-ups that travel reporters turned in to pay for their free junketing. Therefore, don't believe everything you read. However, if the glowing story of Rory Reporter in the *Evening Itch* agrees with more sedate appraisals from other sources, it isn't necessary to assume Rory did the story with a one-hand typewriter peck while the other palm was being crossed by a travel promoter's silver. Most writers are honest; just don't spend your travel kitty for ten glorious days in upper Afghanistan on one article's recommendations.

Recently over a hundred girls from a midwestern high school embarked happily on a several weeks' summer tour of Europe, chaperoned by sedate nuns. When lo! three days after arriving in picture-book Switzerland, the tour promoter who had sold the idea to both Sisters and parents ran out of money and the girls were stranded. They were flown home, "but travel money spent for my daughter's senior-year vacation was irretrievably lost," one parent told me. "Sure, I can sue. The company is in bankruptcy and if I'm lucky I'll get a nickel on every dollar."

There is an easy moral here. Check the reputation, financial strength, and integrity of a tour company before you pay in advance for its blessings.

Even though this sort of thing can happen, it probably won't. Tours remain a low-cost way to have a lot of fun on a relatively little bit of vacation money. Properly used, they represent money stretching at its best.

Suppose you, Sophie, George, and Ronnie want to visit East Nowhere. Since its discovery by Christopher Columbus' third cousin, Bombastus, no one has visited East Nowhere. Travel companies do not package travel to its rugged moun-

tains and mushy plains. How now? All is not lost. Banding together, you, Sophie, George, and Ronnie can do your own tour. Traveling together is cheaper than going singly or in pairs and the do-it-yourself tour is a successful way to lower costs through shrewd money management via chartered bus, prearranged motel accommodation, special rail car, or non-sked airline.

HOTELS AND MOTELS CAN COST LESS

Representatives of George's company travel to meet customers. Although George himself is more deskbound, he qualifies for commercial rates. Not everyone is aware that these can be available for vacation travel to people whose business movements make them eligible.

A commercial rate gives you a percentage off the posted price. Hotels and motels extend this reduction in return for the regularity with which commercial travelers use their hospitality.

"Simple arithmetic," explained a motel owner whom I asked about this. "My place might be full at certain seasons of the year, less full at others, and nearly empty at a few phases of the calendar. A manufacturing plant likes to be able to schedule its work throughout the year. That allows it to provide regular employment to workers, keep the inventory of supplies turning over, and to some degree predict what it will do at any given month or quarter. We're no different. Our rooms are our plant and equipment. We like to keep them busy through all of the twelve months. In order to attract the regular travelers—those who go up and down or back and forth on predictable business trips—we offer reduced rates just as a manufacturer would be willing to have a smaller markup on some volume in order to make regular production certain in the slow months. Hence commercial rates. We extend them to many employees of a firm who as individuals might not travel sufficiently to be "commercial accounts."

A jewelery importer I know calls regularly on accounts in eleven states. "I use commercial privilege when on vacation, too," he says. "Why not? It's available and legitimate."

There are other ways to obtain lessened motel and hotel rates. One is the Family Plan, in use in many places. Here's how a national chain explained it:

> No one can be sure in which hotelman's mind the idea was spawned to "compliment" children when occupying a room with an adult, free of charge. Sheraton first instituted Family Plan . . . about 1956 on a trial run in hotels catering largely, four days a week, to traveling businessmen.
>
> The thought was to try to entice these same customers to return on their own time with their families and, of course, to boost business generally during relatively slack seasons by attracting family groups.
>
> The plan is simple; there is no room charge for children in the same room with their parents; if one or more additional rooms are required for a large family, the single-room rate is charged for each extra room, regardless of how many occupy the rooms.

When Edith attends Faraway U, she will qualify for student rates offered by some motels and hotels. "When we go on family vacations, we can give her a separate room at a separate, lowered rate," Sophie mused. The brochure from which she garnered this idea pointed out:

> Full time students are entitled to special low rates. These rates [are] offered during the following periods:
> 1. Wednesday preceding Thanksgiving through the following Sunday.
> 2. December 15 through January 1.
> 3. July 1 through Labor Day.
> 4. Friday, Saturday, and Sunday evenings throughout the year.

Then there are motels and hotels at which all rates are discounted by comparison with the hostelries that have bell-boy service and other frills.

"I've found a low-cost chain that has air conditioning, in-room television, and most frills that make travel comfortable," Ronnie told George and Sophie. "I use it on trips to the capital and other travel where I have to stay overnight. Carrying my own luggage isn't hard. It might save me as much as $6 per night, plus the amount I'd have tipped a bellman or porter. The swimming pools tend to be smaller at this chain, but that is a hardship only in hot weather and then only for people who like to swim laps of the pool; personally, I'm a bask-in-the-sun-and-dunk-in-the-water man, not a dedicated crawl addict."

WHO NEEDS A HOTEL?

Not the breed of vacationers who go, with more or less luxury, the camping route. If you are one of them, you won't need the ideas below. If not, you may find, as a great number of city types have discovered, that camping is pleasurable and lower in cost than either the luxury or the bargain motel/hotel.

"It's living like a snail," said George when Sophie suggested the idea. "A snail carries his house on his back. So does a camper. He may go in the simplest way—called backpacking. That means he puts his possessions and his shelter in a pack, straps it to his back, and lugs it up mountain and down glen. Or he may go in a caravan. In that case, his possessions are packed behind in either a buslike contraption or in a camper of varying size and facilities towed behind his automobile. His snail hump becomes the back of the bus or the trailer; he travels with his home and his belongings of the moment on his back."

Camping, as George explained, can be a basic Daniel Boone-like existence or it can happen in a caravan as large and luxurious as a motel room on wheels.

Writing about caravan camping in a copyrighted article in the May, 1970, issue of *The Midwest Motorist,* L. R. Whitcomb noted:

A well-equipped motor home costs from $9,000 to $20,000—out of range for most families with growing children. But how about renting one for your family's vacation this year? But before you do, you would do well to read and ponder this story of the Whitcomb family's trials and pleasures.

You've seen it rolling along the interstates, perhaps towing a small car or packing a motorcycle on one of its bumpers. Called a motor home, it has the size and often the shape of an ordinary bus, but inside it's an elongated very small efficiency apartment.

A key feature of the motor home is that in any state in the union the family legally has the run of the vehicle in transit. Not so with travel trailers, and not so with pick-up campers in some states. Imagine the children coloring or otherwise occupied at the dinette table while the wife naps in a full-size bed or prepares dinner as the husband pilots the family toward its happy destination.

Enamored of that vision, I rented one of them for a two-week trip to Key West with my wife and two children, ages 7 and 5. . . .

We paid $195 a week base rental price, ten cents per mile, and gas. The dealer bought oil and propane. Including food and parking expense, our two-week (3,172 miles) vacation cost us $918.

You can camp on public or private lands. The U.S. Department of the Interior, in its Information Bulletin No. 3, *Camping on Public Lands,* points out that

> from the deserts of Arizona to the tundra of Alaska, there are some 457 million acres of public lands. You'll find room to roam here, wide open spaces where you can camp, hike, fish, hunt—or just get away from it all. This is the public domain, that part of the original public lands of the United States still in Federal ownership, lands which haven't been set aside for national forests, parks, and other special uses.
>
> More than a hundred developed campgrounds are now open for outdoor recreationists. You'll find variety, from deserts to forests, sagebrush canyons to snow-capped mountains. These lands are managed for multiple uses by the Bureau of Land Management, an agency of the U.S. Department of the Interior.

In addition, state parks frequently have facilities for low-cost or no-cost camping vacations. Some of the most luxurious facilities are private. In these, you, Ronnie, or the George-and-Sophie family can find things as city-slickerish as those at the best motels, at a fraction of the cost of motelling your way across the country on vacation. Many have swimming pools, piped-in electricity, all the indoor plumbing a camper dedicated to what his rougher brethren call decadence could wish, golf courses in a few cases, and catering establishments which will package a dinner of more or less gourmet quality if the Sophie of your group is too tired to cook on her butane range.

Facility for facility and chuck wagon for motel cuisine, camping is likely to cost less than conventional travel. When you get up to more luxurious campers, however, the differential shrinks. Camping is a good gambit for lessening the cost of fun and travel only if you and your family have a streak of pioneer in your personalities. It is not everyone's idea of pleasure.

CAST YOUR SNAIL UPON THE WATERS

Boating has become a part of life for many in almost any community on or near water. The water might be a mighty river, it can be a lake, it is frequently only a pond. If a vessel will float, it qualifies.

Like the camper, a houseboat is a snail. This one goes on watery paths instead of concrete roads. It needn't have a planned camping spot to stop; any tie-up will do.

In my earlier book *How You Can Beat Inflation,* I wrote:

> In the northern part of my state, the biggest stream running through a town of 80,000 is a bayou 100 feet across at its widest and less than that throughout most of its length. There are fifty people in that small community who own houseboats and who cruise down the winding bayou to a lake 50 miles distant.

A houseboat costs about the same as a camper of equal facility. The houseboat won't go as many places as the camper, but to those it can reach, per-mile costs might be less than for a road snail. "And look at all the fun of living on water!" Sophie exclaimed.

That is a big part of the better-living package that a water snail offers you.

A boat for low-cost fun and travel need not be elaborate. It can be the boat-camper described in a copyrighted article in the Spring, 1970, issue of *Vacations Unlimited:*

> How about a boating vacation and camping trip as far away from home as your time permits, with guaranteed good accommodations any day of the summer without advance notice? And how about coming home from all this with money in your pockets and everyone in the family sorry it had to end?
>
> Impossible?
>
> Not at all, providing you own a gadget I call the "boat camper."
>
> Of course I assume I am speaking to people who enjoy boats and water, fishing, no-smog air, distant places and healthy bank balances. All others are excused to go to their hotels, dress for dinner, bore each other with inane chatter, and at vacation's end, mortgage the homestead to pay for it all.
>
> What is this thing I said you needed? Well, basically it is a boat on a trailer. It could be an outboard runabout of popular size with the addition of a tent you would have fabricated to cover the entire open, or cockpit area, in effect converting the open boat into a cabin cruiser.

LOW-COST FUN AT HIGH-COST PLACES

"Don't go to New Orleans, New York, or San Francisco—the cost is prohibitive."

Have you ever heard that said about the cities above, or about Disneyland in the summer season, Florida during the winter, a world's-fair city when its thing is in swing?

It is true enough, but only if you go the regulation tourist routes. You can have a lot of low-cost fun at high-cost places if you know how to do it.

1. Go Off-season In New Orleans, the tourist rates during Mardi Gras or Sugar Bowl are staggering. Hotel rooms go up by as much as 90 percent. A five-day minimum stay is charged for. "I can't shake the dust of your town from my tires fast enough," one disgruntled tourist told me. His chagrin had a great deal of justification. He also had a great lack of knowledge, for a week earlier or later he could have enjoyed the fine restaurants and seen the sights at little cost.

What is true of New Orleans is also true of many other places, Stay away from any big tourist attraction when it is attracting. Go when it is quiescent. Go off-season. Miami in winter is high. Miami in summer is low in cost.

2. *Frequent Unfrequented Places* Some resorts, hotels, motels, and restaurants cost more because they are "in." Frequently, places which have not received equal notice have food as good and beds as soft at lower charges. Guidebooks, tourist advisories of travel clubs, and the suggestions of knowledgeable local people can help you find the jewel where things are as good but prices not as high.

3. *Let Uncle Sugar Pay Part of the Tab* Ronnie planned to go to Boston. "Trouble is, for a self-employed fellow like me there is no employer's expense account to use. So I'll work things around for the federal tax people to pick up part of my tab," he said to George as the two set out from their apartment house to hit tennis balls on a warm Saturday morning.

"I have been corresponding with one firm in New England about auditing its annual statement. Nothing may come of it, but a call upon the president is a legitimate business expense when I'm so close to his office. Sales calls are deductible business expense even though a sale may not be closed every time out."

Ronnie's message is this: Whenever you can combine some business with your fun, you have a legal way to take part of your travel as a business deduction. How much will depend upon the circumstances. Uncle's tax men won't allow deductions of travel expenses for other members of the family. The business activity must be genuine and related to the way in which you earn your daily bread, butter, and lager beer.

A BARGAIN SECOND HOME

"The cost, George, the cost," said Sophie as they discussed the purchase of an out-of-town property for vacation use.

"It's not high if we pick the land properly," George said.

Often you can obtain public land at prices which, although carefully lined up with appraised values, yield bargains by comparison with the cost of buying land from a real estate firm that is developing its garden paradise on the edge of the metropolis. Frequently, population growth and increasing need for land make such bargain-bought federal lands increase in value so that, in addition to securing a low-cost place for taking Edith, Ethelred, and Frederica on holiday, George and Sophie might realize value appreciation over the years.

Where do you find such land? How do you go about buying it?

In its Information Bulletin No. 4, *How to Buy Public Lands*, the U.S. Department of the Interior explains:

> Land owned by the Federal Government and administered by the U.S. Department of the Interior's Bureau of Land Management is original public domain land which has never left Federal ownership.
>
> Almost all of it is in the public land states of the West— Arizona, Montana, Wyoming, Colorado, New Mexico, Oregon, Nevada, Idaho, Utah, California, Washington.
>
> Small amounts of public land still remain in Alabama, Arkansas, Florida, Louisiana, Michigan, Minnesota, Mississippi and Wisconsin, but land sales in these States are very rare. There are no public lands in Delaware, Georgia, Hawaii, Illinois, Indiana, Iowa, Kentucky, Maine, Maryland, Massachusetts, Missouri, New Hampshire, New Jersey, New York, North Carolina, Ohio, Pennsylvania, Rhode Island, South Carolina, Tennessee, Texas, Vermont, Virginia and West Virginia.
>
> Public land is sold through sealed or oral bidding in Land Offices of the Bureau of Land Management.
>
> Every parcel is appraised by the Government at fair market value. You cannot buy it for less than the appraised price. Don't be deceived by promoters who advertise "free" or "cheap" public land.

Get the very best information available. *Our Public Lands,* a quarterly magazine published by the Bureau of Land Management, carries a listing of public lands to be sold in the near future. The magazine's "Public Sale Bulletin Board" gives a thumbnail description of these lands, including their general location, appraised price, and other information. Send one dollar to Superintendent of Documents, Government Printing Office, Washington, D.C. 20402, for a year's subscription.

"So maybe we don't have to pay a lot for the land, even at 'appraised' values," Sophie said. "Where do we live on it? In an Indian teepee?"

The mobile home is one solution to this problem. Writing about low-cost shelters in an article, "Mobile Homes in New England," Carol S. Greenwald noted, in the May/June, 1970 issue of *The New England Economic Review,* that

> a mobile home is a factory-built, rectangular housing unit which is delivered to the site on its own wheels. As the market has changed from transients to moderate income households, the mobile home manufacturer has redesigned his product. In the mid-1960's the mobile home was enlarged from an 8 x 40 foot trailer to a fairly immobile 12 x 60 foot housing unit. It is commonly said that the difference between a trailer and a mobile home is that the mobile home is not mobile.
>
> Mobile homes are fully, if inexpensively, furnished. Many modern conveniences have been added, including refrigerator-freezers, and wall-to-wall carpeting. While a mobile home has substantially less living area than the average single family dwelling, the living space is similar to that found in many new apartments and is 45 percent greater than the minimum FHA requirements for a two bedroom apartment. Thus, it is a viable alternative to apartments for many households who cannot afford a single family house.
>
> Mobile homes not only cost less because they are smaller than conventional single family homes, they are also less expensive per square foot to build. The National Commission on Urban Problems estimated that conventional construction of a minimal 1,000 square foot home would cost $10 a square foot, while construction costs for mobile homes were $6-7 a square foot, including complete furnishings. The lower cost partly reflects lower quality construction, but more importantly, is also a result of factory production.

Designs for low-cost wood homes, suitable for budget-planned second dwellings, are available at $1 to $1.25 per set from the Superintendent of Documents, Washington, D.C. 20402.

In the May, 1970, issue of *Better Camping*, Stan Meseroll suggested a novel use of the camper as a second vacation home.

> We have had a second home. . . . It's on a beautiful, pine-rimmed, unpolluted, 10-acre lake exactly one hour's drive from the front door of our first home. The land costs us $110 a year. We pay no taxes and no utility bills.
>
> Our second home is our Nimrod camping trailer. The property is a secluded 50 x 75 foot, hemlock-shaded camp-site in a privately managed campground less than two hours from Times Square, New York City.
>
> Sound great? It is. . . .
>
> . . . We visited four campgrounds, all within a two-hour drive from New York City, and found that sites were available in all of them. More and more campgrounds are beginning to offer such sites. One firm in Pennsylvania's Pocono Mountains is even *selling* campsite lots for $495 and up. Costs vary between $100 and $300 per season, depending upon facilities available or desired. Some campgrounds have sites with or without hookups and price them accordingly. Ask about other fees. For example, we pay an additional $20 per season to keep our canoe at the lake launching area. What about daytime and overnight guests? Some campgrounds charge, some do not. Trailerists can, for an additional $25, store their trailers for the winter at our campground.

THE STAY-AT-HOME VACATION

The day was March 17. George and Sophie were discussing what had become, by that midspring date, the top conversational topic in that family. "Sure and begorra," said George, "if t'isn't a foine Saint Paddy's Day. What better time to be thinking of enjoying ourselves? I'll bet we would have a fracas of a time this vacation right here at our eleventh-floor sod hut."

"And why not?" asked Sophie. "Sure it's meself that likes fun and games at home."

Some of the hometown ideas that George and Soph might consider when his expected vacation does roll around are:

■ *Lower-cost golf and bowling.* At night, the lanes charge top dollars. That's when the leagues roll and open lanes for individual bowling are few. During the day and at offtimes such as Sunday morning or Saturday afternoon, owners want the individual bowlers whom they can't fit in during league hours. The per-game discount might be 30 percent.

Anyone who attempts to play golf on weekends knows how hard it is to schedule starting time. Ronnie has found another self-employed soul with whom he plays on Wednesday mornings.

"Not only is the course free of slow foursomes you can't play through, but the greens fees are lower than on weekends," he told George. "I make up office time by working Saturday mornings, and I gain in two ways. I have a better golf day at lower cost. And I have a Saturday for work when the phones don't ring, the salesmen don't call, and the clients don't bring up problems. Perfect both ways."

■ *Try local sports.* In my part of the country, crabbing is a leisurely sport enjoyable to everyone except the crabs. Few vacations have been as pleasurable as a recent week spent crabbing and settling the problems of the world in company with a friend.

Every locality has its equivalent of crabbing. Try the hometown availabilities to pass a pleasurable in-town vacation.

■ *Tour without travel.* "For five years I've been after you to take the walking tour the Chamber of Commerce advises for visitors," Sophie announced as George's vacation drew near. "Since we're staying at home this year, let's enjoy the pleasures that tourists come long distances to have. You'll get your exercise walking with me, me bucko, and if it tires you too much, then you and Ronnie can skip that Saturday tennis set-to. There are a couple of museums I want to see, too. We'll try the *turista* trap right here at home."

■ *The 100-mile round trips.* Plantation homes in the

south, prerevolutionary places in New England, bandit hide-outs in the West, ports on the sea, and waving grain inland—within a hundred miles of every hometown, yours included, there are interesting trips that can be taken in a day. They fill out a hometown vacation that costs less than conventional holidays.

TO RECAP:

1. Travel and fun cost—but not necessarily a lot, if you follow ideas for cutting the price and increasing the fun of vacations.

2. A number of packaged plans are available on airlines in addition to family rates, spouse discounts, youth fares, standby rate cuts, and the like. Even without these, air-travel costs can be lessened if you go tourist instead of first class.

3. For most, the vacation vehicle is the family car. In a number of ways, travel via interstate or scenic highway can be made lower in cost and higher in pleasure.

4. There are special opportunities for low-cost travel aboard buses and trains. Although in the past there has been a tendency to cut schedule frequencies and discontinue passenger runs on the railroads, the trend now is to make the iron horse more pleasant for travelers.

5. Tours and packaged holiday plans give greatest travel bargains. But they should be undertaken only if you genuinely enjoy the company of other people, many of whom you have never seen before and most of whom you will never see again. Togetherness is the essence of tour travel.

6. Hotel and motel rates can be legitimately shaved by gimmicks that include commercial rates, family room plans, student discounts, and the seeking of bargain instead of luxury accommodations. Often the latter are within a whisker of parity with luxury inns.

7. Camping is healthful, full of fresh air and, its cynics say, full of bugs as well. It is also cheaper than conventional

travel. You can find accommodations at every level from austerity to luxury, and from a few pence to many pounds.

8. Boating aficionados say their bag offers cost reductions since the boat is both a means of travel and an overnight lodging.

9. At high-cost vacation spots there are low-cost ways to enjoy the same fun for less if you go during off-seasons and search out the unfrequented places whose prices have not been hiked by popularity.

10. A second home furnishes an all-year retreat. Its cost per year becomes small when considered over the number of years such a retreat can serve.

11. Stay-at-home vacations allow fun in the hometown that a tourist from afar might pay considerable sums to enjoy.

9

Borrowed Bucks and Banks' Services

WE ARE A NATION of debtors, if you believe results of a study recently published by the Survey Research Center of the University of Michigan. An "average" family, which might be yours and mine and is sure to include that of Sophie and George, owes a debt of $1,540. That does not count its tab with the friendly mortgage company. It does include amounts owed for the new car Sophie purchased and the shiny freezer out in the kitchen, along with debt for personal purchases ranging from fur coats and furniture to shoes that Ethelred seems to wear out faster than he can outwear them.

It is possible to base substantial savings upon that average debt. Let's consider arithmetic applied to the $1,540 payable accounts.

Assume that George and Soph have purchased that grand and a half on what has become conventional terms for time payment. That is, 1½ percent a month, 18 percent a year. While they tend to reduce the debt through payments, they also tend, being normal, red-blooded, greedy-for-goods Americans, to run up some additional debt all the time so that the $1,540 stays average throughout the year. The interest charges run to $277.20 in twelve months of toiling to make ends meet before inflation can push them apart.

Now assume that instead of shelling out this usurious 18 percent, as so many of us do without thinking and without shopping for better terms, George smartens up. "Why pay Plainfellow's Big Bargain Store that 'service charge,' as Plainfellow propaganda euphemistically calls its interest rate, when we have a portfolio of stocks sitting in Able Banker Charlie's Eighth National vault. I talked yesterday with Able Charlie. He tells me he will rent us some of the Eighth National's wampum on a secured collateral loan, using these stocks, and charge us only 8½ percent. That's still a lot of rental, but it's cheaper than the 18 percent Plainfellow's credit department gets on time payments.

"Now observe. Paying 8½ percent on a $1,540 loan used to liquidate debts to Plainfellow's Big Bargain Store, and any other operators who hold our notes, means that we'll reimburse Able Banker Charlie $130.90 over the course of a year.

"We save $146.30.

"That new coat you've wanted is yours with such a saving. In effect, we can buy it from Plainfellow's, using money we formerly paid to Plainfellow's for interest."

If you're as average as George and Sophie, such a saving can mount up. But maybe your family isn't average. If your annual income is $15,000 per year, you probably owe something more than George and Sophie's ménage has run up on time. Your debt, according to the University of Michigan's survey figures for a family in the fifteen thou bracket, comes to $2,240. Should you pay for credit at the 18 percent charged (in most states) on time payments and credit-card balances allowed to run more than twenty-five days, you lose $403.20 per year to the people whose money you have employed in such easy fashion.

Now suppose that, like George, you decide to put up stocks as collateral for a bank loan. You approach Able Banker Charlie at the Eighth National Bank. For an opener you invite him to have a cup of coffee at Randy's Restaurant across the street.

"A.B.C.," you say after the waitress has served two cups, spilling half the contents of one and a mere one-third of the other. "Let us have words.

"In my right hand is a packet of stock certificates. You lend about 70 percent of the value of listed stocks. Based on yesterday's closing prices, these are worth $3,500 at present—more than sufficient to cover a loan of $2,240 from your wampum emporium. Deal?"

After discussing such things as interest rate and length of payment, you're likely to end up with the loan you seek. Not having been a math major in your undergraduate days and being, like many of us, afraid of the margin for error when you add and subtract in your head, you put down on paper numbers similar to these:

Borrow $2,240 at 18 percent, pay interest of	$403.20
Borrow, instead, at 8½ percent, pay interest of	190.40
Save	$212.80

With that you can enjoy a lengthier vacation, or buy two coats for your wife, or repaint your kitchen, or make a start toward building a carport you have always wanted to replace the gray tin monstrosity that a previous resident of your home had constructed to house cars narrower than those turned out from Detroit today.

In this chapter we're going to look at ways to borrow money at low (and sometimes at no) cost; offbeat methods of obtaining capital for business purposes without hocking all the future profits in order to enjoy your needed present lettuce; the services a bank offers in addition to storage and rental of moneys and how they can help your money management program without costing you anything; ways your checking account can work without draining away service fees every month; what to do about the credit cards that flood through the mail on so many of us; and how to keep the costs of a Plainfellow's—or any other—time-payment plan within reason when you haven't the packet of stock certificates in George's bank box to borrow against.

BORROW AT LOW (SOMETIMES NO) COST

The scene is the office of Able Banker Charlie, screened off from the view of most bank customers, whose conversations form a background hum. George sits on an upholstered chair; he is about to rise.

"Sorry I bothered you, Able. Didn't know I had exhausted the borrowability of the stocks put up for collateral. It's too bad the market took such a tumble—my stocks did, at any rate. Can you give me a suggestion on raising money elsewhere at lowest possible cost?"

"We've considered stocks, on which banks allow lowest interest because they are easily liquid and can be valued from day to day," Able Charlie Banker answered. "Here are some other ideas you might try." He handed George a list:

■ *Don't be afraid to negotiate.*   Bankers are like other businessmen. Sometimes they take an old customer for granted. Maybe the bank down the street or out in the next county is hungry for business now and will give a better rate to attract your personal or business account.

■ *Use your insurance policies.*   The borrowability of these can be helpful in high-interest times. And not only for individuals. A sizable corporation recently reported that it was able to raise a half-million dollars by borrowing from insurance companies against the cash-surrender values of life policies carried on its top executives.

Written into most life insurance policies is provision for lending by the company against the security of funds already paid in. Rates were set back in a day when 5 percent looked like high interest. They offer opportunity today to people who need funds and don't wish to pay the going skyhigh rates.

"I don't have sizable cash-surrender value in the policy against which I want to borrow," a businessman said not long ago. "But with 80 percent of our needs promised from another source, borrowing on insurance assures the initial capital to swing our larger deal."

■ *Beware compensating balances.* A corporation borrowed $100,000 but had to agree to maintain 20 percent compensating balance. A compensating balance is part of the money you borrow which you must repay, are compelled to pay interest on, but can't use. In this case the practical effect was that a $20,000 balance had to be maintained in the account. The borrower received only $80,000 in *usable* dollars. The company got a favorable break on interest, having to pay 8½ percent, then close to prime rate. The interest was charged on the whole $100,000, making a total of $8,500 interest. If you apply that amount as a percentage of the *usable loan,* you arrive at an annual borrowing cost of 11.6 percent—quite a bit larger than 8½ percent.

You can't always escape this gimmick. But by shopping several banks—do this whether it's a personal loan of $1,000 or a business loan of $1 million—frequently it's possible to negotiate away that compensation trap.

When you can't do so (and this happens), read financial journals for the ads of firms that furnish compensating balances. For a fee, they will move, say, $20,000 to your bank as compensating balance on that $100,000 loan, freeing your $20,000 for use. They charge a fee. But it is not likely to increase borrowing cost as much as maintenance of the compensating balance.

Typically, a fee might run 1½ percent. So if you pay 8½ percent on $100,000, plus 1½ percent on $20,000, your interest cost would be $8,800. That is more than 8½ percent face interest. But it is lower than the percent you'd be paying to borrow $100,000 but use only $80,000.

A banker such as Able Charlie won't always freely discuss the word "discount." He may be loath to talk plainly about compensating balances too. It is important for you and George to know both, for ignorance in either area of borrowing can vastly increase your costs.

Assume the same $100,000 borrowing we discussed before and a two-year payout on a regular schedule of $12,500 each three months. Interest is payable quarterly. Average amount owed during the period would be approximately $50,000. Simple interest charged on this would mean high interest payments at first, with interest declining as the balance declined. It would run approximately $8,500 for the two-year period, or $4,250 yearly on average.

If the lender were to make this a discount loan, however, he would compute interest for two years at the full amount, and deduct this off the top. He would then take $17,000 interest instead of $8,500. Moreover, since interest came off the top you would only receive $83,000 instead of $100,000. Payments would be made quarterly and the average balance payable during the period would be about $41,500. A quick computation of $17,000 interest over two years—$8,500 per year—on an average $41,500 balance yields an interest figure of 20.4 percent.

George has choices outside a bank and so do you if, like our hero of the money management wars, you work for a company which has a federal credit union. You can set one up in any group to which you belong. How? The U.S. Department of Health, Education, and Welfare has issued a brochure called *A Credit Union Can Help* (10 cents buys it from the Superintendent of Documents, Washington, D.C. 20402). In this, HEW points out:

> A Federal credit union is a group of people with common interests who band themselves together for the purpose of solving their money worries. The people where you work or where you worship or where you live have many of the same interests. You know one another. You work and worship together, and you are interested in making your community a better place in which to live.
>
> And, if you're like other people you have money worries. Not all to the same extent, of course. Some of the people you know have things going their way and are able to save some

of their money. But even they need to borrow from time to time, and frequently do.

First, you must have a charter to operate a Federal credit union. You and others who join with you will actually run the credit union. But there is a law called the Federal Credit Union Act that says what a Federal Credit Union may do and how it must be run. Everyone in the field of membership is free to join. This requires only a 25¢ entrance fee, signing a membership card, and opening a savings account with at least 25¢.

The members elect the people who will run the credit union.

A board of directors (usually 5 people) will manage it.

A credit committee (usually 3 people) decides on the loans that will be made.

Another committee (usually 3 people) is appointed by the board to make sure the credit union is run right. This is called the Supervisory Committee.

Your Federal Credit Union will do three things:

- Encourage and help its members to save regularly;
- Give them a place where they may borrow for good purposes at fair interest rates;
- Advise members on how to use money wisely.

Credit union interest rates are supposed to be lower than those charged by commercial lenders. Generally, they tend to be. Before you or George covers the dotted line with a signature and receives proceeds of a loan, however, it is well to also check out competitive commercial lenders such as Able Banker Charlie.

Today it is easier to distinguish true from illusory interest savings than it was a few years ago before the Truth in Lending Law went on the books. You should know this law in order to judge wisely when a low-interest loan offers genuine saving. Our monetary gurus, the financial fathers of the Federal Reserve, have explained in an advisory called *What Truth in Lending Means to You:*

> The law makes it easier for you to know two of the most important things about the cost of credit. One is the *finance charge*—the amount of money we pay to obtain credit. The other is the *annual percentage rate*, which provides a way of comparing credit costs regardless of the dollar amount of

those costs or the length of time over which we make payments. Both the finance charge and the annual percentage rate must be displayed prominently on the forms and statements used by a creditor to make the required disclosures.

Many of us know what interest is—6 percent per year for example. Let's suppose you borrow $100 for one year and pay 6 per cent—or $6—for that money. If you have use of the entire amount for one year you are paying an annual percentage rate of 6 per cent. But if you repay the $106 in 12 equal monthly instalments, you do not have use of the entire amount for the full year. In fact, over the entire year you have the use on the average of only about half the full $100. So the $6 charge for credit in this case becomes an annual percentage rate of 11 per cent.

Some creditors levy a service charge or a carrying charge or some other charge instead of interest, or perhaps they may add these charges to the interest. Under the Truth in Lending Law they must now total all such charges including the interest, and call the sum the finance charge. And then they must list the annual percentage rate of the total charge for credit.

The Truth in Lending Law won't always save you from one trap, however. Sometimes, Able Banker Charlie and other friendly practitioners of the ancient art of borrowing low and lending high will make you a seemingly attractive offer. It might go in this wise:

You make regular deposits during the month, and as long as you replace the money drawn out via the special cheques by the end of the same month, your cheques have cost you absolutely nothing! Actually, you have been paying bills with our money!

Meanwhile, we have been paying you 4.5% interest on your savings which have remained untouched. As you add to your savings, your ability to write cheques against them increases, and the more interest you earn.

If you choose not to make deposits up to the amount of the cheques you have written within the same month, we charge 1% on the difference. (This is an ANNUAL PERCENTAGE RATE of 12%, less than other credit card and similar credit plans in the state.) For instance, if your original deposit was $500, and you wrote cheques up to $400 and only deposited another $350 in that same month, there would be a charge of

50¢ per month, until you deposited another $50 to clear your account. Of course, you could again begin writing cheques against your savings deposit, which has remained untouched!

This looked like a doozy of a deal to George until he discussed it with Ronnie over a couple of before-dinner highballs.

"*That?*" Ronnie asked. "It's good only if you like the idea of paying interest to use your own money. Take their example of a $500 deposit, $400 in withdrawals, and $350 in deposits. They'd be hitting you a 12 percent interest charge (less, of course, part of the 4.5 percent they generously paid to you) for failing to deposit money—not, mind you, for borrowing it."

Quite different (and possibly productive of true savings) is the plan offered by another bank. This bank's advertisement was headlined:

"I've been paying 18 percent service charges!"

The copy explained:

Then I discovered I can charge clothes, furniture, appliances, most anything on my Mr. BOL-Master Charge Card and take 20 months or more to pay with no carrying charges whatsoever! It'll save me $50 to $75 a year. All I need do is maintain $1000 in a savings account on which I get 4½% interest. In addition my money is compounded quarterly from date of deposit and insured by F.D.I.C.

No-interest loans are sometimes available in other ways. When a friend of mine purchased a house, he signed a conventional mortgage note for most of the money required to swing his deal, being careful to observe mortgage reminders we looked into earlier. Then he arranged credit for most of the balance with the man who sold the house.

"This fellow wanted *out,*" he told me. "He had purchased another home for himself and didn't wish to go longer than necessary being owner of two homes, each with a mortgage and each on the property-tax collector's rolls. To make the deal attractive to me, he offered a no-interest loan for the last $3,000."

Distress over duplicate insurance, taxes, and notes is not the only reason a seller might take your no-interest note on part of the purchase price. He could prefer to spread out his receipts for tax or other purposes. He might be able to cajole you into a higher purchase price where you can obtain no-interest money to finance it, thus losing interest income but possibly gaining an amount taxable at lesser capital gains rates.

An offering of that type is not always as attractive from your standpoint as it is from his, however. The seller has converted high-taxed ordinary income into capital gains, should you pay a higher price in order to get lower interest. You could miss out on the deductible item of interest. Should such a deal be offered, balance tax cost against interest saving to see where your loan bread is buttered.

Awareness of the direction of judges' thinking and decisisions can help you to avoid high interest costs. In late 1970, the Wisconsin Supreme Court decided, in a case against a leading national retail firm, that the 1½ percent per month interest charge which it, and so many others, assess on unpaid balances exceeded the maximum then allowed by law in the state. Then the Attorney General of Iowa filed suit against another big national operator to establish a usury limit in his commonwealth. If you watch what is being done in your state, you may be able to chop these charges down to more reasonable size. Perhaps *you* might institute suit. Attorneys will frequently take such cases if they can become class actions in which the attorney, while retained by one client, represents interests of all who pay the charge.

OFFBEAT WAYS TO RAISE BUSINESS MONEY

Phil Phrustration publishes, edits, sells ads for, runs errands on, and generally enjoys the dubious privilege of owning a suburban newspaper. Ronnie visits the office once a week to keep the *Bootville Bugle's* books in shape and to talk over the relative miseries of being a journalist or a journeyman accountant. ("Writing news isn't a business," Phrustration insists, "it's a mistake.")

Among the frustrations of being Phil, one crisp autumn day when the following conversation took place, was the matter of infusing additional capital into the *Bootville Bugle* without, in Phrustration's phrase, "hocking all tomorrow's headlines and my hopes of earthly salvation by paying high interest rates."

"There are a number of things you can do," Ronnie answered. "Have you thought of the Small Business Administration as a starter?"

SBA will do nothing if you want a personal loan or if you can get an acceptable loan through regular banking channels sufficient for your need. But if you can't get a business loan on sound terms and if, despite this inability, the SBA believes you are a worthy risk although your collateral might be insufficient or your business history too short to obtain a commercial loan, SBA people can arrange to get you about 80 percent. Part of the loan might be carried by the bank which turned you down in the first place but which, with Small Business Administration backing, is now willing to take the risk.

Don't be worried about the word "small" in the SBA title unless you have a sizable operation already. For SBA purposes, a small firm is (among other criteria) one employing fewer than 250 people. (You can't qualify, however, if you are a subsidiary of a larger firm which doesn't meet the SBA yardsticks.)

"Then, too," said Ronnie, "there are the people and firms— mostly firms—who provide what is called venture capital to small outfits such as yours. You might have to sacrifice something of your equity in such a deal. But you would (1) raise the money, and (2) frequently get it at low or no interest because of the angle of selling equity."

Once there were only a few venture capitalists. Now it's a popular institutional way of life. One such firm is Greater Washington Investors, Inc., whose president, Don A. Christensen, said in a speech before the Washington Society of Security Analysts:

We are involved in the most exciting business that one could imagine—participating in the creation of what could be tomorrow's Polaroid or Xerox or Digital Equipment Corp. We call this venture capital.

I view venture capital as a melding together of the money and the experience within Greater Washington with the talents and creative energy of an outside management group to create a substantial enterprise.

Greater Washington is a large company, listed on the New York Stock Exchange, as is another sizable firm, American Research and Development. But there are dozens of venture firms like them in all areas of the country. Many are interested in lending to (or buying equity interest from) firms as small as Phil Phrustration's *Bootville Bugle*. Some run as mutual funds, others as sideline corporations of banks. A number are Small Business Investment Corporations; almost any registered SBIC is at least potentially a prospect for a business that wants to raise some capital through equity or equity-equivalent issues.

Ways exist to raise equity capital other than through these specialty firms. You can go public by selling stock to outsiders.

"But that would involve me in all kinds of regulation and red tape and take years to accomplish," wailed Phil.

"Not so," said Ronnie. "Several years ago, the Federal Reserve Bank of Boston commissioned a study of public financing through what are known as Regulation A offerings. You can obtain the full study by writing the Boston Fed and asking for its *New England Business Review* of October, 1966."

The study indicated that most Regulation A offerings came from companies and institutions of moderate size. Said the report:

Although a few issuers had assets of over $1 million, most had considerably less. More than three-quarters had assets of less than half a million dollars; 37 percent had assets of less than $100,000. In terms of owners' equity, the figures were even lower with the median at $80,000.

The typical offering was common stock with expected proceeds of about $250,000. Roughly one-third of the sampled issues were of the maximum $300,000 size.

(Going public this way offers a secondary money management advantage. With a publicly held stock in existence, your own stock holding can furnish collateral for a low-cost loan in future.)

"Then there is business leasing," Ronnie continued.

At the risk of repeating, let's review from the businessman's point of view how leasing can sometimes furnish low-cost money as an alternative to borrowing from Able Banker Charlie or another lender:

Leasing has the tax advantage of making immediate payments deductible where they would perhaps not have been to so great a degree under different circumstances. And leasing frees capital for other uses. Thus if a firm or an individual owned land and buildings worth $100,000, and then sold these to a leasing company, taking back an immediate rental agreement stretching over a long period (this is called saleleaseback), the capital formerly tied up in real estate would be freed for other uses.

SERVICE, ABLE BANKER CHARLIE, SERVICE

Banks offer many services. Some cost nothing over and above the charges you're assessed anyway for Able Banker Charlie's facilities. Other times there are moderate charges, frequently less than you would pay to have the same thing done in other ways.

A typical bank should offer most, probably all, of these savings services: regular passbook savings accounts; Christmas Club; longer-term premium savings accounts; and certificates of deposit for varying periods of time. Note that as long as inflation continues and/or interest rates stay as high as in 1970, banks' savings interest payments are undesirable since higher yields at equal, sometimes lessened, risk can be obtained elsewhere. More on that later. The exception is short-range certificates of deposit. Say you have some money you won't need for thirty days. That's a time period too short to buy a Treasury bill and you couldn't deal in bills for less than $10,000 anyway. On amounts larger than $1,000, many banks will write a 5 percent CD. You thus earn a return from

Able Banker Charlie on money which is momentarily un-
needed.

Checking-account services of most good banks include
regular checking accounts; minimum "free" accounts (more
on these in a moment); special accounts for smaller deposi-
tors; and, if the bank has a tie-up with Master Charge, Bank-
Americard, or another credit plan, checking accounts in
which an overdraft becomes an automatic loan.

The bank probably makes these loans: letter of credit in
which, again by arrangement, checks turn into loans; for
installment purchases or personal notes; commercial business
notes; for farming purchases and farm operation, home
modernization, and mobile-home purchase; and automobile
financing.

Other bank departments will buy bonds for you; invest
your money through trust arrangements; issue cash-any-
where travelers checks; look up credit in faraway cities;
arrange overseas credits and collections through branches or
correspondents abroad; and store your valuables (safe-de-
posit vault service).

Some banks operate travel departments and a few furnish
data processing service, using bank computers, to businesses
in their areas. Research information on area economic prospects is issued by many full-service banks.

You probaly don't need all the aids that Able Banker
Charlie offers. Certainly Sophie and George do not. However,
you—and they—should be aware of what is on tap.

Availability of services is not alone a reason for choosing
a bank. Look over Able Banker Charlie's balance sheet, too, or
ask your friend Ronnie the accountant to do it for you. Even
in these affluent days, there are a few shaky banks. Most of
them offer a full line of customer services. In some cases,
that is how they became shaky.

KEEP THE CHECKING COSTS DOWN

"That's easy," exclaimed Sophie. "I'll just get one of those
deals that Able Banker Charlie advertised in yesterday's

Bootville Bugle. You keep a minimum of $200 per month in the account and all costs are free—he says."

Begin with an understanding of the checking-account varieties we listed a few paragraphs back. Here is how the Valley National Bank of Arizona explains them:

> 1. REGULAR CHECKING ACCOUNT: Service charges are computed according to account balance and number of checks written. No minimum balance required. No service charges on accounts with low balances of $500 or more.
>
> 2. SPECIAL CHECKING ACCOUNT: Your only cost is 10¢ for each check written, and a 25¢ monthly maintenance charge. No minimum balance required. No charge for deposits.
>
> 3. $200 MINIMUM: Keep $200 minimum in your account and write all the checks you want, with never a service charge. If your account drops below $200, you will be charged just $2 service charge for that month, no matter how many checks you write.
>
> 4. LOAN CHECKING ACCOUNT: A "line of credit" up to $3,500, established on your ability to repay. You can write checks anywhere, anytime, up to your full line of credit. And each monthly repayment builds up your reserve—against which you can again write checks.

Type (1) is best if you maintain a hefty monthly balance. It is the costliest of all for those whose average checking account balances run $100 or below.

Type (2) is the cheapest by comparison, although not cheap in absolute fact, if you're a George-and-Sophie family that maintains low balances.

Type (3) appears to be the lowest cost of all for most people. In the September/October, 1969, issue of the *New England Economic Review,* Steven J. Weiss, regional economist in the research department of the Federal Reserve Bank of Boston, noted:

> Most "free" checking accounts are not really free, for service charges are dropped entirely only if the account holder maintains a specified balance during the relevant statement period. Only in cases where the required minimum balance is zero are the checking accounts truly free. The general case is more appropriately described as a "No Service Charge-Mini-

mum Balance" plan (NSC account). Bankers have contrived many variations within the general pattern of NSC account plans. The minimum balance required varies from the ultimate zero to $500 and higher. Some plans specify a required *average* balance rather than a minimum, and a few programs even provide an option, i.e. no service charges are imposed if a customer maintains a specified minimum balance or a given average balance during the statement period.

. . . If an NSC account does not satisfy the balance requirement in a given period, the customer is charged according to an ordinary service charge schedule, or a flat fee, or in some cases a combination of the two. *It is not unusual to find that charges for violation of the NSC balance requirement exceed the service charges that an individual would ordinarily incur under a regular or special checking account plan.* [Italics by author.]

"Here's something to consider," said Ronnie on his next visit to Editor Phrustration. "You have two checking accounts in Able Banker Charlie's Eighth National. The business account balances are more than enough to ensure against banking charges. In the personal account, I see that the bank frequently assesses charges because your average 'float'— that is, the balance available to offset banking charges—is lower than in the business account. Why not talk to Able Charlie next time you are in the neighborhood of the bank and suggest that he combine both floats and both sets of charges into a single assessment every month? That way, I am sure you will be able to escape bank charges on either account."

Ronnie's plan is an eminently feasible one. I maintain three separate accounts with a New Orleans bank. Arrangements provide that the *total* float be balanced against the *total* charges for checks drawn and items deposited in all three accounts. It has been years since I had to pay anything in bank charges even though the balance in one account or another might be below minimum during any given month. Such arrangements must be negotiated. Able Charlie's computer won't take care of them automatically because computers can't tell when three accounts belong to a single customer.

THE CARDS THAT COME IN THE MAIL, TRA-LA

"Look—here are three credit cards I didn't request that came through the mail," Sophie said, throwing them on the table before George. "We don't want them. I'm told that if I lose them and someone else uses them I can be liable. One company even sent a card for which a charge is made and now demands we pay on pain of having our credit rating affected. What will we do, George?"

Sophie's problem is not unique. It is so un-unique that Congress and the Federal Trade Commission have devoted considerable attention to it. Before you feel bound to do something other than ignore the plastic evidence of credulity that sellers send you through the mail, you should know how things stand in regard to this distribution of pseudo-dollars. The following quotations are from a Federal Trade Commission rule which states, "Unsolicited Mailing of Credit Cards Constitutes an Unfair Trade Practice." (The complete report is available from FTC in Washington.)

■ Marketers of products and services such as gasoline companies, department stores and all-purpose credit card issuers have attempted to increase the use of credit cards through distribution . . . through the mails to persons who have not requested such cards or agreed to accept the same.

■ A retail credit card holder is more likely to purchase at a retail outlet honoring his credit card.

■ Unsolicited cards are often lost in the mails and the intended recipient is unaware there is a card or that an account has been established in his name.

■ Such credit cards are often misappropriated and fraudulently used by unknown parties and the intended recipient of the credit card is put to the often considerable burden of demonstrating to the billing company that the goods or services were not ordered or purchased.

■ Billings resulting from fraudulent use of cards or billing errors cause concern among consumer recipients that their retail credit reputations might be jeopardized.

■ As a result of an unsolicited credit card being issued, recipients are put to the burden of returning the unwanted credit card to the sender if they wish to indicate that the card is not desired.

■ Credit card issuers who resort to the use of unsolicited mailings of credit cards may be placed at a competitive advantage over their competitors who do not utilize the unsolicited mailing.

■ Therefore it follows that such practices constitute unfair acts of practices and unfair methods of competition in violation of Section Five of the Federal Trade Commission Act.

Remember that cards sent as renewals of existing, in-use accounts do not come under the FTC's official frown. You'll still owe Plainfellow's on that account you established back in 1967, if only the card evidencing it is new and that card was sent as renewal.

Keep in mind that credit cards are best used for open, current charge purchases. There are cheaper ways of obtaining long-term money than allowing charge purchases to become long-term on which sizable charges are assessed.

TO RECAP:

1. The amount of interest paid on a loan depends upon the kind of lender with whom you deal and, in large part, upon the type of loan. Changing the collateral which secures a loan can sometimes result in a considerably lower interest rate.

2. Interest rates are negotiable. You can change from bank to credit union, finance firm to credit card. You can also negotiate with each lender; you don't have to pay the first rate anyone asks.

3. Some types of lending sources are especially advantageous. An example is a company, church, or other group credit union. Another is an insurance company. Written into many older policies is provision for borrowing at rates that seem bargain-basement in today's inflationary, high-interest era.

4. Where you are compelled to maintain compensating balances, certain little-known lending sources will maintain deposits sufficient to cover the required balances. This frees your full borrowing. A small charge is made for the service.

5. The difference between discount and straight interest should be understood. Both are available from the same sources. On a discount loan, you might pay almost twice as much as in a straight-interest borrowing.

6. Know the advantages that the Truth in Lending Law puts into your hands. Use them to make sure that seemingly good terms are in reality in your favor.

7. Some banks have gimmick accounts. With these, you can find yourself paying interest for the use of your own money.

8. Sometimes sellers extend no-interest loans to clinch a sale. On certain kinds of borrowing these possibilities should be investigated before borrowing from conventional sources.

9. If you own a business and must obtain funds, look into possibilities of going public through Regulation A, minus much of the red tape of an orthodox offering. Venture capitalists are another funds provider.

10. Sometimes business loans on special terms are available with the help of the U.S. Small Business Administration.

11. Banks extend many services. Part of money management is to obtain fullest use of these at lowest—and often no—cost.

12. There are legitimate ways to keep checking-account charges down. It's necessary to weigh the relative advantages of the types of checking accounts modern banking makes available.

13. You should know your rights in regard to credit accounts you did not ask to have. Each year, people lose millions by making good on credit claims that the federal authorities consider unfair.

10

Increase Income without Working Harder

"So far so fair, but we have not gone far enough," said George.

"For this money management bit to bear its best fruit, we should do something about increasing our income as well as getting more for our outgo. Preferably without too much more work on my part."

The ideas outlined earlier for living better on the same money can indeed improve your life patterns. But, as George pointed out to Sophie that dull, gray winter evening after the children had retired and just before the late, late movie had come on, "It is even better if we can add some lettuce to the income we already have. That gives a two-way scope for money management."

Ideas you or George can use to increase income without

increasing (greatly) the amount of work needed to reap such income will be the subject of this chapter.

The suggestions which follow assume that you, like George and Sophie, have some extra cash to invest. It is not necessary to have a lot of backlog money. The Plainfellow family are big investors, but American capitalism has been built upon the capital of small- to medium-sized families such as George's, yours, and mine. Statistics of the New York Stock Exchange show that 30.8 million people now own stocks. Probably as many own real estate which brings them some income (it might be only an extra apartment in the family castle).

Even small amounts can make worthwhile contributions to the better living we're after. After counting up all extra cash and then wisely holding back enough in reserve so that he would not be pushed to the wall if medical or accidental catastrophes should strike, George found that he could put about $1,000 to work. On that he might expect to earn $80 to $90 yearly, depending upon the manner in which it would be invested. "Doesn't look very large," he admitted, "but that income will purchase an extra couple of days' vacation, buy me a new suit, repaint a room for us, or go toward tuition charges in a better grade school for Edith, Ethelred, or Frederica. Even $80 to $90 is certainly worth striving for when striving takes the form only of making an investment."

Having a thou at work in stocks, bonds, or mutual funds does not seem difficult. "But in real estate?" Sophie asked. "We could hardly buy a house with that amount."

"True," replied George. "But real estate is a field in which the leverage is very large. In many cases, small downpayments swing goodly parcels of mud and brick, and the small amount can certainly furnish downpayment for improving a piece of property to enhance its rental potential."

(The ideas which follow are not intended as detailed outlines for investment. You will find those in an earlier book of mine, *Nine Roads to Wealth,* which shows how to make that little stake do a lot and which gives closer attention to methodology of investing.)

LOOK INTO WALL STREET'S WARES

Stocks represent ownership of a corporation. If ABC, Inc., has 50 million shares outstanding and you hold 100, you're a 1/500,000th owner of the business. A *bond* is an I O U. When the I O U is unsecured it is called a *debenture*. Owners of *preferred* stock have the right to receive dividends before any can be paid to the owners of common stock (but the common usually offers the widest participation in company growth). Sometimes preferreds and debentures can be exchanged for common at their owners' option; these are called *convertibles*. A *warrant* is an out-and-out option. Speculators like warrants because these tend to go up or down faster than common stocks, but it is well to know that warrants receive no dividends and are risky at all times.

Mutual funds are among the most interesting vehicles in which small investors can put their money. These were described in my earlier book *How to Make Money with Mutual Funds;* the book tells how to select funds for varying investment objectives. A mutual fund is a pooling of the capital of many investors with the purpose of securing, for each, diversification of risks and professional money supervision that he could probably not otherwise purchase with the money he has available.

Generally, stocks yield a lesser return today than do bonds. Nevertheless, there is a rationale for buying stocks as opposed to bonds. It is not always applicable, despite the enthusiastic claims of aficionados of the equity concept. It makes sense for some people all of the time and all of the people some of the time. The equity argument goes something like this:

It is an age of inflation. You might receive a 9 percent return on a bond and with that 9 percent buy a sport coat or a new kitchen table. In three years you still receive the same absolute dollars. Inflation has eroded prices in the meantime. Now your dollars buy, instead of a sport coat or a kitchen table, a pair of slacks or a kitchen chair. Add another three years and the dollar erodes still more. Now you can buy a plate to set on the table and perhaps a necktie to wear under your shabby old sport coat.

In stocks, inflation might affect the corporation whose blue-edged certificates you purchased; it makes the profits and dividends rise in dollars even if not in buying power. You may not be ahead, but at least you'll still be able to buy the same table or pay for the same sport coat of Harris tweed in the men's department of Plainfellow's store.

And if things go *very* right, your corporation might prosper to a greater extent than inflation causes dollar deterioration; you might thus buy, in three years or six, a complete kitchen set instead of a table alone, or slacks plus the Harris tweed sport coat with money Funnybone Corp. pays out as dividends on its blue-edged certificates.

Dividends on stocks, as already mentioned, are likely to be lower in immediate yield than the return on bonds, however. Keep that in mind. And don't be bemused that growth in Funnybone's dividends is inevitable. Many a good corporation has seen inflation blow up its costs while shrinking its markets and the result has been decreased, rather than increased, earnings. For George, that might mean a pair of socks instead of a sport coat. For Sophie, a new place mat instead of a kitchen set.

So why not bonds on which the yield can't drop?

A good question.

Bonds, as noted, are I O Us. These might be issued by corporations and can vary in quality from the impeccable notes of a blue-chip outfit to the shakier (and usually higher-yielding) promises to pay issued by firms such as Phil Phrustration's *Bootville Bugle* which, following the success of a Regulation A stock offering engineered by Ronnie, sold bonds direct to an institutional investor who later pushed some off on the public market.

Debt instruments include Treasury obligations of Uncle Sugar, divided into *bills* (maturities ranging from three months to a year), *notes* (maturities going up to five annums), and *bonds* (longer-term maturities). There are the bonds and notes of semigovernmental bodies such as the Federal Land Bank, Federal Home Loan Bank, and the Federal National Mortgage Association, whose friends call it Fannie Mae from the initials FNMA.

Governments also issue savings bonds. These are the little dinguses on which you pay one price and collect another (example: the $25 bond for $18.75). Savings bonds are lousy investments. Their interest rates are miniscule. You would do better using a savings account in Able Banker Charlie's Eighth National.

A drawback to investing in government is that, except for savings bonds, Uncle Sugar's I O Us are not issued in small denominations. Some are in minimum hunks of $10,000. Financiers' ingenuity gets around this, however. One New York bank now buys in big amounts and sells interests in its holdings to people with $500 or more to invest. Perhaps such a plan exists in your community. Ask Able Banker Charlie about it.

Exempt from federal income tax on the interest paid to bondholders and often from income levies in the state where they're issued are municipal bonds. This broad term covers the obligations of states, cities, counties, taxing bodies such as bridge authorities, school boards, industrial districts, and the like. Like corporate bonds and unlike Treasuries, these vary widely in quality. Some are backed by the full faith and credit of the area offering them. Some are called revenue bonds; certain revenues, as from a toll road or a particular tax, are dedicated to paying the interest and retiring the principal.

It is true that bonds offer a steady rather than a growing yield. But they can have a kicker in high-interest times. If prevailing rates go down, bond prices, as a corollary, must go up. Here's a simple example: Flysheet County has issued tax-exempt municipals bearing a 3 percent coupon. They came out in easier money times at par, called 100 but in reality meaning $1,000 per bond. Later, times tightened and, alas for holders of Flysheet County's gilt-edged debt, the bonds were selling down at 60 where they yielded 5 percent prevailing as an immediate return from investments of similar ratings.

Enter George.

George buys at 60 in the hope that in a few years interest rates will become easier. They do. Back to par go Flysheet County's 3s of 1980. They yield 3 percent on market price once more. *But they are still paying 5 percent on the amount George invested.*

Here is George's best kicker: He bought the bonds at 60. At 100, each $600 investment for the once-deflated, discounted Flysheet bond has grown to $1,000, the price at which the bonds had been issued in happier, easier times.

George has a big yield plus a big profit.

If, that is, times ease and Flysheet 3s of 1980 go back to par. If money tightens instead, the bonds will go still lower and George will have a capital loss instead of a gain.

You buy bonds if money rates are high and you believe they will go down. That causes bond prices to jump. You refrain from buying bonds and sell any Flysheet 3s in your bank box if money rates are already low but you fear they might go higher. That would cause bond prices to decline.

Some bonds allow you to enjoy the best of both the bond and stock worlds. Convertibles, as we have noted, are issued as bonds (sometimes as preferred stocks) and can be changed at the owner's option into stock on set terms and at set times. These as a rule pay a little less in yield than do straight bonds, but often more than the common stock into which they can be changed if Funnybone Corp. has a good year and its stock in consequence enjoys a substantial rise.

Mutual funds invest in stocks or bonds or both. They are run by pros, as noted earlier. Professional investment managers are no more uniformly skilled at their trade than are professional football players, medical doctors, or sanitation engineers. Some are smarter than others. You'll want to look at both the dividend and growth records of a mutual fund to determine whether its pro jockey is one of the fast-with-a-whip operators who get the most out of money entrusted to them, or one of the plodding drivers whose nags furnish background for the kind of race-track tickets bettors tear up and toss to the winds.

Mutuals might invest in special industries or special areas of the world. They may go for go-go performance, or instead concentrate upon steady production of dividends for their shareowners. You should know their thing as well as how effectively they do it.

And you must look into the load picture.

Load is a commission tacked on to the front end of a mutual fund. Net asset value—the current worth of the whole portfolio divided by the number of shares outstanding—is the start of fund valuation. Some funds are sold at this figure. They are called no-loads but you can't buy them as easily as the load funds since dealers understandably push mutuals on which they make the most money. A load fund computes a sliding-scale commission which begins at 8¾ percent. If you buy one of the latter, your percentage yield on an investment is lower since less of your saved capital goes into buying shares, some being diverted to make the dealer-broker and his salesmen a bit richer.

A few funds are called closed ends. These have set numbers of shares and are traded on stock exchanges where you buy them from other investors instead of from issuing companies, and pay stock exchange commissions for doing so. Such commissions are lower than mutual fund loads unless you buy a very large amount of a load fund. However, at the rate New York Stock Exchange member-firms are rewarding themselves for inefficiency by jacking up commission rates, this may not always be so.

One kind of closed end has special interest to both income and capital gains investors. It is called a dual fund. My book *How You Can Beat Inflation* explained:

> These result from an unusual concept in investing methodology. The dual fund has two classes of investors. To the half who have elected to invest for income go all of the dividends, etc., which accrue as yield on the investment of the whole portfolio. The investors who opt for capital growth receive no

income whatever. But they get all of the appreciation and profits which accrue to both halves of the portfolio.

The point of all this is leverage. With 100 percent of the capital working to give income to only 50 percent of the stockholders, the income half of a dual fund has added financial muscle. And with all of the capital gains (if any) being added to the accounting of per share asset value of the other half of the combination, extra leverage muscle is applied to the accounts of those in search of growth.

Whether you utilize bonds, stocks, or mutuals to increase your income, you had better do some homework first. In the case of an existing security, you ask Friendly Broker Ferd for a Standard and Poor's report or look it up in *Moody's Industrials* or *Moody's Handbook*. In the case of a new issue similar to the debentures sold by Phil Phrustration's *Bootville Bugle*— also in the case of a mutual fund—you ask to see the prospectus. Most prospectuses and stock/bond reports measure no more than 5½ by 9 inches. But their importance is beyond measure.

Look for:

1. *How much potential dilution?*   The existence of warrants, convertible debentures, or preferred stock can bring, in future years, a reduction of earnings which is the base for dividends and the statistic on which professional analysts will judge the stock's desirability. (Example: There are one million shares now but existing preferred stock can be converted later to an additional million shares of the common. If the profit should double in coming years, but each share of preferred be converted, then the per-share earnings would stay exactly still. The result would probably be no increase in stock price or in dividend.)

2. *What is the earnings record?*   A company able to bring down to net profit less than 1 percent of sales in the past is not likely to become suddenly brilliant with the addition of new capital from a stock sale. "I know of no light able to show my way into the future but the lamp of experience," said a sage. He was right; past results don't guarantee equal future performance, but they help to form a judgment on future probability.

3. *Is the balance sheet in good shape?*   Where the balance sheet of assets and liabilities shows a shaky existing setup with management skirting the brink of bankruptcy, addition of the sought-after new funds may solve the problem and bring Funnybone Corp. to new prosperity. But that is not a good thing on which to bet if your aim is conservative investment.

4. *To what purpose will new capital be put?*   This is vital. I have seen instances where the new money resulting from a stock sale was used to pay for advertising and product inventory. Those are proper uses for day-to-day funds, not for permanent capital. Unless the advertising is wildly successful and new inventories move smartly, such a company will be likely to need more, then still more, capital in times to come. Permanent capital should be put to long-time usage.

5. *What percent will the public own?*   Management's presumed expertise is worth something over and above its existing stake in the capital structure. But where the public is expected to put up 95 percent of capital after completion of an offer and receive for it only 5 percent of ownership, things are obviously out of line and you should cogitate carefully before joining the group which puts up the big end of the money and receives the short end of the stock.

6. *Who has underwritten the issue?*   The underwriter is a firm which brings out the issue. Most new issues trade over the counter at first. An underwriter big enough to make a market in the stock is necessary; otherwise you'd be buying a stock you couldn't sell later because no market exists without a firm ready to make the future market. Look for a reputable name.

7. *How much experience do officers have?*   I recall the prospectus of a new mutual fund which hopefully planned to invest its shareowners' money for profits. "It's appalling," I told a client. "No officer has more than six months' experience. Most are just out of school. I would not buy it." A year later, the fund had lost over 40 percent of the money investors had put into it.

8. *Are aims realizable?*   "This publishing company should corner the Air Force book market," a client was told by an

enthusiast for one new stock issue. While this was its aim and hope, as events turned out the company quickly lost to more experienced publishers. That this was probable could be seen in the prospectus, which revealed past sales of only $5,000 per year.

When you have made your choice, it isn't necessary to have a lump sum for investment. Wall Street, in its kindness, consideration, and desire to generate commissionable volume, has invented accumulative plans. These allow you to put small sums to work, gradually increasing the income base for money management to bring you better things without harder work.

Members of the New York Stock Exchange offer a Monthly Investment Plan which permits investment of as little as $40 every three months. Here is how one large investment firm explains the MIP to its customers:

> Let's say that you find you have $75 a month that you want to invest in stocks. Your first step is to select a common stock that suits your needs. Suppose the stock you want to buy is one that costs $30 a share. There was a time when you could buy only full shares of stock. Then, if you had $75 to invest and wanted to buy shares of a $30 stock you had to decide whether to buy two shares, pay the commission, and put the balance back into your pocket, or buy three shares by adding to the $75 you originally intended to invest. Under the Monthly Investment Plan you can buy stock by the dollar's worth instead of by the share.
>
> The next step is to fill out a Monthly Investment Plan purchase order and mail it with your check. Your stock is then purchased for you. The only requirements are that you must be at least 21 years of age and that you declare your intention of investing with any amount of money from a minimum of $40 every three months.

Accumulative plans in many sizes and shapes are also offered by mutual funds. While an investor can withdraw from the MIP without penalty, some of the mutual fund plans are contractual and a few are arranged so that if an investor withdraws in the first year or two, he will find that a sizable portion of his funds has gone into salesman's commissions. It is well to read a contract carefully.

Because bonds are individually so high in price, there are no organized accumulative plans for putting away I O Us of Uncle Sugar, the states, and the corporations.

Whether you buy bonds, stocks, or mutuals to do your income-increasing bit, think about something called plow-back. On the face of things, this seems to negate the objective of increasing income because, by reinvesting dividends and interest payments into more shares or additional bonds, the money can't increase living standards here and now.

"But immediate money isn't everything," George pointed out when Sophie raised the objection. "Tomorrow always comes, but it is not always better than today. Plowing back helps to build an estate which might ensure that tomorrow will indeed be a time for better living."

This was explained in *How You Can Beat Inflation:*

> Let's say your capital purchased common stocks. Assume that the stock you bought for $2,000.00 is worth $3,000.00 at the end of twelve months. Your capital growth of 50 percent is a very enviable thing. This stock, let us say, also paid a dividend of $150.00 during the year. You can take the dividend money and buy a big dinner for your friends to celebrate your financial coup of the year or purchase some new clothing.
>
> Or you might plow it back by using the dividend disbursement for purchase of more stock. You purchase $150.00 worth of extra shares. Another year rolls around and at the end of it you are pleased to discover that your capital has again appreciated by 50 percent, thanks to your wise selection of a stock likely to go up in the latest year. The holding is now worth $4,725.00. It would have been worth only $4,500.00 if you had not possessed those additional plowback shares on which to go after further growth.
>
> In mutual funds plowback of at least one kind of disbursement is necessary, or you will drop back. Mutuals pay out two kinds of "income." One of these is true income. It is based upon dividends received by the fund. The other is usually called a "capital gains distribution." Unless you reinvest by taking fresh shares rather than cash, you will—using an investment sense of the words and not a tax sense—be spending your capital itself rather than the fruits and monetary berries it has produced.

"When you buy stocks and mutual funds, there are ways to get more for the money," Ronnie noted as he and George downed cold glasses of beer following a Saturday-morning tennis session.

"One way is to buy high-priced stocks. Your commissions are lower in buying 100 shares of an $80 stock than in purchasing 1,000 shares of an $8 stock although both transactions involve $8,000. Wall Street's outmoded methods impose commissions on the round lot of 100 shares rather than the total dollar amount. Brokers push the low-priced stock idea; that's where they make the biggest commissions.

"In mutual funds, go for a no-load over a load fund *if* its objective is what you seek and *if* it has a record of accomplishment and prospects of continuing to perform as well as the load fund. Also seek closed-end funds on the Big Board. Commissions are lower than on load funds except for very large transactions."

One of the interesting ways to use mutuals is in equity funding. This was explained in a March 16, 1970, article in the *California Financial Journal:*

> Mutual funds and insurance are sold in a coordinated program whereby both the mutual fund and insurance premium dollars are invested in a mutual fund. The mutual fund shares are then pledged as collateral for a loan to pay the insurance premium.
>
> Upon completion of a 10-year program, the loan is repaid by the sale of mutual fund shares. Any appreciation from the investment in excess of the amount owed is profit. In other words, the equity funding program applies leverage, to permit the investment of after-expense dollars plus insurance expense dollars for possible profit.
>
> We believe that if the market enjoys an upward trend, an equity funding program would not only keep pace with inflation, but result in a profit in spite of inflation; the program could turn an expense into a possible profit.

A phrase in that last paragraph should be noted: "If the market enjoys an upward trend." Funding is a good idea only when that upward trend is at work. This fact is cited because funding, despite claims, is not a guaranteed way to the country club where Plainfellow and his economic equals meet every weekend.

REAL ESTATE

"I like the land," said Sophie. "Maybe I'm a peasant at heart. Or maybe it's just the attraction of owning property you can see, feel, and pay for the repairs on."

"Don't you know better than to end a sentence with the preposition 'on'?" George asked.

"Don't you know Winston Churchill's reply to a clerk who pointed this out?" replied Sophie. "Churchill said, 'This is an impertinence up with which I will not put.' If Churchill won't, neither will I. Let's get back to the land."

In real estate investing, you can buy raw land or property which will bring you a rental income. The raw land investor hopes that something will come along, or he expects to be able to force it to come along, making his land more valuable. He then expects to sell at a profit, taking his money management increment in the form of a capital gain. The buyer of rental property may (and probably does) also cherish this hope of selling out later at a profit. But he mainly wants to make money month by month through rentals.

Consider raw land. In *How You Can Beat Inflation* I pointed out four criteria experienced land buyers seek before signing to own a parcel of dirt:

1. Is something afoot? Can I logically envision the coming of a new development which will increase the value of this land in the future over what it is today without my having to invest anything except mortgage payments in the interim?

2. Can value be added to this land? It may look like a swamp or desolate mountainside now. But a usable idea can bring extra value.

3. Is a city expanding in the direction of my proposed land purchase?

4. Has this land a potential industrial use due to its proximity to water, transportation markets, raw material source, or skilled labor?

There is a great deal of money to be made—more than enough to overcome inflationary inroads on your lessening currency—in buying and reselling raw land. There is still more to be made by developing that land yourself. People of moderate means can do this, thanks to the leverage of borrowed money.

Many people believe that raw land with price potential has to be in the desert or swamp. Not so. There is great potential in urban land, too. Slum clearance and improvement of our civic environment are large among America's targets.

In buying rental property, the rule of thumb is that, after allowing for reasonable vacancy of perhaps 15 percent, your property should pay back a tenth of its cost every year. Example: Should George buy real estate to rent, investing $15,000 total price (downpayment might be as little as $1,500), the gross return from rents should be about $1,500 per year.

In this area as with stocks, you or George can keep and spend that $1,500 rent, or plow it back. If you plow it back you're building up a capital asset which, if all goes well, will pay you more tomorrow.

Take George's $15,000 rental property bought on $1,500 downpayment. George gives a $13,500 note. Rental income runs about $1,500. This finances notes to the mortgage company and leaves around $500 a year for plowback. Assume he escapes taxation because the mortgage interest, upkeep costs, etc., are immediately deductible expense, and with depreciation of the structure on, say, a fifteen-year table (allowable because the building is not new), you have a small net *loss* for tax purposes which can be used to reduce income taxes on money from other sources such as your regular job or your business. But you possess the income which accrues after mortgage costs and running expense even though you escape taxation on it. In three years, you have accumulated another $1,000 stake. The depreciation will be used to lessen the taxable cost base of the house, and eventually, if you sell it, you will pay capital gains rates on the amount of profit. With a stake accumulated from cash flow, you go out looking for a similar house. If successful, you soon have two income producers, and shortly you're searching for a third piece of income-producing real estate.

One rule for success is to avoid single-family dwellings. Two-family is better, four- or six- family better still. That way you won't be hurt if one unit goes tenantless for a time.

Don't spare the expenses for keeping your place up to date. Competition is tough. People will live in an old structure, but not in rundown quarters.

Successful landlords say you should not let rents become delinquent. Be tough with the tenant who can't pay and let your contributions to United Fund or another cause take care of your charity obligations. If leasee Henry Hairbrush doesn't have the money on the first, he isn't likely to have it by the fifteenth. By the first of next month Harry will owe you for two months and it will be twice as hard to get your money. Real estate ownership is intended to be a method for expanding income, not housing the friendless. Welfare was invented to serve that end.

Finally, don't buy in a dilapidated neighborhood unless it is one where landlords are sprucing up. Things usually go from rundown to worthless.

In *How You Can Beat Inflation* I wrote this about the cash-flow advantages of real estate as a sideline income producer:

> Real estate investments permit you to take a variety of deductions which are very real in a business sense but which do not reduce the cash flow—the vital, in-the-pocket sums reaching you. It is possible to make a seemingly high income return become almost negligible on the tax return. However, since you have deducted it in great part for depreciation, the writeoff reduces the taxable cost base of a property. You therefore pay a greater capital gains tax upon eventual sale. But you escape the higher tax bite of ordinary income rates. This feature does not apply to raw land.

Changing tax laws might make that provision less or more attractive over the years. Always consult an attorney, CPA, or other tax adviser.

Few people know about the mortgage trust, another kind of real estate investment. This allows George and Sophie, Ronnie, you, or me to get in on the sometimes-sizable returns paid on mortgages. You don't have to lend tens of thousands of dollars to do so.

The following is extracted from a prospectus offering

2,550,000 shares of beneficial interest and $24.5 million of 6¾ percent convertible subordinated debentures. A "unit" consisted of 30 shares of beneficial interest and $300 principal amount of debentures. The offering pointed out:

> The Trust has been established to provide investors with a diversified portfolio of real estate investments. The Trust's long-range investment policy is expected ultimately to emphasize equity investments in real estate and, to a lesser extent, long-term first mortgage loans, often coupled with equity participations. However, during the early phases of its operation, expected to last for at least a year or more, equity investments will not comprise a significant portion of the Trust's investment portfolio; during this period its portfolio will consist predominantly of short-term construction loans.

A FRANCHISE?

In late years a popular way to invest has been to purchase a franchise. This allows George to operate a fried chicken parlor, hamburger joint, crime control lab, boutique, pet registry, or whatever. He and you can obtain franchises to get into almost any business under a nationally advertised name umbrella. Some franchises have proven big money-makers.

But all involve your own work and sweat.

If you own real estate, you may have to collect rents, supervise tenants, clean up, or paint up. If you buy stocks, bonds, or mutual funds, you will need to acquire facts in order to buy the right ones, and you should invest some continuing study time along with your initial cash.

But a franchise is a business. No business runs well if its owner is absent. Look into a franchise investment only if you plan to switch full-time into that field or if you have sufficient extra hours. Sophie might take on management of the franchise instead of going back to her teaching job.

A franchise is less an investment, defined as something in which the money works for you, than a business, definable as a deal in which you work for money.

This description of franchising was given by the U.S. Small Business Administration in a publication, *Management Development Program on Franchising* (available from the Superintendent of Documents at $1.25):

> In the more commonly understood sense, franchising is taken to mean the licensing of an individual to conduct a specific type of business according to a predetermined pattern developed and perfected by the franchisor.
>
> The franchised establishments which operate within a particular franchise system are usually identified as members of a group. They operate under a common trade name—for example, Chicken Delight, Dunkin' Donuts, MacDonald's, and so on. Their business operation, their establishment's appearance, their merchandise—even their operating procedures are standardized to a very high degree. In their efforts to maintain a standardized image and marketing approach to the general buying public, the franchisors usually retain a strong, formalized system of control of the business operation. In this type of franchise, the responsibilities of both parties —franchisor and franchisee—are spelled out in the franchise contract, and are usually considered to be of mutual advantage to both parties.

Nothing about investment there. A franchise is an operating business. Enter one if you wish; it is a good way to make a sometimes large living. But understand what you are doing.

TO RECAP:

1. Investment of extra cash can add to the family income without increasing the family breadwinner's working hours. Extra cash for this purpose should not be needed when unexpected catastrophe or expense arises. The income and profits from even small investment amounts can make worthwhile contributions to better living.

2. Stocks are shares representing ownership of corporations. They are likely to pay smaller immediate income than bonds, but if a corporation prospers over the years its dividend payout can increase.

3. Bonds represent indebtedness of corporations, states, municipalities, and the federal government. Some bonds sell at discounts; these could rise in value when easier money returns. Yields of 7 percent to 9 percent are sometimes available in high-grade bonds.

4. Income from some bonds is tax-exempt. Other bonds can be converted later into shares of common stock.

5. Mutual funds pool the money of many investors. They give diversification that people with small capital cannot otherwise obtain, and they furnish professional management that likewise could not be retained by smaller investors. Mutual funds can be found to fit every investment objective.

6. Read prospectuses and applicable financial reports before making an investment decision. Otherwise you might find yourself in the position of the legendary horseman who mounted a steed and rode off in all directions at once.

7. You should be wary of mutual fund accumulative plans which assess a heavy first-year commission, penalizing those who withdraw before completing the plan.

8. Plowback of dividends and/or interest can help to build a bigger stake. It won't contribute toward a higher immediate income but might make you richer tomorrow.

9. Equity funding combines insurance with mutual funds. If the fund shares go up in value, you can build a paid-up insurance plan while also achieving an increased estate.

10. People who invest in raw land do so with hope that, by proximity to community growth or because of other factors, value will be added to the land and it can be sold at an increased price. Raw land seldom brings in immediate money.

11. Rental property can produce income in itself. If you live in part of a house and rent out another portion, rentals sometimes equal mortgage payments and you achieve full ownership at no out-of-pocket cost.

12. Plowback of real estate income can add to the value of holdings. This is done at the cost of immediate monthly rentals, however.

13. Mortgage trusts allow small investors to participate in

real estate lending. Many also accumulate equity in land and buildings.

14. Franchising has become popular. Before going all out for a hamburger heaven or a lab to combat crime—franchising opportunities are found in every facet of business—you must know that you are going into a business which requires your time rather than an investment in which money works for you without more than brief supervision.

11

The Consumer Watchdogs

CONSUMERISM in the America of the Seventies means that we have adopted the concept of 'buyer's rights.'

I believe that the buyer in America today has the right to make an intelligent choice among products and services. The buyer has the right to accurate information on which to make his free choice. The buyer has the right to expect that his health and safety are taken into account by those who seek his patronage. The buyer has the right to register his dissatisfaction, and have his complaint heard and weighed, when his interests are badly served.

Who said that?

Some loudmouth from the New Left?

A troublemaker who doesn't like the free enterprise system?

A wild-eyed professor who was sore because he once made a bad buying decision?

A Naderite? A Maoist? A militant?

A nut, obviously.

Wrong.

Those were the words of Richard M. Nixon, President of the United States, embodied in an official message on Protection of Interests of Consumers. Mr. Nixon sent them to Congress on October 31, 1969, with his recommendations for legislation to sharpen the teeth of consumer watchdogs.

You're a consumer. So am I, so is Ronnie, so are George and Sophie.

If we are to manage money wisely and live better as a consequence, we have to recognize the gyp situations, avoid them where we can do so, know what can be done about those we don't manage to avoid, and be acquainted with all the avenues for consumer protection which exist to make the gyp drain on our dollars less than it used to be.

Some of the dangers that beset people who buy things today are staggering. Happily, watchdogs have been trained to eliminate dragons that endanger our pocketbooks. Most, not all, of these watchdogs are ethical and honest. A majority are able. It's well to know who they are and what they do.

THE HAZARDS

But first a look at the abuses that make money management harder than it was in Grandpop's simple world only a few decades ago.

1. *Guarantees, for Example* When the old medicine-man pitchman told your grandfather that his product was guaranteed not to wear, tear, rust or bust, Grandpop may or may not have believed him. It didn't matter. The peddler was over the county line and away by morning, and if trouble arose there was no one to whom a complaint could be taken. Today, there are supposed to be guarantees that the gaurantee is good. These aren't always operational, however, and although the seller may not have moved on by the time his product wears, tears, rusts, or busts, you are sometimes no safer than old Granddad. Or are you? It depends upon how well you know your rights.

If a product is sold across state lines or through the mails, or otherwise comes under jurisdiction of the kindly great white father in Washington, then strictures of the Federal Trade Commission apply. Here is the law of the Medes and Persians as interpreted by Federal Traders in a booklet, *Guides against Deceptive Advertising of Guarantees:*

> In general, any guarantee in advertising shall clearly and *conspicuously disclose—*
> (a) *The nature and extent of the guarantee.*
>   This includes disclosure of—
>   (1) what product or part of the product is guaranteed,
>   (2) what characteristics or properties of the designated product or part thereof are covered by, or excluded from, the guarantee,
>   (3) what is the duration of the guarantee,
>   (4) what, if anything, any one claiming under the guarantee must do before the guarantor will fulfill his obligation under the guarantee, such as return of the product and payment of service or labor charges;
> *and*
> (b) *The manner in which the guarantor will perform.* This consists primarily of a statement of exactly what the guarantor undertakes to do under the guarantee. Examples of this would be repair, replacement, refund. If the guarantor or the person receiving the guarantee has an option as to what may satisfy the guarantee this should be set out;
> *and*
> (c) *The identity of the guarantor.* The identity of the guarantor should be clearly revealed in all advertising, as well as in any documents evidencing the guarantee. Confusion of purchasers often occurs when it is not clear whether the manufacturer or the retailer is the guarantor.

It is not easy to run out on these rules now that the county line has been extended to the national border. FTC orders can hit the retailer as well as the manufacturer. In a recent case, consumers found that manufacturers refused to make good on guarantees of watches bought through a national chain. "Not our goods," said the manufacturers. "The works have been removed and cheaper movements placed inside cases bearing our names. We can't make restitution or repairs on such a deal." The FTC then issued, and the retailer agreed to, orders prohibiting this practice.

"So don't assume we have lost out when there is conflict over whose guarantee applies to a piece of defective merchandise," George warned Sophie. "Somebody is at fault. Let's find him."

The auto industry, which many believe could win any unpopularity contest hands down, has come under particular fire for its warranties. Even car dealers sometimes say that manufacturers' warranties are unclear. They claim on occasion that manufacturer compensation for warranty work is not enough. This becomes an excuse for poor or skimped warranty repairs.

"Any car buyer should know the exact terms of his warranty," stressed an attorney with whom I discussed this. "And he should demand strict fulfillment. Whether the dealer receives sufficient or insufficient compensation from the manufacturer is a matter between manufacturer and dealer. The buyer doesn't enter into it and should not be compelled to suffer."

2. How Believable Is Advertising? In one eastern city in the early days of television, TV program ratings were made by checking water pressure. "When an unpopular program came on, people left their sets to use the plumbing, wash the dishes, make a drink. The water pressure dropped. The higher the pressure, the higher the program rating," one researcher explained. During commercial messages, the water pressure was very low. "Who wants to look at commercials?" this man asked. "Who believes them anyway?"

That is a good question in this gimmicked world. How believable *is* advertising?

Generally, it is very believable. Advertising is like other commercial things. A sound, reliable firm puts out sound, reliable ads. But not all advertisers are sound and their advertising is often unreliable. Knowing what goes on in mass selling helps if you want to manage money for better living.

Today, many of the big, seemingly sound and reliable firms are under fire. An example was the marbles-in-soup controversy involving a nationally advertised food brand. The FTC labeled as "false advertising" TV commercials using marbles to show that the advertiser's soup ingredients would not sink to the bottom.

"If that were the worst consumer advertising complaint, we'd be in good shape," Sophie said sharply. "Are our consumerism watchdogs devoting all their time to children's games?"

3. *Insurance That Doesn't Always Insure*   When my family was away on vacation one recent year, our house was robbed. Over $400 in cash was missing, along with other things. The insurance adjuster explained: "There is a $100 deductible on this policy. Then there is a $100 limit on cash losses." The company proceeded to wash out the $100 deductible against the $100 cash limit, paying only for our loss of other objects. If this had been computed by taking the full loss, deducting the initial $100, *then* taking $100 of cash loss, payment would have been larger.

"You can depend upon an insurance company to find a way to make its payment small," said an attorney to whom I mentioned this. "And you can depend upon some of them to take months over a settlement. The hospitalization claim of one client did not have a single disputed item. Yet the company delayed payment for half a year!"

Does insurance really insure? Many people, saying that it does not and that state regulation of insurance companies is often inadequate, demand that a federal eyeball be applied to insurance firms' methods and accounting. Especially bitter are many residents of the Mississippi Gulf Coast towns of Bay St. Louis, Clermont Harbor, Pass Christian, Long Beach, Gulfport, and Biloxi whose homes were demolished in Hurricane Camille of 1969. Wrote Ronny Caire (not to be confused with George's neighbor, Ronnie), publisher of *The Owl* newspaper, in a May 12, 1970, front-page article:

> Many visitors driving along U.S. 90 on the Mississippi Gulf Coast ask the question, "Why is rebuilding going so slowly? The hurricane happened over eight months ago."
>
> Mainly the answer lies with insurance.
>
> Some insurance claims have not been settled between the insurance companies and the property owners to provide funds for rebuilding.
>
> Many owners' policies have been cancelled by insurance companies and windstorm insurance is unavailable within 1000 feet of the water. Without this insurance the property owners cannot secure financing from mortgage companies and building and loan associations for rebuilding. Others, of independent means, do not wish to build and have storm exposure without insurance coverage.

Camille victims, many without compensation for their losses, found existing policies canceled and new, higher rates in effect. Their wails over the accounting methods insurers pursue have found echo in other parts of the country. Since these accounting methods affect policy costs everywhere, it is well to know what might be used in computing the charge Ira the insurance agent makes when he sends a bill for *your* protective coverage.

"Part of your premium dollar is put into a reserve fund," an insurance critic told me, "and part in an operating fund. The company tries to ignore the 'reserve' portion—even the income from investing it—and expects insurance commissions to allow it rates which permit a profit only on part of the income received for protection. A national magazine a few years ago computed that one large underwriter which had reported operating losses for five straight years nevertheless had a growth of over *$10 billion* in net worth during that time."

The insurance companies have an answer in part to this. They claim that rates go up because the things they insure— particularly products of the auto industry—are so low in quality that they deteriorate almost without being damaged.

"That's correct," Ronnie said when George brought up the subject one evening after the scotch had flowed freely. "Bumpers used to be protective devices. Now they are only decorative. Hit one a light blow and it crumples. The insurance companies are right when they say that part of the blame for high policy costs lies in the lofty repair charges necessitated by those fragile cars coming out of Detroit."

"Whether you blame things on the auto boys or the insurers, something needs correction about rate making and policy payoffs," said George. "Let's drink to a little light being let into the insurance setup. Lower rates and faster settlements. Cheers."

4. Quackery Is the Cruelest   The day is past when horse liniment was peddled as a cure for cancer and everything-pills were offered to gullible people in the backwoods. But peddlers who prey upon the simple have not vanished. They yearly mulct millions, using more sophisticated appeals. Theirs is the cruelest consumer racket.

The U.S. Food and Drug Administration, watchdog on the quackery front, says this about present-day practices:

> Worthless drugs include "cures" for baldness among men, which is incurable; chemical "face peels" that promise new youth but may bring permanent disfigurement; "prompt relief" from colitis through laxatives which can seriously worsen this condition; drugs that "melt away" fat without dieting—when dieting is the only way known to medicine to reduce weight. Most cruel and dangerous of all are the "effective treatments" for diabetes and cancer. In diabetes, they can cause coma and death; in cancer, the patient is robbed of the one element that can save his life—valuable time during which really effective treatment could still be administered.
> ... The electrocardiograph records the action of the heart; a special gauge shows the blood pressure; X-rays record abnormalities within the body. But there is no machine which can diagnose or treat different diseases by simply turning a knob or flashing lights; no apparatus can reduce excess weight by vibration; no glove or bracelet can "cure" arthritis with "electricity" or "uranium ore." Sometimes quackery even

involves legitimate devices. It is practically impossible to get properly fitted eyeglasses or dentures by mail order, for example.

Quackery follows certain well-defined patterns. If your answer is "yes" to any of the following questions, it is very likely that you are one of the thousands of people who are victimized by quacks each year.

Is the product or service offered a "secret remedy"?

Does the sponsor claim that he is battling the medical profession which is attempting to suppress his wonderful discovery?

Is the remedy sold from door to door, by a self-styled health advisor, or promoted in lectures to the public, from town to town?

Is this "miracle" drug, device, or diet promoted in a sensational magazine, by a faith healers' group, or a crusading organization of laymen?

Does the promoter show you testimonials on the wonderful miracles his product or services have performed for others?

Is the product or service good for a vast variety of illnesses, real or fancied?

If you suspect that you are the victim of quackery, there are a number of things you can do:

See your physician or inform your county medical society.

Get in touch with the Food and Drug Administration, either at its District Office in your area, or in Washington, D.C.

Ask the Better Business Bureau about the reputation of the promoter.

If the drug or device was promoted through the mail, inform your local Post Office.

The Federal Trade Commission has noted that "nobody knows how much quackery costs in the United States today, but at hearings conducted by the subcommittee on frauds and misrepresentations affecting the elderly, a unit of the U.S. Senate's Special Committee on Aging, testimony indicated the cost ran into the hundreds of millions each year. Subcommittee Chairman Senator Harrison A. Williams, Jr., in commenting on the cost, said: "It seems to me there are losses that go far beyond the original purchase price for the phony treatment, useless gadget, the inappropriate drug or pill. How can we measure the cost in terms of suffering, disappointment, and final despair? Do we really know how many

Americans are quietly using therapy or products that can give them neither cure nor the hope of cure?"

5. How Safe Is It?   "In this day of close scrutiny of every product, most things should be safe, even if not every one is a good buy," said Sophie as George read over labels in their medicine cabinet. "*That* shouldn't be a problem in money management."

"Wish you were right, my lovely wife, but you are not," said George. "If we eat unsafe foods or buy an unsafe tire or ride in an airplane not properly maintained, we can lose health and maybe life. Don't say that is outside the area of money management, because it costs a lot when you're maimed or sick. It even costs a lot to die and be buried. Here—read what an expert says."

On March 5, 1970, Charles Edwards, M.D., Commissioner, Food and Drug Administration, testified before the National Commission on Product Safety. Commenting upon the flammability, pressure generation, and toxic, corrosive, irritating qualities of some "safe" products, Dr. Edwards reported:

> We estimate that there are annually 20,000 deaths and 20 million injuries associated with products *covered by the law* [emphasis mine].

His report did not include the checks on tires, auto fixtures, bus standards, airline scheduling and inspections, and other activities of the U.S. Department of Transportation which annually uncover many defects and unsafe parts and practices associated with our systems for getting from one place to another.

6. Is Wall Street Secure?   Only by virtue of repeated bail-out operations were the New York Stock Exchange member-firms able to make investors safe from losses when some of their sizable, formerly prestigious fellows went down the drain in 1969 and 1970. One day, bailing out the shaky firms may prove too big a task. Even when the Exchange's assessment funds make good a firm's bankruptcy so that investors' stocks and cash balances are secure, it can take months before the unfortunate investors win clear.

"I have instructed my broker that all stocks must be transferred to my name and mailed to me," Ronnie commented as he and George discussed the problem over afternoon coffee. "True, it's easier to let the broker keep securities in 'street name'—that is, credited to me as a bookkeeping operation the same way Able Banker Charlie's Eighth National credits cash deposited in an account. When I hold the stock certificates I need a safe deposit box, since lost certificates are difficult to replace. And I have the problem of keeping track of things that Broker Bill used to do for me.

"However, the cost of a bank box is small by comparison with what would be entailed should Broker Bill go broke. I'm not letting him keep my cash balance in the account any longer, even though he pays a small monthly interest if I do so. Risk outweighs the advantage."

HOW TO YELL AND BE HEARD

Sophie, George, and Ronnie—and you—do not have to battle alone against these and other hazards to finance. You can call upon the consumerism watchdogs.

Some of them are in government. They have teeth with which they can threaten offenders. Others are the ombudsmen of business and industry. Their teeth aren't as big or as sharp as the fangs possessed by watchdogs of government.

Here are the words of a governmental watchdog, Leslie Dix, then with the Committee on Consumer Interests, headed at the time by Betty Furness. Mr. Dix was testifying at National Consumer Protection Hearings before the Federal Trade Commission in November, 1968:

> Consumer problems result not alone from the fringe of un-ethical business in our views, but from some of the general practices of legitimate business.

Consumer concerns also include the social and economic cost of inferior quality, both to the public and to the government. Environmental rights are also being thought of and characterized as fundamental consumer rights, for if we foul our planet further so as to make it uninhabitable, all other consumer issues will become meaningless. . . .

What the consumer asks and what the government has been taking steps to assure, an open competitive marketplace of informed buyers and sellers, is but to make the textbook concept of the free enterprise system a reality. The consumer is the true beneficiary of a free and truly competitive business community. Improvement in the quality of the marketplace, enlightened and equitable measures to insure stability, growth and flourishing of the free enterprise system are the goals of the consumer revolution.

We must recognize that government protection of consumer rights in the marketplace is a necessary corollary to the government's long-accepted role as protector of the ethical man. We submit that these objectives are as American as the Fourth of July.

Business is becoming concerned, too. Not long ago, the U.S. Chamber of Commerce made a serious study entitled *Business and the Consumer*. It made twelve recommendations:

1. Manufacturers, distributors, and all businessmen concerned with consumer goods and services should seek constantly to upgrade both product quality and marketing methods. In this connection, adoption of model corporate codes of consumer relations should be seriously considered.

2. Manufacturers should simplify and modernize their warranties.

3. Manufacturers should seek means by which warranty fulfillment by dealers and others involved in providing servicing under warranties can be made more attractive so as to improve quality and speed of performance of such servicing.

4. Manufacturers should set up a simple system for providing customers feed-back on products and product servicing under both warranty and non-warranty terms.

5. Improved training programs should be devised for sales and service personnel with particular emphasis on informing sales personnel of product capabilities and limitations to

avoid overselling the product with consequent adverse customer reactions.

6. Wherever possible, sellers should price their products on an objective unit basis, such as weight, volume, and standardized ingredient content to permit easier price comparisons by consumers. In addition sellers should expand information regarding safety, performance and durability of products.

7. In the sensitive area of product safety, business should seriously consider such mechanisms as federal certification of voluntary standards as well as notification and recall systems for defective products. There is also a demonstrated need for expanded systems of product accident data collection and consumer information on safety.

8. Business should take more forthright and specific positions and action against fraud and deception, especially as practiced in sales to low-income consumers.

9. Business should actively support efforts to broaden the participation by other groups, including consumers, in voluntary product and service standards-making.

10. Business, in cooperation with local chambers of commerce and other appropriate organizations, should undertake to recast Better Business Bureaus as a consumer ombudsman to coordinate and strengthen manufacturer-seller-customer complaint, information, and warranty performance communication systems. Enactment by the states of uniform laws to deal with fraudulent, deceptive, or misleading business practices would be desirable.

11. In cooperation with local chambers of commerce, Better Business Bureaus should provide basic consumer economics information to customers who request assistance and who indicate ignorance of how the market economy works.

12. Business should intensify its efforts in product development to anticipate the social consequences of the use of its products in order to forestall consumer complaints about environmental pollution, congestion, public safety, health and public morality effects.

An important difference exists between the recommendations of the U.S. Chamber of Commerce and strictures of governmental watchdogs on the federal, state, and local levels. The Chamber's well-meant, generalized recommendations are just that—recommendations. They can be flouted. Every day, chamber members do so. Governmental rulings tend to be more specific and a lot harder to flout because the government watchdogs can bite. Frequently, they do.

Washington's watchdogs include:

■ The Federal Trade Commission, whose far-ranging activities have crossed our money management path before. The FTC views itself as a kindly cop on the corner, more interested in the happiness of the block than in catching one of its residents redhanded. Don't be fooled. The FTC watchdog does bite. Here's its description of the kindly cop bit:

> Although the Commission has specific responsibilities for law enforcement, this does not alter the agency's fundamental purpose to guide business, rather than to prosecute violators. The Commission's staff has never been even remotely big enough to undertake detailed surveillance of all business operations under its jurisdiction. Nevertheless, with the help of complaints by injured business competitors and duped consumers, plus the identification of problems by a watchful Congress, other agencies of Government and the Commission's own staff, it would be surprising indeed if troublespots were not quickly identified. It is then the Commission's function to bring whatever actions provide the best remedy, mindful of the public interest and its own dominant mission to illuminate and prevent violations of the law rather than to punish transgressors.

In all of this there must be a public-interest angle. Who decides whether public interest is involved? Not you. The kindly cop does so. The FTC beat includes antitrust violations as well as anticonsumer frauds. If you have been had by one of the latter, Federal Traders say these are steps to be taken:

> Protest directly to the seller (if you can find him!). Possibly the misrepresentation was done without his knowledge, in which case, he can take steps to assure against its repetition. There is even a chance he might square himself with you.
>
> If, however, the fast-buck operator shrugs you off, you can carry your indignation further by registering your complaint with the organizations in your community devoted to maintaining proper conduct for business. A good example is the Better Business Bureau. And certainly your cause would be

served if your complaint, backed by hard facts, went to the newspaper or radio or TV station that carries advertising for the product. It wouldn't take many such letters to deprive the huckster of his innocent readers and listeners. Truth in advertising is too important to these media to risk gaining a reputation for carrying phony ads.

A third line of defense is your local government. This is particularly important because most of the things you buy are marketed only locally, and the seller is not engaged in interstate commerce. The result is that you have to depend not on the Federal government but on your city or state for protection. Nearly all of the states have statutes aimed at misrepresentation of products and services. And in some states these laws are enforced with vigor.

Certainly it behooves you to find out what kind of state (or city) protection is available to you. And if none is, you might want to help improve the situation.

Your fourth line of defense is the Federal Trade Commission. Congress gave it the broad responsibility to halt "unfair methods of competition in commerce and unfair or deceptive acts or practices in commerce." Thus, not only were all the known deceptive practices outlawed but any new ones that might be invented. Other responsibilities of the FTC include policing the labeling of furs, woolens and other textile products, and guarding against the sale of dangerously flammable wearing apparel.

■ When the transgression against your pocketbook occurred in Mel's and Sal's Plaza supermarket where we shopped through an earlier chapter, your complaint might belong with the Food and Drug Administration. An advisory, *How the FDA Works for You,* tells the scope of its consumer protection regulation:

> The Food and Drug Administration protects the health of American consumers by insuring that: foods are safe, pure, and wholesome; drugs and therapeutic devices are safe and effective; cosmetics are harmless; and that all these products are honestly and informatively labeled and packaged. The Administration is also empowered to see that dangerous household products carry adequate warnings for safe use and are properly labeled; counterfeiting of drugs is stopped; and that hazards incident to the use of various types of consumer products are reduced. FDA administers the Nation's basic food and drug law—the Federal Food, Drug, and Cos-

metic Act—and also the Federal Hazardous Substances Act, the Tea Importation Act, the Filled Milk Act, and the Import Milk Act. FDA also enforces those parts of the Federal Caustic Poisons Act and the Fair Packaging and Labeling Act which apply to foods, drugs, and other products within FDA jurisdiction.

In pricing, FDA points out that "the law prohibits use of misleading terms." FDA investigators tend to feel that Sophie is being misled if Mel and Sal label something "jumbo pound" or "giant quart" since, they note, a pound is a pound is a pound and the same can be said for a quart—or any other size or weight which is not enlarged by the modifying word applied to it.

If you feel that there is something fishy besides tuna in the can on the Plaza store's shelf, or that drugs being handed out by the friendly corner pharmacist are not all that the doctor ordered, you can yell "cop!" and FDA should respond. According to a fact sheet:

You can complain either in writing or by phone to the nearest FDA District office, or directly to the Food and Drug Administration, U.S. Department of Health, Education, and Welfare, Washington, D.C. 20204. FDA has 17 District offices and 93 resident inspection stations throughout the country. In major cities, you can find the address of the nearest FDA office in the telephone directory under "U.S. Government, Department of Health, Education, and Welfare, Food and Drug Administration."

1. Report your grievance promptly.

2. State clearly what appeared to be wrong.

3. Describe the label of the product and give any code marks that appear on the container. (In the case of a canned food, these are usually embossed into or stamped on the lid of the can.)

4. Give the name and address of the store where the article was bought.

5. Save whatever remains of the suspect product or the empty container for your doctor's guidance or for use in case of an investigation.

6. Hold any unopened container of the product bought at the same time.

7. If an injury is involved, see a doctor at once.

8. Also report the suspect product to the manufacturer, packer, or distributor shown on the label of the product and to the store where you bought it.

■ Plagued with a problem car or trouble concerning any of the extra appurtenances from the Detroit factory? The U.S. Department of Transportation may be interested. Thirty-six closely typed pages were required to list its compliance report of a single recent month.

■ Finally, there is the Committee on Consumer Interests. This office has garnered more publicity than other federal efforts, partly because it has been headed during two administrations by ladies with a flair for the flamboyant. The chairman under Lyndon Johnson's reign was Betty Furness. She was succeeded by Mrs. Virginia Knauer, soft-spoken but diligent along Press Row as well as in the shoddy shops of the ghettos.

In its June, 1970, issue, *The Spectator* quoted Mrs. Knauer:

> Briefly, my job is to represent the consumer to the President, to the Congress, and to the various Federal Departments. We have proposed legislation to the President for his consideration, we have testified before the Senate and the House on consumer measures, and we have appeared before some Federal Departments on rules and regulations affecting consumers. We are in constant contact with business organizations on behalf of the consumer, and we are in daily touch with various consumer organizations throughout the country, helping them in whatever way we can. We also have a very active education division which is now preparing consumer education guidelines for use by grade and high schools throughout the country. . . . In general, you could say we serve as a catalyst and coordinator.

The Special Assistant to the President has a different task from those of watchdog agencies. She advises and coordinates. They act directly. Yet if enough people get in touch with this Presidential assistant, new regulations and legislation might result. In regard to the consumers' insurance gripes we examined earlier, Mrs. Knauer noted in *The Spectator* interview that "we have many complaints about the high cost of insurance. The complaints vary, of course, with specific types of insurance. But generally they fall into these categories: cancellation of insurance without reasonable cause, forcing the consumer to seek insurance from the so-called 'special markets' at higher rates; discrimination in providing insurance, some on a racial basis and some on the basis of the geographical location of the applicants; rate discrimination, based on the charges that the rating programs and classifications offered by insurance companies are too refined and, accordingly, discriminatory; charges that rates are too high on the basis that companies are making inordinate profits and are not passing them along in the form of rate reductions."

The Committee on Consumer Interests will put you on the mailing list for its monthly *Consumer Legislative Monthly Report* (write Room 6026, New Federal Office Building No. 7, Washington, D.C. 20506). This describes legislation introduced into or pending in both houses of Congress. You and your neighbors can pressure the congressmen and senators who represent you to push through consumer-protection laws you consider important.

Special consumer offices such as that of the Presidential advisory committee are being established in cities, counties, and states. New York's Department of Consumer Affairs is the best known. This outfit bites. Often hard. The scope of its legal clomp includes criminal penalties against offenders and group actions on behalf of all who have lost out to an illegal badger game. Once a judgment has been obtained under such an action, every consumer able to prove that he was nicked can get his money back and the offender must reimburse the City of New York for the time its legal servants spent in court and the costs they incurred.

In a prepared statement read at an FTC hearing on November 22, 1968, Commissioner Gerald M. Weinberg of the New York City Department of Consumer Affairs stated:

> Our Department is no longer a remote, unknown quantity to the people in our many neighborhoods. They have learned to

know and deal with our local representatives. They have an immediate outlet for their questions, complaints and frustrations. They have an opportunity to help and be helped, and to become part of their own government.

One of the most popular of all new operations emerging from our encouragement of community involvement has been the telephone complaint and inquiry service established in our agency by Mayor Lindsay. This particular program evolves from the employment by our agency of the same theory used by the medical profession.

It is evident to all of us that if doctors had to spend their time visiting every resident of the City in an effort to determine which ones were ill or had any troublesome symptoms, not only would there be little time to treat the sick, but even the initial coverage would become an impossible task. By the same token, we recognize the possibilities involved in an arrangement whereby consumers—yes, and businessmen too —bring their troubles directly to us for examination, advice and action.

"Why don't we have such a setup?" complained Sophie. "Let's all get together, march to City Hall, and demand establishment of a local Department of Consumer Affairs."

Not all consumerism watchdogs are governmental. There are self-appointed guardians of your rights. Some—certainly not all—of them are able and effective.

■ The ubiquitous Ralph Nader has tilted verbal lances against many of what he considers enemies of the people, ranging from the auto industry to his fellow watchdogs in the Food and Drug Administration. You can write to Nader in Washington if you have a problem. His bark, if he chooses to use it, is very loud.

■ Another barking watchdog is Robert Choate, Jr., who achieved instant fame with a fight against breakfast foods that, he said, contained little nutrient value.

■ The American Medical Association and American Dental Association can take action against quacks in their fields, seeking a court order when they consider the health of the public in danger. Cynics say that their most biting actions are against people who endanger the prerogatives of their members rather than the privileges and needs of the patient group.

▪ Better Business Bureaus are supported by community commercial interests. Many minor cases of fraud—some major ones as well—have been cleared up by the quick attacks of these business-supported watchdogs. Nearly every community has a BBB.

▪ Many complaints are settled by company managements. Top-level bosses have on occasion been appalled by outlandish claims and/or shoddy practices of those under them. However, don't count too strongly on the president of Funnybone Corp. to rush to your defense if you find one of its products bad and the local dealer unwilling to do anything. However, it's worth a try. The *Business and the Consumer* recommendations of the Chamber of Commerce indicate an awareness at top levels that consumers won't be pushed as easily as their daddies were.

TO RECAP:

1. The rule once was caveat emptor—let the buyer beware—but things are swinging to a state of *caveat vendor* in which the seller had better behave as well as beware. Consumerism is one of the new movements of the times. Out of this movement come new safeguards for your money and opportunities to make purchases represent true value.

2. Guarantees must mean something. If they don't, you can make a vendor mend his shoddy ways.

3. The sometimes-sharp ways of insurance agencies and companies are coming under fire. Increasingly, watchdogs stand ready to hear legitimate complaints against an industry which—whether deservedly or not—has come to rank with auto manufacturers on the most hated list.

4. Fake cures are the cruelest consumer racket. They sap health as well as time and money. Remedies exist on all levels of government, and private groups such as the American Medical Association and American Dental Association put down quackery that was common in our grandfathers' days.

5. Unsafe products are another dollar drain. Like quack cures, unsafe products and business practices cost lives in addition to money. Know the people who enforce safety rules and appeal to them before injuries happen.

6. Bananas on the sidewalk and poorly serviced equipment are not the only unsafe things that derail a sound money management plan. In Wall Street, formerly sound, prestigious firms fail. Unscrupulous operators mark up corporate earnings and mutual funds' asset values.

7. If your community has no department of consumer affairs that can bite wrongdoers as well as issue warning barks, you can work with neighbors and civic groups to have protective legislation passed.

8. Business, too, is concerned with protecting the consumer's dollar and has set up agencies such as Better Business Bureaus to help defang defrauders. The business community's efforts seem to work best against its smaller members.

12

Wrap-up

IT WAS A DULL WINTER EVENING. Edith and Ethelred were busy on homework. A television epic had captured Frederica's attention. George, Sophie, and Ronnie gathered in the living room.

"Here's to the better life," said George, raising his glass. "These have been good adventures in the lands of money management opportunity. Feller named David Markstein wrote them all down. Mainly, as the fictional Huckleberry Finn said of Mark Twain's reports on Tom Sawyer, he told the truth. Cheers!"

Index